A History of
Developmental Psychology
in Autobiography

Developmental Psychology Series

Series Editor, Wendell E. Jeffrey, U.C.L.A.

Communication Development During Infancy, Lauren B. Adamson

Reading and Writing Acquisition, Virginia Berninger

The Development of Peer Prejudice and Discrimination: Evolutionary, Cultural, and Developmental Dynamics, Harold D. Fishbein

Moral Psychology, Daniel K. Lapsley

How Divorce Affects Offspring, Michael R. Stevenson and Kathryn N. Black

A History of Developmental Psychology in Autobiography, Dennis Thompson and John D. Hogan, editors

Human Auditory Development, Lynne A. Werner and G. Cameron Marean

Forthcoming Titles:

Social Development: The First Three Years, Celia A. Brownell

The Social World of Adolescence, Ana Mari Cauce and Nancy Gonzales

Parents and the Dynamics of Child Rearing, George W. Holden

The Ontogeny of Creativity, Stanley Kuczaj and Virginia Kirkpatrick

Friends, Peer Groups, and Child Development, Gary Ladd

Neuropsychology of Infant Development, George F. Michel and Celia L. Moore

Minority Children in American Society: Issues in Development, Diane Scott-Jones

Young Children's Logical Reasoning, Susan C. Sommerville

Infant Assessment, M. Virginia Wyly

A History of
Developmental Psychology
in Autobiography

edited by

Dennis Thompson
and John D. Hogan

WestviewPress

A Division of HarperCollins*Publishers*

Developmental Psychology Series

Copyright © 1996 by Westview Press, A Division of HarperCollins Publishers, Inc.

Published in 1996 in the United States of America by Westview Press, 5500 Central Avenue, Boulder,
Colorado 80301-2877, and in the United Kingdom by Westview Press, 12 Hid's Copse Road, Cumnor
Hill, Oxford OX2 9JJ

A CIP catalog record for this book is available from the Library of Congress.
ISBN 0-8133-3078-5 (hc.)   ISBN 0-8133-3079-3 (pbk.)

The paper used in this publication meets the requirements of the American National Standard for Per-
manence of Paper for Printed Library Materials Z39.48-1984.

10   9   8   7   6   5   4   3   2   1

Contents

Preface

Developmental psychology is not well represented in textbooks in the history of psychology. When G. Stanley Hall appears, for instance, he is more likely to be remembered for his role in the founding of the American Psychological Association (APA) than for his contributions to the child-study movement. Even Sigmund Freud, perhaps the most influential of all developmental psychologists, is apt to be cited mostly for his contributions to clinical psychology rather than for his theory of development.

Part of that neglect is due to the traditional focus on experimental psychology in psychology's history. Since many components of developmental psychology have not lent themselves well to the experimental method, the field has taken on a secondary status in some quarters. The way in which that lower rank came about is an interesting story in itself, and that story still needs to be told. Fortunately, the status of the specialty has been upgraded in recent years. There are at least two reasons why.

During the last two decades, there has been an explosion of interest in the history of psychology, and that renewed interest has resulted in a reevaluation of many parts of the field. In the process, neglected areas have been looked at with fresh eyes—including developmental psychology. Historical overviews of the specialty have become more available (e.g., Birren & Birren, 1990; Cairns, 1983; Dixon & Lerner, 1988), and there is occasionally a volume devoted entirely to some aspect of the history (e.g., Cravens, 1993). Recently, as part of the APA centennial, a publication was released that was one of the boldest attempts to date to summarize the previous one hundred years of the field (Parke, et al., 1994).

The status of the field has also changed because the scope and manner of developmental psychology itself has changed. In the beginning, the leaders of psychology were also leaders of developmental psychology (e.g., Hall and Baldwin). Soon, however, their paths began to diverge. Many developmentalists were content with their approach and did not consider themselves "experimentalists" in the sense of directing research where variables were manipulated. As a result, the separation between mainstream psychology and developmental psychology became greater. But that period of separation did not last. Soon there were many changes that revivified the specialty, including the work of Lewin, the growth of "experimental child psychology," the enhanced interest in infancy and the elderly, and the rise of new conceptions and models. Once again, developmental psychology became part of mainstream psychology.

Perhaps a third problem with the identification of developmental psychology lies in its definition. The meaning of the phrase "developmental psychology" is different for different people. In its most general sense, it refers to the continuity of psychological functioning across the human life span. (At one point there was an attempt to have it encompass development across all phylogenetic levels.) This definition simply recognizes the chronological range of the specialty. It is not meant to incorporate the assumptions of the so-called life-span approach, which looks at development across the life span with a particular view: for instance, that each part of development is an opportunity for genuine development, or that no part of the life span is more important to development than any other part.

There are those who would truncate even the chronological aspect of the definition. For instance, it is common practice in some quarters to use the phrase "developmental psychology" when the meaning is more properly "child psychology." Note, for instance, the formal title of Division 7 of the American Psychological Association—the Division on Developmental Psychology. If it were truly a division of developmental psychology, would there be a need for APA Division 20—the Division of Adult Development and Aging? And incidentally, how many APA members belong to both divisions? The answer: not very many.

The problem of definition is not a trivial one, and it speaks to a related issue—the increasing specialization of the field of psychology itself and the splintering of interest within its specialties. If there is any single thing that has characterized the field in the latter part of the twentieth century—besides its sheer size and growth—it is continuing specialization. George Miller, the noted cognitive psychologist and former APA president, referred to psychology as an "intellectual zoo" (Miller, 1985, p. 40) and argued that "every large psychology department is a small college unto itself . . ." (Miller, 1985, p. 42). Nowadays, even members of the same specialties are likely to have a hard time understanding one another. But in our history we have common ground, and it is a part of this history we wish to examine in this text.

The Genesis of the Book

This book grew out of an interest in the history of developmental psychology, or perhaps more properly, an interest in contemporary developmental psychology in historical perspective. In one sense it is simply an attempt to bring some aspects of the field to an interested audience. We believe strongly in the power of the biographical approach to simultaneously entice and inform. In the long run, we think that such an approach provides a more accurate view of the way in which research and inquiry is developed and conducted. Certainly it adds a dimension that is entirely absent from the traditional scientific journal article. But we also believe that the leaders of the field themselves—including aspects of their personal lives—are a significant part of the field. We wanted to provide a place where information about some of them would be available.

There was a conscious model for this undertaking, a series called The History of Psychology in Autobiography, which was begun in 1930 under the editorship of Carl Murchison of Clark University. To date, there have been eight volumes in the series, the most recent of which was published in 1989 (Lindzey, 1989). In those intervening sixty years the series has catalogued the life and work of more than one hundred extraordinary contributors—from James Mark Baldwin and Mary Calkins to William Estes and Eleanor Maccoby. Along the way, it has built up a repository of some of the richest biographical material in the discipline, which by now contains much material that surely would have been forgotten if the series had not come into being.

Some developmental psychologists have been included in past editions of the series, perhaps most notably Jean Piaget, Arnold Gesell, Sidney Pressey, and Eleanor Gibson. Still, the presence of developmentalists seemed to us to be relatively infrequent. Moreover, there was no guarantee that the series would continue—it has already been through five publishers. Perhaps most important, we thought that the specialty deserved a book of its own. We were aware that two volumes containing autobiographies of clinical psychologists had recently been released (Walker, 1991, 1993), and they served to whet our appetite. Developmental psychology has a unique voice and we wanted that voice to be heard.

The Contributors

We began our project by making lists of people we thought were the most important living contributors to developmental psychology. Although we were impressed with the accomplishments of many younger contributors, we were reluctant to include them on our final lists. We reasoned that some chronological distance was necessary in order to evaluate the strength of contributions. Further—and we hope this isn't simply an ageist perspective—we believe age provides a view that younger contributors would rarely attain, no matter how accomplished. That view includes an ability to take the day-to-day occurrences in life and work and locate them in a larger life context.

We also made an attempt to sample from different areas within the specialty. Certainly we wanted people who had worked in different periods across the life span. We also thought it was important to have some international representation. It is becoming clear to us that developmental psychology, like many other areas of inquiry, is acquiring more and more international links, and we wanted the biographies to reflect that enhanced scope.

But despite all these self-imposed "rules," we were flexible. When our lists were compiled, we circulated them among some of our associates and began soliciting their opinions. Before long, we narrowed the lists down to a much smaller list of potential authors. Soon we were ready to begin writing to people on our list and asking for their participation.

To our surprise, we began receiving acceptances almost immediately. Our informants were anxious to tell their stories. We received some declinations—a few who felt they had already told their stories in some other source; a few who felt they weren't ready to tell their stories; and a final few, sadly, whose health would not permit them to undertake the project. Still, we were exhilarated with the acceptances and with the range of interests they represented.

In our initial contact we had laid down some guidelines. We wanted the autobiographical piece to be both personal and professional, and we provided a rough outline of the suggested topics. However, we were careful not to be too rigid in our format, and this flexibility was a central concern of ours. We wanted the story to be told in the manner and style of the informant. We wanted his or her voice to be the dominant one, not ours. And so we did not press for uniformity either in the initial outline or in the final editing. We had to face some realities regarding the length of the piece and citations, but even in that we tried to be as pliant as possible.

A Final Note

One of the obvious benefits of working with such accomplished individuals is that the editing demands were relatively slight. That was not a surprise. All the contributors have written extensively, and several have been involved in major editing projects of their own. The surprises, if there were any, came from the diversity expressed in the individual essays. Even within our somewhat restricted age range and choice of specialty, the voices of developmental psychology are distinct. The view of the field and the manner in which it was entered and practiced exhibit as much diversity as there are contributors. And yet there seem to be at least two things that all the contributors have in common—a personal style that would have to be called "inquisitive," and a feeling regarding their contributions that would have to be labeled "satisfaction," or something close to it.

We invite you to share in the life experiences and accomplishments of these gifted contributors to developmental psychology. We hope you find their essays to be as rich and rewarding as we did.

Dennis Thompson
John D. Hogan
November 1995

References

Birren, J. E. & Birren, B. A. (1990). The concepts, models, and history of the psychology of aging. In J. E. Birren and K. W. Schaie (Eds.), *Handbook of the psychology of aging* (3rd ed., pp. 3–20). San Diego: Academic Press.

Cairns, R. B. (1983). The emergence of developmental psychology. In P. H. Mussen (Ed.), *Handbook of child psychology, Volume 1* (4th ed., pp. 41–102). New York: Wiley.

Cravens, H. (1993). *Before Head Start.* Chapel Hill: University of North Carolina Press.

Dixon, R. A. & Lerner, R. M. (1988). A history of systems in developmental psychology. In M. H. Bornstein and M. E. Lamb (Eds.), *Developmental psychology: An advanced textbook* (2nd ed., pp. 3–50). Hillsdale, N.J.: Erlbaum.

Lindzey, G. (Ed.). (1989). *A history of psychology in autobiography, Volume VIII.* Stanford: Stanford University Press.

Miller, G. A. (1985). The constitutive problem of psychology. In S. Koch and D. E. Leary (Eds.), *A century of psychology as science* (pp. 40–45). Washington, D.C.: McGraw-Hill. (Reissued in 1992 by the American Psychological Association).

Parke, R. D., Ornstein, P. A., Rieser, J. J. & Zahn-Waxler, C. (Eds.). (1994). *A century of developmental psychology.* Washington, D.C.: American Psychological Association.

Walker, C. E. (1991). *The history of clinical psychology in autobiography, Volume 1.* Pacific Grove, Calif.: Brooks/Cole.

Walker, C. E. (1993). *The history of clinical psychology in autobiography, Volume 2.* Pacific Grove, Calif.: Brooks/Cole.

1

Louise Bates Ames

Birth, Family Background, Early Years

I was born in Portland, Maine, in 1908, the oldest child of Samuel L. and Annie E. Bates. I had two brothers, John and Silas. Looking back, I appreciate that I must have had a rather unusually privileged childhood—as of course did many who grew up in that time and place.

Life was for the most part, for many of us, serene and secure. The area of Portland in which I lived (Deering) housed an extremely homogeneous population—mostly WASPs. In fact, at our elementary school a very large proportion of the children (some said as high as 75 percent) had parents who had attended the same school. The major diversity actually seemed to be a matter of what church one attended, and most people did belong to one church or another.

Ours was a very close-knit neighborhood. School, church, and shopping areas all were within walking distance, and "everybody" knew everybody. This may in part have accounted for the good behavior of the children—anyone attempting to get away with anything was inevitably spotted by some familiar adult.

My father, Judge Samuel L. Bates, was a very firm disciplinarian. We accepted this, in fact took it for granted, since we admired him vastly. We thought he knew everything and could solve any problem. This notion was shared by many people in town, and to some extent I basked in my father's reflected glory. "Oh! Judge *Bates's* daughter," people would say, as later they might comment, "Yes, she works with *Dr. Gesell!*"

Our family atmosphere was more intellectual than emotional. Ours was a bookish household. We spent many a pleasant evening by the fire, our parents reading to us, until, or even after, we were able to read for ourselves. Also, since my father was a devoted naturalist and there were plenty of woods available, both in Portland and in South Brooksville, where we spent summer vacations, we spent a good deal of time with him in the woods learning about trees and flowers.

Our lives flowed along rather evenly, with the understanding that we would do well in school and eventually go to college and on to professional lives. I was in the fifth grade when the notion hit me that it would really be fun to be a secretary, but since I would be going on to college I supposed I should choose a profession. I chose law, and from then on during summer vacations spent a good deal of time in my father's office.

I attended Leland primary school, Longfellow grammar school, and Deering High. My choice of a college was influenced more by the high school than by my parents. They both had attended normal school but not college and so had no special affiliation. Our high school for some reason favored Wheaton College in Norton, Massachusetts, and I spent my first two college years there.

College and Graduate Education

Wheaton turned out not to be a happy choice. I did not enjoy it, and they were not entirely satisfied with me. In the middle of my sophomore year, at my own suggestion, I arranged to transfer to the University of Maine for my junior and senior years.

Maine and I were a much better match. At Wheaton there was a good deal of talk about people's coming out parties and whether or not they were going to Europe for the summer. At Maine people asked one another if they had a job for the summer, and I knew some students who came to college with as little as one hundred dollars (all their families could spare) and earned the rest of what they needed.

The level of instruction, too, seemed far superior at Maine. In fact, the contrast in one area was so great that after a course in psychology at Wheaton I was so bewildered as to what it was all about that I vowed never to take psychology again. At Maine, the psychology courses under Dr. Dickinson, head of the department, were so superior that when an early marriage made it seem impractical for me to pursue my idea of being a lawyer and working in my father's office, I decided to choose child psychology as my profession.

The University of Maine turned out to be a good choice in many respects. To begin with, I had a wonderful time. Wheaton had been more or less a convent— no riding in cars even in the daytime, and no being off campus (with or without boys) after 6 P.M. Maine was a holiday in comparison. We really did enjoy ourselves, and I learned a lot.

My undergraduate courses, especially psychology but also other courses, were interesting and comfortable. And after eloping in my senior spring and taking a year off to pursue parenthood, my husband and I returned to campus in the fall of 1932. I worked half-time and studied half-time, ending up in the spring of 1933 with a master's degree in psychology and a minor in education.

Among the courses I perhaps enjoyed the most were project courses in psychology. In these projects I could choose what I wished to study. Before marrying, I had carried out a project on dreams. After marriage, I completed a second project comparing dreams during pregnancy with dreams during nonpregnancy.

Possibly my most useful bit of study at Maine, however, was the work I did toward my master's thesis—"Growth of Motor Coordination in One Child from Birth to Two Years" (Ames, 1933)—in which I used my own daughter[1] as my subject. With my great personal enthusiasm for language, I would have preferred to have studied language. Dr. Dickinson discouraged me on the grounds that Mc-

Carthy and others had adequately covered this area. Actually, my work on motor behavior fit in more effectively with the work I was to do at Yale than language would have, so it turned out to be a happy choice.

Not so fortunate was my graduate work at Yale, which was neither pleasant nor productive, so it's perhaps best to comment on it only briefly. For detail, see my autobiographic chapter in C. Eugene Walker's *The History of Clinical Psychology in Autobiography* (Ames, 1993).

Though I went to Yale to study child behavior with Dr. Gesell, it was not possible to get a degree in child behavior or even clinical psychology. In fact, no courses were offered in either field. I was forced to get my Ph.D. in experimental psychology. Yale's position appeared to be that any proper psychologist would be doing experiments, in all likelihood experiments of such an esoteric nature that we would need to be able to make our own equipment (thus our classes in "shop").

Both assumptions were ludicrous as far as I was concerned, and I did not star. In fact, at the end of the first year, Dr. Roswell Angier, then head of the psychology department, called me in and asked me, "Why don't you go away, Mrs. Ames? You will never become a psychologist and even if you did no one would hire you."

During the years in which I was a student at Yale, Clark Hull and his students were the dominating force in the psychology department. Their contempt for clinical and child psychology was not hidden. Hull and his students, especially Kenneth Spence and Neal Miller, who with their "neobehavioristic" theories of conditioning and learning dominated psychology at Yale, did not appreciate Dr. Gesell and his work.

Enough said. I endured the requirements of the psychology department and thoroughly appreciated my work as research assistant to Dr. Gesell. The good more than balanced the bad, and in 1936, at the end of three years, I did receive my degree.

Research: The Early Years, 1933–1950

Though a modest amount of my time in my years at Yale was spent in clinical work, for the most part my work with Dr. Gesell was primarily in the field of research. Few researchers can have been offered a more fruitful opportunity. Dr. Gesell, himself enamored with the cinema and its possibilities in the study of infant and child behavior, assigned me to an analysis of the massive amount of film material that had been gathered at the Yale Clinic of Child Development.

My first research thus was conducted almost exclusively by the method of cinemanalysis. Perhaps the significance of this was in my doctoral dissertation, "The Ontogenetic Organization of Prone Behavior in Human Infancy," published jointly with Dr. Gesell (Gesell & Ames, 1940). This thesis demonstrated that infant behavior does indeed develop in a patterned, predictable way.

However, the study had far more than this rather predictable outcome. It demonstrated to our surprise that behavior does not develop in what we had expected to be more or less a straight line—the infant when first placed prone on a flat surface being pretty much flexed as to arms and legs and gradually, age by age, becoming more extended. Instead, as my notes suggested, "Oddly enough this 20 weeks infant is more flexed than he was four weeks earlier." Time and again this kind of seeming regression was noted.

It was also noted that ages when arms and legs were adducted seemed to alternate with ages when they were abducted—again a lack of straight-line development. These rather simple observations eventually led to what Dr. Gesell termed a principle of "Reciprocal Neuromotor Interweaving" (Gesell, 1939).

My observations about prone behavior, and Dr. Gesell's conceptualization of this observation, fit with a notion that Dr. Frances L. Ilg of our staff was developing through the 1930s. Her concept was that just as each human being has his or her own individuality that is in some ways unique, so does each age level have its own individuality. Thus, a two-and-a-half-year-old child is not simply a bigger and more mature two-year-old but is in many ways a quite different personality. A three-and-a-half-year-old is not simply a bigger and more capable three. But rather, fitting in with our newly developing theory of Reciprocal Interweaving, ages of equilibrium seemed systematically to alternate with ages of disequilibrium as the child grows older, and also ages of inwardized behavior might alternate systematically with ages of outwardized behavior.

This notion of the way behavior develops caught on rather slowly, but now in the 1990s it is rather generally accepted by scientists and parents alike—some of whom may not even be familiar with the name Gesell. The phrase "the terrible twos" (incorrect in that it tends to be the two-and-a-half-year-old who actually is in a state of disequilibrium) is today part of common parlance.

At any rate, it does seem fair to say that this now common way of looking at child behavior had its roots in this early study of prone progression, in Dr. Ilg's inspiration that each age level does have its own individuality, and in Dr. Gesell's combining these notions into his now accepted theory of Reciprocal Interweaving.

Our findings were eventually written up in three books for parents—*Infant and Child in the Culture of Today* (Gesell, Ilg, Ames & Learned, 1943), *The Child from Five to Ten* (Gesell, Ilg, Ames & Bullis, 1946), and *Youth: The Years from Ten to Sixteen* (Gesell, Ilg & Ames, 1956).

Though professional people who are environmentally oriented have for the past seventy years or so objected vigorously to much of our work and to our basic notion that much of any individual's behavior is determined by his or her body, for some reason our descriptions of the various ages seem not to have aroused much antagonism. Not only parents but many psychologists and educators seem to accept this basic concept.

This lack of opposition is very likely due to the fact that our books that deal with the kinds of behavior to be expected at the various ages have been directed primarily to parents rather than psychologists. Parents for the most part are interested in information and advice that fits their own experience and that "works." They tend to be less contentious and less opinionated than professionals.

Though many people like to think of the broad sweep provided by viewing age changes for a long range of behavior—one to five, six to ten, ten to sixteen—it gradually became evident that most parents were primarily interested in obtaining information about *their own child's immediate age.* Thus, with the help of our attorney, Harriet Pilpel, and with the permission of Harold Grove, then our editor at Harper & Row, we began what turned out to be our most widely accepted series of books for parents. Titled, perhaps rather unimaginatively, *Your One-(Two-, Three-, Four-, Five-, Six-, Seven-, Eight-, and Nine-)Year-Old,* these are as of this writing our best-selling books, and books that do not seem to arouse the kind of opposition to our work that some of our other publications have elicited (Ames, Ilg & Haber, 1976–1987).

Your Ten to Fourteen-Year-Old (Ames, Ilg & Baker, 1988) is a revision of our earlier *Youth: The Years from Ten to Sixteen,* originally published by Harper & Row. That book, when revised at the request of the publisher, was rejected by a feminist editor on the grounds that it was "sexist and old-fashioned." We then extracted this book from Harper and shaped it into *Your Ten to Fourteen-Year-Old* to cover the upper ages of our Delacorte series.

This rather long digression from my own early research is included here to illustrate the continuity of much of the work of Dr. Gesell and his staff. One idea or bit of work so often led to the next in a seemingly inexorable progression over many decades. It also seems important because, even as of this writing, the current versions of these books for parents are being translated into Polish, German, and Chinese.

Going back to my earliest research, I should note that cinemanalysis offered an ideal method for determining the ways in which the early motor behavior of the infant (at that time a rather unknown territory) developed. Cinema records permitted the analyst to observe the same behavior over and over again, thus enabling him or her to note fine points that may indeed have been missed at the time the behavior was first observed.

At any rate, in addition to my work on prone behavior, seven other studies (for a complete listing see Ames, 1974d) were carried out between 1937 and 1945. Most of these were published in the *Journal of Genetic Psychology* or the *Genetic Psychology Monographs.* Several were also made into edited films. Other research studies published in the years before 1950 (when the original Gesell group left the university) covered such topics as "The Gesell Incomplete Man Test" (Ames, 1943), "Variant Behavior as Revealed by the Gesell Developmental Examination" (Ames & Ilg, 1943), and an analysis of imaginary companions in the young child (Ames & Learned, 1946).

A subsequent small group of studies was carried out in our nursery school and focused on observations of smiling behavior and the development of the sense of time and space and the sense of self (for a listing see Ames, 1974c). *Children's Stories,* a book about children's stories as revealing their emotional interests, was also published (Ames, 1966).

I was in an unusually favorable position so far as publishing was concerned since Dr. Gesell was an editor of both the *Journal of Genetic Psychology* and the *Genetic Psychology Monographs*. And though filmmaking was not something I would ordinarily have aspired to, it came about quite naturally as a result of my cinema studies. It was Dr. Gesell's suggestion that, after analyzing our film, both 16 mm and 35 mm, to find out how some certain behavior developed, it would be useful for me to put selected footage together to demonstrate behavior I had already described in print (for a listing see Ames, 1974b).

My very first film, published in 1938 by the *Encyclopedia Britannica,* had to do with my dissertation topic, prone progression. It was called *How Behavior Grows: The Sequential Patterning of Prone Progression.* The second, *The First Five Years of Life,* was put together in 1940 and covered characteristic behavior in the fields of motor, adaptive, language, and personal social behavior in the first five years.

The year 1941 showed quite a flurry of filmmaking, with the following titles represented: *Similarities* and (a second film) *Dissimilarities of Behavior in a Pair of Identical Twins.* I edited three more films that year: a film covering the first ten years of life of one of our research subjects, Justine Ford; a film on oral behavior patterns; and a film on visual fixation in early human infancy.

In 1942 there was a further film on vision—*Successive Localizing Visual Fixation in Early Human Infancy.* The year 1943 saw just one film, *Patterning of Leg Behavior in the Supine Infant: A Comparison of Supine and Prone Postures.*

In 1944 I edited a series of films on home behavior: *The Baby's Bath, Bottle and Cup Behavior, The Conquest of the Spoon, Self Discovery in the Mirror,* and *Early Play.* In 1946 there were two further films, *Laterality I* and *Laterality II.* And in 1948 one more, *Reciprocal Neuromotor Interweaving.* These last three mark the end of my editing of films. When our program left Yale, we were not permitted to take our films with us, bringing an end to that work. However, I was privileged to assist as one of a group that, along with Dr. Gesell and under the auspices of the Office of Naval Research, produced a half-hour color film titled *Embryology of Behavior.*

Working with Dr. Gesell

Dr. Gesell was a very stern man, demanding of himself and of those who worked with him. He did not suffer fools gladly, and the atmosphere at the clinic was extremely formal. He did not encourage staff members to chat with one another; in fact, he preferred them not to be out of their offices.

I admired him vastly and considered it a privilege to work for him. Somebody once asked me at what point I decided to remain at the clinic. I never *decided.* I felt that this was where I belonged. Dr. Gesell was not warm personally—at least not to his staff—but he was an inspiration to work for and was gratifyingly accepting of our ideas.

Fortunately, as he once put it, "Mrs. Ames and I work well together." He once complimented me by saying that he considered me to be "very logical and rational, for a woman." Happily, I am of a generation that did not take such statements amiss.

Many people throughout the world, myself included, considered him to be the leading expert in his field. I believed that, and this belief was supported by the reactions of the hundreds of visitors who came every year to observe and hear about our work. It should be noted, however, in speaking of Dr. Gesell's extremely formal manner, that after members of his staff left the university and stayed together, continuing his work without salary and at their own expense, his manner toward us became much softer and gentler. One might almost say that he was genial.

At any rate, his reaction to the closing of the clinic was remarkably stoic. Like the rest of us, I suspect that he was totally shocked and surprised and somewhat disbelieving. However, he behaved through those difficult times with remarkable dignity. He once advised me, "Don't be angry at the university, Mrs. Ames. Administrations come and go and things may well change."

He was correct in this belief. It did take several decades and there was indeed bitterness. However, largely through the skill and goodwill of Dr. Donald J. Cohen, current director of Yale's Child Study Center, a very solid, and to me surprising, rapprochement has been arrived at between the center and the Gesell Institute.

Reunion of Yale's Child Study Center and Dr. Gesell and his Work

This rapprochement is perhaps best described by Dr. Cohen in his 1993 annual report to the University.[2] In this report he noted that the Child Study Center was founded at Yale by Dr. Arnold Gesell in 1911, he being the first of its four directors. After discussing some of the theoretical reasons why a split came about and Dr. Gesell and his group then left the university, he noted that in the years since 1950 the field of child and adolescent psychiatry had changed and that there was room within our eclectic house for inner life and outer behavior, developmental factors and maturation, environment and genes. Indeed, the basic concepts of developmental psychopathology and research on gene-environment interaction were rooted in both worlds. It seemed to virtually everyone within the center that it was time for a rapprochement and restoration of Dr. Gesell to his rightful place in the pantheon of child development at Yale.

And so it has come about that Dr. Gesell is now considered to be the first director of the Child Study Center (though it was under his leadership known as the Clinic of Child Development). An Arnold Gesell professorship, now held by Dr. Linda C. Mayes, has been established at Yale. We have also established a postdoctoral Gesell fellowship as well as a Louise Bates Ames postdoctoral fellowship at Yale, both supported by Gesell funds. Additionally, I have been returned to the Yale faculty as lecturer and assistant professor emeritus at the Yale Child Study Center. Finally, a Gesell Clinic in the center will be the focus of longitudinal studies of children with developmental vulnerability such as prematurity.

Research: The Later Years, 1950–1975

The vigorous research emphasis that characterized our years at Yale did diminish somewhat once our program left the university and founded the Gesell Institute. We had been invited to leave Yale chiefly, as far as I know, because it was Yale's wish to become increasingly psychoanalytical in emphasis and we, with our determinedly biological emphasis, were definitely an obstruction.

We could not in all conscience go along with a philosophy that, at that time, tended to blame parents or other aspects of the environment for behavior and abnormalities. We were never comfortable with the notion that schizophrenic behavior was caused primarily by a "schizophrenogenic mother," or that autistic children behaved coldly toward other human beings because they (the children) had been rejected by their parents to begin with.

At any rate, our work at the Gesell Institute did continue to have a research emphasis. My own contributions in the years from 1950 to 1970 or so were along three different lines: first, projective techniques; second, constitutional psychology; and third, school readiness.

Projective Techniques

My work with projective techniques, especially with the Rorschach, is, of all my studies except perhaps my original study on prone progression, that which has interested me most. To begin with, though much of our work at Gesell was indeed a group effort, I have not been primarily the idea person. But the Rorschach research was my idea.

When we first encountered the Rorschach we were not much interested in it. It seemed complicated and difficult, and also we found that according to customary Rorschach scoring and interpretation, many children whom we considered to be quite normal appeared to be extremely troubled.

Our, I believe somewhat original, idea was: Just as many other behaviors develop in a patterned, more or less predictable way, and often children respond to various situations in a manner that would be considered atypical for the ordinary adult, so might the Rorschach response change as the individual grew older, and the more or less atypical response of normal young children might be one that in the adult could be, and was, considered abnormal.

This notion was laughed out of court by Seymour Sarason of Yale, who taught the Rorschach course I was required to take in order to become a member of the Society for Projective Techniques (of which I eventually became president). Also, some investigators, such as Kathy Wolf of Yale, insisted that the Rorschach test could not and should not be used with children. Milton Senn, also of Yale, insisted that since the Rorschach was a test of the unconscious, and since Mrs. Ames did not believe in the unconscious, she should not be using the Rorschach.

However, these handicaps aside, we did proceed as a group to study the Rorschach response in children two to sixteen years of age. In our opinion, results of our research lived up to our expectations. The Rorschach response did appear to change somewhat predictably with age, and quite normal young children did quite typically give responses that would, indeed, be considered abnormal in the adult.

Our Rorschach books, of which we are really quite proud, include: *Child Rorschach Responses: Developmental Trends from Two to Ten Years* (Ames, Learned, Métraux & Walker, 1952); *Adolescent Rorschach Responses* (Ames, Métraux & Walker, 1959); and as part of an investigation of old age, *Rorschach Responses in Old Age* (Ames, Learned, Métraux & Walker 1954). (This set of three Rorschach books was revised and republished in the 1970s by a different publisher, Brunner/Mazel).

The Rorschach was especially useful as one of the basic techniques I employed in further efforts to evaluate the emotional, intellectual, and developmental status of the aging. My work on aging was published in several papers, the most substantial of which perhaps was "The Calibration of Aging" (Ames, 1974a). (This particular paper was published in relation to my receipt of the Bruno Klopfer Distinguished Contribution Award in 1974.)

A second, beautiful, projective technique that very nicely supplements the Rorschach is the Lowenfeld Mosaic. This test, according to its originator, Dr. Margaret Lowenfeld, who herself taught it to us, gives a basic notion of how any given child *functions,* in contrast to the Rorschach, which tells how he *experiences.* Our contribution here, quite predictably, was a book providing norms for age changes in the Mosaic response that may be expected in the child from two to sixteen years of age (Ames & Ilg, 1962). A third projective technique that was used briefly but that we did not keep as a permanent part of our testing procedure was reported by Dr. Ilg and me as "Responses of three to eleven-year-old children to the Horn-Hellersberg Test" (Ames & Hellersberg, 1949).

Constitutional Psychology

A major area of investigation on which we spent vast quantities of time, money, and enthusiasm was the area of constitutional psychology, with the help of and following the method of Dr. William H. Sheldon. Dr. Richard N. Walker was in charge of this work over a period of maybe two decades. This was not my project, though I worked with Dr. Sheldon, his assistant Barbara Honeyman, Dr. Ilg, and Janet Learned in setting it up.

For many years we somatotyped all of our basic research subjects as well as children in our nursery school. We ourselves, and the parents concerned, found the concept that behavior is a function of structure and that one can tell a great deal about any individual's behavior potentials from measuring his somatotype extremely useful. Before we finally gave up on somatotyping, we had very probably the largest collection of child somatotype photographs of any group in the world. Unfortunately, this concept—that individuals differ from one another and that any of these differences are biologically determined—has always been extremely unpopular with many, and as of this writing it has fallen virtually into oblivion. Our own research has been discontinued. One can only hope that it may be revived eventually, even if not by us.

School Readiness

One further major area of research carried out at the Gesell Institute had to do with the matter of school readiness. This concept was first introduced by Dr. Gesell in 1919, when he pointed out that "there could be nothing more unscientific than the unceremonious, indiscriminating, wholesale method with which we admit children into our greatest social institution, the public school . . . I suggest a psychophysical entrance examination of every school beginner" (Gesell, 1919).

This idea lay dormant until the late 1950s and early 1960s, when Dr. Ilg and I turned our own attention to the area of education, an area that had so preoccupied Dr. Gesell several decades earlier. In the 1950s Dr. Ilg and I observed that many boys and girls referred to us because they were suffering from so-called learning disabilities (the then-popular term that followed brain injury and brain dysfunction and preceded Attention Deficit Disorder) appeared to be perfectly normal, intelligent children who were simply overplaced in school. That is, they had started too soon.

Checking on this possibility, we discovered that the last one hundred children we had seen on our school service did fall into this category. They were quite normal children but were developmentally young for their ages, had started school too soon, and were thus overplaced. It seemed reasonable to us to believe that they were having trouble in school not because they were learning disabled but merely because they were in the wrong grade.

Fortunately, the Ford Foundation agreed to support a three-year research project to be carried on in the Hurlbutt School in Weston, Connecticut. Our findings there agreed with those in our own clinical service—a substantial number of these children did appear to be in a grade ahead of the one for which their maturity or developmental level suited them.

This study was carried on by Dr. Frances L. Ilg, Dr. Richard J. Apell, Dr. Richard N. Walker, and myself. Results were published in a monograph—*School Readiness as Evaluated by Gesell Developmental, Visual and Projective Techniques* (Ilg, Ames & Apell, 1965), and more substantially in one of our major book publications—*School Readiness* (Ilg & Ames, 1964).

This book, aimed primarily at educators and psychologists, presented our basic thesis that children should be started in school, and subsequently promoted, on the basis of their behavioral age, not their age in years, and not their IQ or reading ability. We recommended that all children before entering school be given a behavior test that would determine their behavior level. We recommended that, ideally, all children be fully five years of age *behaviorally* (regardless of their birthday age) before entering kindergarten. It was, and is, our assumption that behavior or developmental age can be effectively measured through the use of the Gesell Developmental Scale.

This seemingly modest area of investigation, like our work on the individuality of the ages, and our work with projective techniques turned out to be probably of more significance than we anticipated. The whole concept of school readiness, as we have noted was first mentioned by Dr. Gesell in 1919 and picked up by us in the 1950s and 1960s, has now become one of the major areas of interest and activity of the Gesell Institute.

We have now trained a group of Gesell lecture staff members to administer our readiness tests in schools throughout he country and abroad, or to teach others to do so. Some figure that at one time in the 1980s, perhaps 20 percent of schools in this country were run "developmentally." Our aim was to see that all children entering our public or private schools should be examined before their time of entrance to determine readiness. We consider that starting a child at the "right" time, especially not starting him or her too soon, is perhaps the single most important thing a parent can do to insure or at least encourage school success. Our method of spreading this work has been to give workshops for teachers and psychologists by our own local staff or by members of our national lecture staff. As of this writing, some twenty such workshops are being given.

Clinical Work and Administration

Though I have thought of myself primarily as a researcher, especially in the early years, a good deal of my professional time for the last half century has been spent in clinical work with children. This work is described in full detail in an autobiographical chapter titled "Louise Bates Ames: Child Development and Clinical Psychology" (Ames, 1993).

So far as administration goes, as one of three founders of the Gesell Institute I have had a reasonable number of administrative responsibilities through the years. From the beginning date I have been a member of the board of directors. I was president of the board from 1971 to 1987.

So far as the institute as a whole was concerned, I was in the first two decades director of research. When Dr. Ilg retired in January 1972, Dr. Richard J. Apell and I became codirectors. This codirectorship continued until March 1, 1978, when by action of the board I was appointed acting executive director. I continued in this position until September of that year, when Dr. Sidney M. Baker became director. The title of my position varies from time to time. At present I am associate director.

LBA as a Media Psychologist

Many of the interesting aspects of my career have occurred more by accident than design. Back in the early 1950s, to the best of my knowledge, we did not have the group of individuals now known as media psychologists. Certainly it was not my aim to become one.

Newspaper Column

However, while we were a part of Yale and after we left the university, Dr. Ilg and I were in considerable demand as lecturers both to professional and parent groups in this country and abroad. It was at one such lecture, held in Darien, Connecticut, in the spring of 1952, that a man in the audience, Mr. Robert M. Hall, came to me and said, "I wish I could give you some money." Of course I asked him what he had in mind. He said he was a newspaper syndicator and it had been his dream to have the Gesell Institute (or at least the Gesell people) write a column for him. But, he said, Dr. Gesell would not even give him an interview and he knew that Yale would not permit this kind of activity anyway.

I was able to tell him that we were no longer at Yale and that Dr. Gesell was no longer the institute's director. Very quickly plans were made. Dr. Ilg and I agreed that we would write a daily column if he could sign up at least thirty newspapers. He did so, and in July 1952 we started our daily newspaper column, "Child Behavior," which soon was being published in sixty-five of the largest papers in the country, spanning the United States from Portland, Maine, to Portland, Oregon, and including such distinguished papers as the *New York World Telegram,* the *Boston Globe,* the *Washington Post,* the *Pittsburgh Post-Gazette,* the *Philadelphia Bulletin,* the *Los Angeles Times,* and many others of which I think fondly.

This column provided us not only with funds to keep the institute going but also with an unusual opportunity to present to the public our own non-Freudian point of view. Writing the columns was not especially difficult—we had plenty of material to share with the public. However, answering the mail was rather demanding. At times I sat at my desk until midnight, responding to the plaintive pleas of parents. These letters were not entirely easy to answer, because many began with the comment, "My pediatrician does not know how to handle this problem, so I am turning to you." Thus it was not just a matter of acknowledging the mail—it was, in many instances, a question of trying to solve someone's real child-behavior problems.

It is probably true that in those more conservative days Yale would not have allowed us to write a newspaper column. Certainly had Dr. Gesell still been the director of the institute he would not have approved. It was only some years later, after (or so it seemed to us) we had tested the waters, that perfectly "respectable" professional people, including Dr. Spock, began writing in magazines for the general public and appearing on television.

At any rate, I considered it a privilege to have daily newspaper space available for propounding our basic (Gesell) biological point of view. That the column probably did have an effect is suggested by the fact that Dr. Milton Senn, who had taken Dr. Gesell's place at Yale, once allegedly commented, "Mrs. Ames is the most dangerous woman in the United States because people not only believe what she says in her column but think it helps them."

Television

The column was well received. One of our most enthusiastic papers was the *Boston Globe.* Although with most papers, the syndicate's and my dealings were with promotion personnel, in the case of the *Globe* I was dealing directly with

John I. Taylor, the grandson of the founder. He invited me to give a series of lectures in towns around Boston as a "gift" from the paper. He accompanied me to these lectures. They were successful, and as a result he developed the notion that it might be a good idea for me to undertake a television series.

Television was very new in those days and, of course, just in black and white, and there was no taping. Nearly all shows, as far as I remember, were broadcast live. At any rate, Mr. Taylor took me over to Station WBZ in Boston, where we conferred with John Stilli and others of the management. John Taylor said he thought it would be a good idea for me to have a weekly television program on child behavior. They asked if I had had any experience. He said no, but that I could do it all right. They asked what kind of program we envisioned. I responded that since I felt I could go to Boston only once a week, I would not be available for rehearsals, so it would have to be a live, unrehearsed show.

They said this was a rather difficult type of program to do, but John Taylor agreed with me. So a week or two later (in the spring of 1953) I gave the first of what were to be thirteen weekly television programs. WBZ used its Studio A, a small theater. Anyone wishing to be a part of the audience arrived at the *Boston Globe* office and was brought out to the studio on a bus. The program consisted of the audience asking me questions, which I would answer. The master of ceremonies was a very capable veteran television man, Arthur Amidon.

The first thirteen-week series was successful enough that the program was continued for two years, and a weekly radio show was taped just following the program. One viewer, who apparently came to television late, once told me, "I used to hate you on radio but then when I saw you on television I realized that your voice went with your face."

WBZ liked the program because it got good ratings in the New England area and also because it "did them good" with the Federal Communications Commission as a program of presumably useful content. At the end of two years the studio told me it could not afford the entire program anymore, but for another year I was a guest on a variety program called *Swan Boat* (the performers were introduced to the audience while sitting in a boat that resembled the famous swan boats of the Boston Public Garden). This project at WBZ was successful, fun to do, and very profitable.

Since that early beginning in Boston in the 1950s, I have done a good deal of radio and television. Among the more rewarding series was one of twenty-six programs at Station WEWS in Cleveland, Ohio, that was taped at the instigation of Donald L. Perris, at that time assistant manager of the station. These programs were taped in Cleveland over a series of weekends and then distributed to stations around the country.

My next extended and serious television undertaking was a series of daily half-hour programs, taped again at WBZ in Boston and titled *Playmates/Schoolmates*. It was a nursery school on the air. It was initiated by George Moynihan, the original producer of my 1953 Boston series, who by then was a vice president of Westinghouse Broadcasting Company. The format was that of an actual nursery school. The children played for twenty minutes with their parents watching the play on a monitor in another part of the studio. In the last ten minutes of the program I appeared on the set with the parents, who asked questions either about what they had seen or about anything that interested them about their children. The message of the program was primarily that children do not need to be taught or instructed in nursery school, in addition to our usual message that behavior changes from age to age in a patterned and somewhat predictable way. These programs were aired on all the Westinghouse stations: Boston, Philadelphia, Baltimore, Pittsburgh, and San Francisco.

Through all these years, from the early 1960s to the present, I have also very frequently appeared as a guest on such popular talk programs as *The Mike Douglas Show, The Phil Donahue Show, The Oprah Winfrey Show, Sally Jessy Raphael, AM Chicago, Kennedy and Company,* and many others. I have always found being on television to be a lively, interesting activity and a wonderful way to give our developmental message about children to many people who might otherwise not come in contact with it.

Magazines and Journals

Like many psychologists these days, I have also written a good number of articles for popular magazines. Perhaps the most rewarding of these relationships was from 1971 to 1974, when I was a contributing editor of *Family Circle,* providing a monthly article for the magazine.

In spite of this popularization, however, through the years, especially in the early years, most of my articles were published in such journals as the *Journal of Genetic Psychology* (of which I was an editor for some time after Dr. Gesell's retirement), *Genetic Psychology Monographs,* and the *Journal of Projective Techniques.* Also, I was one of the original editors of the *Journal of Learning Disabilities* and continued as an editor from 1968 to 1986. During that time I contributed numerous articles and editorials.

Mentors

A mentor is customarily considered to be someone who inspires, encourages, and supports a student in his or her endeavors. My three mentors—Drs. Charles A. Dickinson, Arnold Gesell, and Frances Ilg—all did that and much, much more. They determined the profession I chose, provided an unparalleled working environment, and offered the inspiration that I—a steady but not particularly creative worker—much needed.

Dr. Dickinson

Dr. Dickinson, head of the Department of Psychology at the University of Maine in Orono, was the person directly responsible for my becoming a psychologist. I had transferred to Maine after two years at Wheaton. While at Wheaton I had taken an introductory course in psychology. It was somewhat of a disaster, and I ended up with a firm resolve never to look at psychology again. Dr. Dickinson changed all that, not by proselytizing but merely by being an unusually good teacher. After an initial course with him I took all the others offered. And when I married in the spring of my senior year, making my plan to become an attorney and join my father's firm in Portland, Maine, seem impractical, in looking for a more flexible profession that might be pursued wherever my family ended up, I chose psychology.

Dr. Dickinson not only inspired me to become a psychologist, but he transferred to me his own (unfulfilled) ambition to study with Dr. Gesell. It was his enthusiasm for Dr. Gesell and his work that led me to apply to the Clinic of Child Development at Yale for a fellowship or assistantship so that I could work there for my Ph.D. (happily, Dr. Dickinson lived long enough to see things go well for me at Yale and to meet Dr. Gesell in person).

Dr. Arnold Gesell

To anyone familiar with Dr. Gesell and his work I need not elaborate on the effect that he and his thinking had on me in the years from 1933 to 1948, when I worked as his personal research assistant. Dr. Gesell was unquestionably an inspiring mentor, though admittedly a hard taskmaster. He expected perfection of himself and of those around him. However, the opportunities he offered in the way of inspiration, in opportunities for new and innovative work, and by introducing me to scholars worldwide and their work were unparalleled. He was always extremely receptive to and accepting of my own work and ideas.

He also opened up to me the world of cinematography, a method that is not only extremely revealing of the secrets of developing child behavior but that I found so congenial that I ended up as curator of the Yale Films of Child Development. When I left the university in 1950, Dean Long and Mark May offered me a permanent assistant professorship as curator of the Yale films in return for the physical ownership of the films, about which there had been some question. At the end of one year, though the university kept the films, the assistant professorship vanished into thin air.

At any rate, Dr. Gesell's influence on my professional life was, during my years at Yale, virtually total, as can be gleaned from the number of our joint publications in my bibliography. Though the university forced me to obtain my degree in experimental psychology, I have never for a minute regretted going to Yale and working with Dr. Gesell.

Dr. Frances L. Ilg

Virtually every individual notion and idea proposed by Dr. Gesell as well as his basic philosophy were extremely congenial to my own way of thinking. Equally congenial was Dr. Ilg and her way of thinking. She was by far the most creative person I have ever known. She had more new ideas in any season (sometimes in any day or week) than many have in a lifetime. Some of these ideas, admittedly, were a little far out, and as Richard Walker of our staff once commented, she was often right for the wrong reason. But her inspirations were what kept a more pedestrian worker like me active and reasonably productive. Her especially effective ideas, so far as my own work was concerned, helped address the matter of the *personality of each age level,* and to the whole field of *readiness or unreadiness for school.*

It is a clear testimonial to Dr. Ilg's strength, vigor, creativeness, and enthusiasm that when Yale University decided to dispense with Dr. Gesell's clinic, Janet Learned and I had the courage to join with her in founding the Gesell Institute to carry on his work. Without her we would never have begun.

Individuals or Movements Opposed to Our Work

My friend Dr. William H. Sheldon, of constitutional psychology fame, once told me that most people thought he and his work were either better or worse than was actually the case. Few saw it, or him, as they really were. The same might be said, in a way, of the Gesell work. We do indeed have many admirers who have found our work extremely helpful. There are others who scorn it and oppose it violently.

The cutting edge here seems to be the individual's basic attitude toward the inevitable and probably permanent heredity-environment debate. Those who in the main believe that, as has been said, "anatomy is destiny," that to a large extent we behave as we do because of the bodies we have inherited, and that behavior is a function of structure tend to feel favorably toward the Gesell work. Those who insist that it is the environment that primarily determines behavior oppose us. Thus, back in the early part of this century, John B. Watson, who allegedly believed that the environment can make any child into anything, had a certain influence on some. Later on there were those, such as the well-known J. McV. Hunt, who believed that by doing the right thing one could raise any child's IQ by many points. Others of this environmental persuasion include Benjamin Bloom, O. K. Moore, and Burton White.

Nearly all on both sides of this argument did at least admit that the other factor (whether genetic endowment or environment) did have a certain influence. Dr. Gesell himself often made courteous reference to the importance of environment, as in his statement that "environmental factors inflect and modify but do not determine the progressions of development" (Gesell & Thompson, 1934).

At any rate, it takes no paranoia to be quite certain that the majority of individuals, groups, or movements that opposed most aspects of our work vigorously and often viciously, standing in the way of grants or other sources of support, were nearly all (though not all) those who had great confidence in the all-powerfulness of the environment and the relatively minor role heredity can play.

Certainly in the first thirty or so years of Dr. Gesell's work, the playing field seemed somewhat even. Vigorous (and seemingly exaggerated) as were the claims of the environmentalists, Dr. Gesell had not only his own brilliance and effective work but the support of Yale University behind him. Of the sometimes well over a thousand professional visitors a year who came to observe our work, the majority were complimentary. Those who insisted that the whole thing was nonsense were relatively few, though they did exist. Dr. Gesell once advised me, "Mrs. Ames, don't get so angry at these people. If we are right they will know it one day. And if we are wrong you are wasting your energy."

However, trouble was brewing. Quietly and not so quietly, Freudian forces were gathering strength, and to the surprise of many, certainly ourselves, when the time came for Dr. Gesell to retire in the late 1940s, those favoring a Freudian point of view prevailed at Yale University. A successor to Dr. Gesell was chosen and, allegedly, given five years to "get rid of" Dr. Gesell's staff, and five more years to make his own work known.

Though now, fifty years later, Freudian forces have for the most part backed off on the idea that it is the parents' behavior (the "schizophrenogenic mother") that causes schizophrenia and that it is the emotional coldness of the parents that causes the lack of social responsiveness in the autistic child, in the 1940s through the 1960s these notions did prevail and were of course antipathetic to us. The Gesell Institute, which Dr. Frances L. Ilg, Dr. Janet Learned (Rodell), and I founded to carry on and expand Dr. Gesell's work, was based on a strictly biological point of view.

Our first nearly fatal opposition came from the National Institute of Mental Health (NIMH), which had assured us that if we wished to strike out on our own in order to complete the adolescent sector of our so-called trilogy (Gesell, Ilg, Ames & Learned, 1943; Gesell, Ilg, Ames & Bullis, 1946; Gesell, Ilg & Ames, 1956), it would give us grant money to carry on this work. We did found the institute and did begin our work on the teenagers. Then NIMH turned us down, as did other sources of hoped-for funding.

Next, a major bit of our research, one that engaged our staff, efforts, and money for many years, was our work on constitutional psychology. With the help of Dr. Sheldon and his staff we set up a major investigation of somatotyping over a period of several decades. Unfortunately, this project, along with nearly all of Dr. Sheldon's work, was rejected by most psychologists, one assumes largely on the grounds that its basic premise, that behavior is a function of structure and that different bodies behave differently, is incompatible with much current thinking.

Currently, many environmentalists also oppose the major part of our work—our effort to have children start school and be subsequently promoted on the basis of their behavioral age, not their age in years, their intelligence level, or their reading ability. Our position is that perhaps at least a third of school failure might be prevented if school placement and promotion were based on the child's *readiness* for the grade in which he or she is placed. Environmentalists loudly and all too often effectively oppose what are called developmental placement programs. They insist that if any school provides a developmentally appropriate curriculum, it does not matter whether the children are ready or not (we, of course, vote for readiness *and* a developmentally appropriate curriculum). This seemingly theoretical difference of opinion actually influences the way schools are run, and in our opinion, lack of attention to readiness is the cause of much school failure.

Two other major areas in which we met with vast opposition cannot be blamed on the environmentalists but rather on the fact that we came down on the unpopular side of issues that are politically very sensitive. The first had to do with our decades-long work on vision. Since what we would contribute to a study of vision would be a study of the function rather than the structure of the eye, we were forced to choose to work with optometrists rather than with the more popular and better-accepted ophthalmologists. Though relations between these two groups have markedly improved in recent years, at that time their feelings toward each other were very hostile. Ophthalmologists castigated Dr. Gesell for his choice, threatened to take away our license,[3] and support funds became very difficult to obtain.

Another area in which we received even greater opposition had to do with our practice of medicine. In 1978, under the directorship of Dr. Sidney M. Baker, the Gesell Institute established a medical department. To our own satisfaction and delight, Dr. Baker practiced what is known as orthomolecular medicine. Once again we had chosen a highly unpopular course. Even today, though we believe that orthomolecular medicine is gradually coming into its own, there has been vast opposition to it on the part of the American Medical Association and much use of the adjective "quackery." A well-known member of the Yale medical faculty still insists that there is no connection between what one eats and one's health and behavior.

In recent years there has arisen something of an objection to the use of projective techniques, especially the Rorschach Inkblot Test. Though this was at one time one of the most widely used and most respected of the psychologist's tools, many experimental psychologists objected to the technique because, they claimed, it could not be proven to be either valid or reliable. Though we ourselves consider it a veritable X ray of the personality and use it consistently, one of our major applications for funds for studying behavior in old age was rejected primarily on the grounds that one of the instruments to be used was the Rorschach.

One final area of our work that has not been accepted or used as we had hoped is our battery of tests that we believe indicate the level of intactness or deterioration of function in the elderly. Some of the staff in institutions where we gathered data, especially Dr. Kurt Pelz, former director of the Masonic Home in Wallingford, Connecticut, actually grouped and housed residents according to our scale. However, psychologists working with the elderly, notably K. Werner Schaie, maintained that with the elderly, as with children, behavior does not change with age but rather that a sixteen-year-old would behave differently from a fifteen-year-old *because he was born in a different year.* An environmental interpretation if ever there was one.

In general, it seems to have been parents rather than psychologists who have found our work not only acceptable but useful (their most common comments about our books are "You could have been right there in our house" or "You could be describing my child"). Our insistence on the importance of the child's biological background and the fact that we have in several instances chosen the unpopular side of highly controversial issues has cost us among professionals.

How the Gesell Work Is Currently Faring

The preceding section makes it quite clear that many aspects of the Gesell work have met with substantial opposition through the years. However, in general as of this writing, the climate for acceptance of the Gesell position seems increasingly favorable. One handicap to our work has been the fact that many followers of Piaget have behaved as if it were a question of Piaget or Gesell—as if there were no room at the top for both. This strong pro-Piaget, anti-Gesell feeling that has prevailed in some quarters for several decades is now seemingly dying out. Many Piagetians now admit that both men made substantial contributions and held positions that were not contradictory.

A small step in the direction of furthering an area of investigation that we ourselves have used and consider extremely important, constitutional psychology, has been made in the work of Stella Chess. Her basic thesis is that children differ from one another at least to a large extent because they are temperamentally different, that is, are born different. Unfortunately, Chess does not agree that these genetic differences are rooted in body structure. But at least her work shows a certain respect for the genetic basis of behavior.

As noted earlier, many parents in this country and abroad do believe in the Gesell work because it describes their children as they themselves see them. And to some extent teachers, too, find our work helpful (this acceptance by educators is admittedly not universal). One basic aspect of the Gesell findings that has for substantially more than half a century been well accepted by many (even though in some instances by the somewhat derivative acceptance of changing our material very slightly and presenting it under another label, as in the case of the Denver Developmental) is the Gesell Normative Assessment Scale, sometimes known as the Gesell/Yale norms. Revised frequently since they were first published in 1925, these norms are currently being once more revised by Gesell and Yale researchers.

An important factor in the acceptance of our work appears to be a change in the atmosphere of developmental psychology (I may be overly optimistic about this, and admittedly my sample is small). But at least to some extent the bitter personal antipathies and antagonisms that during much of the century have existed between child-behavior specialists with different points of view seem to be diminishing. A striking example of this change is the already mentioned evolving positive relationship between Yale's Child Study Center and the Gesell Institute. Also, as in years past, countries other than the United States continue to show substantial interest both in our book publications and, in some instances (as for instance currently in Thailand) in our normative scales. In general it seems safe to say that the Gesell work is enjoying much greater popularity now than it has at any time since our very early days at Yale.

Reflections on the Future of the Field

It is somewhat presumptuous for anyone over eighty to fantasize about the field. I, like many octogenarians, am not as informed as one might wish about the *present* state of developmental psychology. Like many others, I have fallen somewhat behind in keeping up with the literature. However, if *Child Development,* the voice of the Society for Research in Child Development, is to be taken as more or less typical, much effort, paper, and ink have for some time been extended on research efforts that to some extent have not turned out to be particularly enlightening.

Certainly our field has come an unbelievably long way in the past century. In the early 1900s there was virtually no systematic body of information about child behavior. Today there is almost more information than one can keep up with. We have also emerged from beneath a very dark cloud that prevailed in the 1940s to the 1970s—the all-pervasive insistence of government people (NIMH), mental hygiene clinics, and nearly all departments of psychiatry, that parents are largely responsible for all sorts of deviant behavior, as for instance schizophrenia and autism.

A big improvement has been that the field of clinical psychology is now accepted and established—students are permitted to attain their graduate degrees in this field. This seems a tremendous victory for any psychologist who cares about human behavior. It has now become respectable to study the actual behavior of real live children. Admittedly, those who specialize in cognitive behavior sometimes seem not to get much farther down than the neck, though perhaps most would agree with Gesell's insistence that "mind manifests itself in everything the individual does." Though some experimental psychologists still reject test measures and test results that cannot be proved to be valid and reliable (admirable concepts but sometimes hard to prove), it is hoped that a majority of child specialists now deal with the real behavior of real children in real life.

An interesting and, to me, encouraging trend is suggested by Emily Bushnell and J. Paul Boudreau of Tufts University (Bushnell & Boudreau, 1993). These authors note, "As this special section in *Child Development* celebrates there has been a dramatic resurgence of interest in motor development during infancy." This having long been an area of my own particular concern, I naturally welcome such a resurgence.

At perhaps the opposite extreme, there has, happily, been a substantially increasing concern to relate what we know about child behavior to the severe problems of the inner cities, as in work currently being carried out at the Yale Child Study Center and elsewhere. Such theoretical papers as Sandra Scarr's (1993) "Biological and Cultural Diversity: The Legacy of Darwin for Development" have much to offer, especially for people new to the field.

I personally find some of the work of medically trained investigators like Doris Rapp (1991), who relate child behavior, especially aberrant behavior, to nutrition and especially to allergic reactions to certain foods, particularly helpful. Dr. Rapp's approach to such behavior problems as the currently labeled Attention Deficit Disorder, as exemplified in the book *Is This Your Child?* seems to me to show much promise. In fact, it may well be together with investigators in other fields, especially those trained in medicine, that some of the most effective work in our own field may be accomplished.

I am basically optimistic about the future. However, a combination of theoretical conflicts and politics still offers hazards for parents, psychologists, educators, and the children they care about. There are still, in my opinion, all too many who will not admit that children inherit their bodies, and that those bodies to some extent at least limit what the children can do or become. Add to this the civil libertarian position that nobody can be kept out of anything, that to do so infringes on his or her civil rights. Thus many schools are doing away with special classes for the gifted and talented as well as special classes for children with severe problems and are mushing everybody together into so-called mainstream classes. Unfortunately, political considerations often determine what kind of research and educational practice can be funded and permitted.

The increase of knowledge in many fields, in medicine for example, is truly awe inspiring. Whether we as a field, even if permitted, can begin to approach this kind of increase in understanding and usefulness is in my mind a serious question.

Notes

1. This same daughter, Joan Ames Chase, grew up to follow in my own professional footsteps. She received her Ph.D. in psychology from the University of Maine, coauthored with me a book, *Don't Push Your Preschooler,* wrote several articles, and did research on school readiness. My granddaughter, Carol Chase Haber, M.A., a school psychologist, is a coauthor of several books (Ames, Ilg & Haber, 1976–1987).

2. For more detail on Dr. Cohen's report, see Ames, "History of the Gesell Institute," privately published, 1994.

3. A somewhat empty threat because no such license existed.

References

Ames, L. B. (1933). *Growth of motor coordination in one child from birth to two years.* Unpublished master's thesis, University of Maine.

Ames, L. B. (1943). The Gesell Incomplete Man test as a differential indicator of "average" and "superior" behavior in preschool children. *Journal of Genetic Psychology, 62,* 217–274.

Ames, L. B. (1966). Children's stories. *Genetic Psychology Monograph, 74,* 337–396.

Ames, L. B. (1974a). The calibration of aging. *Journal of Personality Assessment, 38,* 505–529.

Ames, L. B. (1974b). A series of films. *Journal of Personality Assessment, 38,* 520–522.

Ames, L. B. (1974c). A series of papers based on nursery school observation. *Journal of Personality Assessment, 38,* 522.

Ames, L. B. (1974d). A series of seven papers on motor behavior, based on cinemanalysis. *Journal of Personality Assessment, 38,* 520–521.

Ames, L. B. (1993). Louise Bates Ames: Child development and clinical psychology. In Eugene Walker (Ed.), *The history of clinical psychology in autobiography, Volume II* (pp. 67–99). Pacific Grove, Calif.: Brooks/Cole.

Ames, L. B. & Chase, J. (1974). *Don't push your preschooler.* New York: Harper & Row.

Ames, L. B. & Hellersberg, E. (1949). Responses of three- to eleven-year-old children to the Horn-Hellersberg test. *Rorschach Research Exchange and Journal of Personality Assessment, 13,* 415–432.

Ames, L. B. & Ilg, F. L. (1943). Variant behavior as revealed by the Gesell developmental examination. *Journal of Genetic Psychology, 63,* 273–305.

Ames, L. B., & Ilg, F. L. (1962). Mosaic patterns of American children. New York: Hoeber.

Ames, L. B., Ilg, F. L. & Baker, S. M. (1988). *Your ten- to fourteen-year-old.* New York: Delacorte.

Ames, L. B., Ilg, F. L. & Haber, C. C. (1976–1987). *Your one-year-old.* New York: Delacorte. (A series of books through *Your nine-year-old*).

Ames, L. B. & Learned, J. (1946). Imaginary companions and related phenomena. *Journal of Genetic Psychology, 69,* 147–167.

Ames, L. B., Learned, J., Métraux, R. W. & Walker, R. N. (1952). *Child Rorschach responses.* New York: Hoeber.

Ames, L. B., Learned, J., Métraux, R. W. & Walker, R. N. (1954). *Rorschach responses in old age.* New York: Hoeber.

Ames, L. B., Métraux, R. W. & Walker, R. N. (1959). *Adolescent Rorschach responses.* New York: Hoeber.

Bushnell, E. W. & Boudreau, J. P. (1993). Motor development and the mind: The potential role of motor abilities as a determinant of aspects of perceptual development. *Child Development, 64,* 1005–1021.

Gesell, A. (1919). Mental hygiene and the public school. *Mental Hygiene, 3,* 4–5.

Gesell, A. (1939). Reciprocal interweaving in neuromotor development: A principle of spiral organization shown in the patterning of infant behavior. *Journal of Comparitive Neurology, 70,* 161–180.

Gesell, A. & Ames, L. B. (1940). The ontogenetic organization of prone behavior in human infancy. *Journal of Genetic Psychology, 56,* 247–263.

Gesell, A., Ilg, F. L. & Ames, L. B. (1956). *Youth: The years from ten to sixteen.* New York: Harper & Row.

Gesell, A., Ilg, F. L., Ames, L. B. & Bullis, G. (1946). *The child from five to ten.* New York: Harper & Row.

Gesell, A., Ilg, F. L., Ames, L. B. & Learned, J. (1943). *Infant and child in the culture of today.* New York: Harper & Row.

Gesell, A. & Thompson, H. (1934). *Infant behavior: Its genesis and growth.* New York: McGraw-Hill.

Ilg, F. L. & Ames, L. B. (1964). *School readiness.* New York: Harper & Row.

Ilg, F. L., Ames, L. B. & Apell, R. J. (1965). School readiness as evaluated by Gesell developmental, visual and projective techniques. *Genetic Psychological Monograph, 11,* 61–91.

Rapp, D. (1991). *Is this your child?* New York: William Morrow.

Scarr, S. (1993). Biological and cultural diversity: The legacy of Darwin for development. *Child Development, 64,* 1333–1353.

2

James Emmett Birren

Conventional histories of science tend to portray the sequence of findings: what was accomplished and discovered. In this pattern, histories of psychology usually present pictures of an orderly development and accumulation of information and a logical flow of ideas. Little is said about the twists and turns in individual lives that play a role in shaping careers and the growth of scientific knowledge. In contrast, autobiographical histories of science indicate why certain pursuits were undertaken as well as mistakes and dead ends and, if the authors are candid, reveal the role of chance in research careers.

Personal Background

Chance is clearly evident in my life. At my birth on April 4, 1918, I promptly fell on the floor in the delivery room, causing consternation for the doctor, nurse, my mother, and presumably for me, who turned purple. Years later, reconstruction of the event with my mother established that she was aware of what had happened, because the ether she had been given had worn off. After my delivery she was conscious of a dispute between the physician and the attending nurse. Apparently the nurse had not put an umbilical cord clip in the obstetrics bag, and the physician complained that he would have done better had the charwoman assisted him. The nurse left the room to find a clip while the doctor in his anger went looking for one in the other direction. Meanwhile, I had been left lying on a small table adjacent to my mother, from which I was pulled by the expulsion of the placenta. When they returned to the room, I was an inconvenient mess on the floor. My mother said, "I will never forget the look on the doctor's face when he saw you lying on the floor." My mother also told me that as she left the hospital with her baby, the nursery attendant mentioned that I was "better now." All these events left uncertainty and the question in my mother's mind: Better than what?

I have the impression that the family did not expect me to survive the fall from the delivery room table. In fact, the doctor must have been so rattled that he did not record my birth. Twenty years later, when I needed evidence of my birth, I discovered there was no recorded birth certificate. The doctor was still alive at that time and signed my handwritten birth certificate application. I became a rare individual in that my birth certificate is in my own handwriting. This event characterizes one of the underlying themes of my life: I have to do it myself.

I had a brother, Raymond Phillip Birren, who was two years older and much sturdier, taller, and muscular than I. While I was by no means small at six feet, he towered above me. Perhaps I might have been taller had I not been dropped on the floor at birth!

My mother and father were simple folks, both children of immigrants from western Europe. My mother's family came from the Rhine area in Germany and bore the name Kolkmann. My father's family came from Luxembourg with the name Birren, the meaning of which appears to refer to pears. Historically, *Birren* appears on a Roman map of England dating from the time of the Roman Hadrian, who had built a wall across northern England. The name on the map may have been of a farm, a pear orchard, or some settlement. The puzzle in my mind is whether the name was carried from the continent to England by Roman troops or whether it was carried by troops to the continent from England.

My father's family was Roman Catholic and my mother converted from Protestantism to marry my father. I was baptized in Saint Benedict's Church in Chicago, the same church in which my parents were married. My father, I believe, was in the second graduating class of the church's elementary school, which was near where his family lived in northwest Chicago. My father told me tales of his swimming in the Chicago River when it was a winding rural stream. Later it became an integral part of the Chicago sewage system. He also told me of his walks along the riverbank cutting trees for winter firewood.

When I was about four and a half, my father moved his family to a then rural area west of Chicago called Saint Charles. Unlike Chicago, where I was confined in a small apartment or small outside area, I could wander out of our small country cottage, and my mother did not need to worry about me. I made acquaintances with the farmers in the area and could get rides down Main Street on the farmers' horses and wagons. I found that the world was a wonderful place to explore. My confidence in people, places, and events may go back to that period of childhood exploration.

As I recall my elementary school education, there were no teachers who took an exceptional interest in me or, on the other hand, took an extreme dislike to me. There were few, if any, nursery schools or kindergartens in the area, and most children jumped from neighborhood play into first grade. My brother, who was in third grade, had the task on the first day of taking me to school. He left me outside the door of the first-grade room, where I remained standing until the nun, Sister Gregory, opened the door and asked me what I was doing there. I must have muttered the right words, for she took me into the class and pointed me to a seat. I was formally enrolled in Our Lady of Mercy School, to which my parents paid one dollar a month tuition. Adjacent to the school building was a playground area where the school had an annual carnival for fund-raising purposes since the one dollar a month did not pay much in the way of expenses.

The carnival's Ferris wheel intrigued me so much that I went back to our family apartment, took the tiny chest in which I saved coins, and went back to the carnival and bought a whole series of tickets. I sat out my time at the carnival riding on the Ferris wheel. In second grade, I invited a neighboring girl out to have a chocolate soda, which cost a dime. Her mother was surprised but agreeable to my invitation. I remember sitting side by side with the girl on a high fountain stool having a soda for some mysterious compulsive reason I did not understand.

By the time I was in third grade we moved farther northwest, and my brother and I went to Our Lady of Victory School. I became more intrigued with the mysteries of the church and wanted to be an altar boy and perhaps a priest. This fantasy was derailed, for my brother's reputation preceded me. I still feel Raymond was much brighter than I, but he was also much more belligerent. The nuns had ignored his left-handed predispositions and made him write with his right hand. I believe the forced change in his handedness contributed to his belligerency in the classroom.

When Raymond was in fifth grade he could roller-skate to the public library, about three-quarters of a mile away, and get a collection of books. For some reason there was little restriction on him, and the books he checked out opened my eyes to reading, although I did not have much grasp of the facts of life. My brother would occasionally do nice things for me, but he would not have much to do with me; I was the "little twerp."

After the school day the kids went home, changed clothes, and poured out of the apartments and houses into the empty lots to play. To their comfort, parents knew very little about what the boys were doing and the risks they were taking. How boys grow up, drop their animal-like behavior, and become reasonable people is beyond me (or do they?).

All of us had nicknames in those days. "Skinny" lived up the block and my brother was "Lefty." For a short interval I was called "Dreamy" because of an offhand comment made by a teacher. Teachers in the public school were required to write some descriptive comments about the students. One day a group of us clustered around Ms. Doyle's desk and asked her what she had written. She candidly told us, telling me that I had a tendency to be dreamy.

My religious upbringing presented me with a major problem in my early teens. My father was indifferent about his Catholicism, though my mother, as a convert, pursued her obligation to have my brother and me educated as Catholics. I entered into a long and fretful relationship with the Catholic Church in my teens. My brother Raymond and I were sent to Catholic schools until we moved far out to the northwest corner of Chicago, when we went to a public school. My brother and I often played baseball with the neighbor boys after school or street hockey on roller skates, among other pants-tearing activities.

At about age fourteen I began to find myself at odds with what the nuns had taught me, and it seemed to me that I became involved in a deep struggle with the church. The scary fairy tales that the nuns had told us to keep us disciplined as children had repercussions. We had been told that God could read every mind and he always knew what we were thinking and doing. We had to be clean in thought and deed or we would burn eternally in hell; the ground itself would open up and swallow us.

As a young boy I dutifully wanted to become an altar boy and then a priest, but later, when tension arose in me, I apparently felt that I had to break with the church or be broken myself. When I was twenty-one I retreated to a psychoanalyst's couch to resolve the internal warfare between my tendencies and my upbringing. My mentor at the Chicago Psychoanalytic Institute was Dr. Martin Grotjahn. He began to encourage me to become a nonmedical analyst. However, World War II broke out and changed his plans as well as mine.

I graduated from the Prussing Elementary School in June of 1932 and that fall entered Carl Schurz High School. The high school was so crowded that it had satellite groupings of portable buildings in three different areas in the northwest portion of the city. These buildings were self-contained metal teaching huts, and each had a heating stove in one corner to keep the room liveable in the cold Chicago winters. Connecting these huts was a series of wooden walkways that were elevated about a foot and a half off the ground to keep our feet out of the snow and water.

I entered a technical course at the high school since I thought I would be an engineer. In addition to the technical courses, I took the college prep courses. At the end of the first year we were transferred to the main building, which was about two and a half miles from our house. I had made a friend during that first year, Al Edahl, and we would occasionally walk home in order to save the seven-cent streetcar fare. If we accumulated enough savings, we could get a hamburger for ten cents.

One of the impressive things about the high school was its size and facilities, with three gymnasiums and two auditoriums. In the main auditorium the school had installed a pipe organ. I doubt if there are many public high schools today with a pipe organ. The tech-boys went through a sequence of well-equipped wood, pattern, forge, foundry, and machine shop classes. Looking back, I am startled to realize that we cast molten brass and steel objects in the foundry. Today, the mere idea of casting molten steel (at 3,000° Fahrenheit) in a high school shop sends shivers down my spine. In forge shop we learned to pound white-hot metal into useful objects under the beetle eyes of a short, round teacher. The discipline required and the risks involved using the old-fashioned methods of forging are staggering. Each student had his own coal-burning forge, where he made his fire and kept the temperature correct for heating the metal. We had anvils, tongs, and sledges to beat the reluctant metal into shape. Today, somewhere in my crowded garage, I still have a hammer, wrench, calipers, and other things I made in these shops.

Since no one in my family had gone to college, there was no clear pattern for me to follow. When Raymond graduated from high school, he decided to go to the local junior college. That seemed to pave the way for me, but there was no parental pressure for it or against it. I also decided to go to the Wright Junior College, and I continued my interest in technical subjects. At that time I had a fantasy about going on to the University of Illinois for a degree in engineering after I finished junior college. The country was still in an economic depression, however, and getting an engineering degree did not seem to be a useful step. So with two years of math, science, and other subjects, I entered the Chicago Teachers College, reasoning that I might at least get a steady job teaching school. At Teachers College, my first intellectual awakenings occurred. One of the instructors of zoology, to stimulate our interests, had us subscribe to a journal of genetics. Other instructors began to show more interest in me, and I responded.

One of the influential teachers was an art instructor, Arturo Fallico, who stirred my interest in philosophy, although I had not taken a single course in it. Together we created the Philosophy Club. Earlier, in high school, I had been president of the Engineering Club, and in junior college I was president of the Engineering Club. But those experiences were more passive; the Philosophy Club was something entirely new.

When I had turned twenty, two friends and I decided to lease a gas station. I went to school during the day, one of us went to night school, and the third was working a day job but needed extra money. We began our investment by collecting four hundred dollars from our personal savings to buy supplies. We paid ourselves the handsome sum of twenty-seven and a half cents an hour! Our gasoline sold for $1.05 for seven gallons. Oil was fifteen cents a quart. At these prices there was not much profit in our sales, though other costs were low. Across the street we could buy a hot beef sandwich with mashed potatoes and gravy for twenty-five cents.

I bought a used car for fifty dollars and had a collection of people that I would drive back and forth to Teachers College on a ride-sharing basis. One of the riders played in a band on the weekends to earn a few dollars. One day he fell to talking about a popular drummer, Gene Krupa. He surprised us all by telling us that Krupa used marijuana. We were curious, and he told us more about the drugs that were beginning to be used before World War II.

Another instructor, David Kopel, responded to my growing interest in psychology and suggested I volunteer for a summer as a research assistant at the Elgin State Hospital to learn new skills and ideas. The suggestion led to a break in my regular summer employment tradition, in the gas station I operated with two other friends. Following Kopel's suggestion, I went to Elgin State Hospital, where my eyes were opened. The hospital was a high-level professional organization, with Dr. Phyllis Whittman in charge of the psychology department. I learned to administer intellectual tests, participated in staff meetings, and watched a neuropsychiatrist, a German refugee, perform postmortem examinations of cadavers.

Another eye-opening experience for me was becoming acquainted with a group of divinity students who were in residence at the hospital. These were very bright students, some from Ivy League schools, who came out of very different backgrounds, and I was caught up in a new culture of language and personal behavior. The man who was coordinating the group was Richard Eastman, a young graduate student in English from Yale University. Eastman subsequently finished his Ph.D. at the University of Chicago and later became chairman of a Midwest university English department. In retrospect, it seems strange to have an intellectual door opened while working at a mental institution, but this time was my doorway into a style of life that I had never before experienced. I was so motivated by the summer experience that I decided to go on to graduate school in psychology at Northwestern University. Dr. Whittman recommended me to Northwestern, and I was admitted in the summer of 1941. But by then the war clouds were already gathering.

My brother Raymond and I had to register in 1940 for the military draft with the selective service. Both of our numbers came up in the summer of 1941, but Raymond was deferred because he had a perforated eardrum. When I was called in to the local draft board for my physical examination, I discovered the exams were held in an empty store. Thin partitions were put up so the various local doctors could examine the draftees. As I sat waiting, I heard them discussing my status. My brother had been deferred and therefore they did not want to defer me, even though I was a graduate student at the university. They also noted that I had a very fast pulse, tachycardia, which was moderately disqualifying. Later, I realized that any young person being examined under those circumstances and listening to the discussions through the thin walls would not only have a fast heart rate but perhaps some other symptoms as well. In any event, I was given a short-term deferment to continue my studies at Northwestern University.

My wife, Betty, and I met in a graduate class on schools of psychology at Northwestern University in the summer of 1941. Thus began a relationship that has lasted over fifty years.

As a graduate student in the Department of Psychology, I gravitated toward Robert Seashore, who seemed to have an affinity for mechanical devices and liked measurements of motor skills. Employed as his assistant, I found myself making some instruments for measuring hand tremor and reaction time. We seemed to understand each other; he knew how to use my mechanical skills and encouraged me to develop some matching verbal skills. My intellectual ability profile at that time would have been high spatial, high quantitative, and low verbal.

Robert Seashore was a good mentor for me. Since he was interested in mechanical things, he helped me make a transition from "things" to "ideas." He had a strong family orientation and once told me that a man was only one-third alive until he got married, and not wholly alive until he had children.

War broke out on December 7, 1941. That Sunday morning, Betty and I had gone into downtown Chicago to have lunch with her father, because he was passing through from Cleveland. He brought rumors about war, which sensitized us to the fact that the probability of war was not a product of a news announcer's enthusiasm. On that day, many of the graduate students were in an old house that contained the offices of the psychology department. It was a wooden structure that had in the basement a shop, and the many bedrooms in its three floors were converted into offices. That Sunday afternoon the graduate students clustered around the radio and heard the news that war had broken out. About an hour later one of the professors came through and told us there was nothing to it, "don't worry." How wrong he was. By the end of the term the graduate students were scattering into the military services and shipping out.

Shortly after Pearl Harbor there was a great move in the psychology department to do war-related research. Andrew Ivy, chairman of the physiology department, had contacted Seashore to develop a project that would measure the use of amphetamines to relieve fatigue. The motivation for the research was apparently derived from the North African war. The war there was being fought between the British and the Germans under General Rommel. Rommel pursued the British at an unusual pace as they retreated. That is, the Germans would drive for hours beyond the usual day. We were told that amphetamines had been discovered in some of the captured German gear, which may have contributed to that army's ability to stay awake long hours and yet perform efficiently.

Ivy and Seashore had organized a project on amphetamines and fatigue at Fort Sheridan, Illinois, with three graduate students. A physiologist, Stanley Harris, a psychologist, A. C. VanDusen, and I, together with Seashore, went into the field at Fort Sheridan to measure the effects of fatigue and the counteracting effects of amphetamines. Soldiers went on long forced marches followed by continuous guard duty, requiring twenty-four hours of wakefulness. We measured them on a series of sensory motor tests such as a photoelectric hand-eye coordination test or aiming test, an auditory-reaction-time test, and a measure of hand tremor. The troops were given alternately one of four types of capsules: a sugar placebo, caffeine, and two types of amphetamines.

This research was quickly expanded to measuring the same behavioral characteristics in tank drivers under forced wakefulness at Fort Knox, Kentucky. We then went to the army desert camp in Indio, California, where troops were prepared to go to Africa. All of this was a vast new experience for me: the travel, military camp life, and the necessity to adapt to the conditions of tent life in the desert. While in the desert VanDusen developed heat exhaustion under the dehydrating 120° Fahrenheit temperatures, and I had a touch of it for one day. Obviously, there was no air conditioning in our tents. Professor Seashore went on all of our trips, participated in the measurements, and seemed to like the novel circumstances of our travel and living arrangements.

Eventually, all of our results were analyzed and passed on to the appropriate authorities. Clearly, the amphetamines combatted sleepiness. Caffeine did also, but it tended to produce hand tremor. After the data collection was over and the project came to an end, Dr. Ivy told me that I would have to either enter the military or go to medical school. Ivy had both a medical degree and a Ph.D. The medical degree, he said, was so that he could tell administrators to go to hell when he needed to. He felt he could always go into practice as a physician. That did not seem like a good enough reason for having two advanced degrees to me, so I elected to follow the military route. I was commissioned an ensign in the Hospital Corps of the U.S. Navy and told to report to the Naval Medical Research Institute in Bethesda, Maryland, in June of 1943. I was extremely lucky. Not only was it a privilege to get such an assignment, but it happened before I had completed my Ph.D. I had already filed my master's thesis, but I was the least educated and experienced person among the group of first-class scientists I was assigned to join. In addition, it was particularly odd to go immediately from civilian life to military life overnight.

My papers for my navy commission were processed in the spring of 1943, and on June 5 I left Betty's family home in Cleveland on a train for Washington, D.C. I boarded the train in civilian clothes and got off the train a very uncertain young man in a military uniform. A few weeks earlier I had been sworn in to the naval reserve. Things could move quickly in those days. I stayed in a downtown hotel one night and the next day reported for duty to both the commanding officers at the National Naval Medical Center and the Naval Medical Research Institute.

The Navy Years

The transformation of James Birren during the three years at the Naval Medical Research Institute was startling. There were scientists from major American universities carrying out research projects related to the navy war effort. The chief of my unit was a biophysicist, Harold Blum, a professor from the University of California at Berkeley. Also in the unit was a Ph.D. in psychology from Yale, M. B. Fisher, a young physiologist with a Ph.D. from Berkeley, M. Morales, and a physicist from Johns Hopkins University, Richard Lee. I was assigned to many different projects, ranging from the study of motion sickness to the effects of oxygen deprivation to visual dark-adaptation.

One major project was research on men's response to climate changes. The U.S. Navy had ships that were primarily intended to sail in the cool waters of the North Atlantic. In the Pacific, ships were sailing closed up under high external temperatures, which led to excessive internal heat and humidity. The navy was concerned that sailors could develop heat rash in response to the high heat and humidity, with consequent infection. Because of fire hazard, the men's bunks had to be covered, which led to the accumulation of moisture in the mattresses and sheets. This was an ideal circumstance for developing heat rash, irritation, and infection. It was also thought that the buttoned-up ship conditions required by wartime emergencies and high heat led to behavioral exhaustion among the crew. Because of this, the navy was beginning to experiment with ways of cooling the ships, and our research task was to determine if cooling improved the efficiency of the men.

I was collaborating with investigators with different styles of methodology and different personal behavioral patterns on a wide range of research projects. We were required to file research reports analogous to research papers, with references and statistical analyses of the data. Within three years I probably participated in about two dozen reports. Sometimes I was the last of six authors; occasionally I was the first or the sole author. My involvement in projects seemed to depend on the principle of propinquity: Was I around when a project began and did I have any relevance to the subject matter, especially as my statistical expertise was reasonably up-to-date at that time?

One project involved my collaboration with a dentist, Commander Carl Schlack. He had gotten duplicate records of dental examinations conducted in boot camps in the United States, and this data was analyzed by region and other variables (Schlack & Birren, 1946). One of the surprising findings was that Boston had the highest number of dentists per capita and its young sailors also had the poorest teeth. This convinced me that although dental repair work is important, prevention is vital and can easily be neglected. This principle I think can be generalized across most medical areas. *Time* magazine reported on the findings from the navy dental study based on our *Science* article and referred to me as a dentist!

I was once assigned to work with a physiologist from Columbia University, Barry King, on the evaluation of an artificial resuscitation device. Dogs were used to test the efficacy of the machine. I knew nothing about animal experimentation, but one learns fast under wartime conditions.

Time went fast and brought along new experiences, such as traveling from Boston to Halifax in a convoy of ships going to Europe. We were studying seasickness aboard landing craft (LSTs, or landing ship, tank), and we tried to evaluate the effects of antiseasickness remedies on the troops headed to Europe.

Later, I was assigned with three other colleagues to a battleship, the USS *Washington*, undergoing repair in Bremerton, Washington. We were to go into the Pacific theater of operations, but the war ended before we could leave port. Instead, we sailed from Bremerton through the Panama Canal to the Navy yard in Philadelphia. En route, my colleagues and I made many observations about the types of factors involved in sick call, what it was like being in the sixteen-inch gun turrets during firing practice or in the fire-control center of the ship. I learned that the guns were not fired like a shotgun, with a single pull of a trigger, but rather the command to fire was released to a mechanical computer that calculated the optimum firing time in relation to the roll, pitch, and scend of the ship, along with target characteristics involving its range and speed. A shell was fired when the computer achieved a solution to the equation. I was impressed by the similarities of the gun-firing process to the central nervous system regulation of motor behavior, involving not only our intentions to act but the complex input of the vestibular apparatus, vision, and cerebellum in modifying the output of our motor system.

It was sobering to see a huge shell placed in the rifle and the large bags of powder rammed, and it was awesome to be in the turret of sixteen-inch guns as they fired. The loud noise was outside; inside, it was more of a thud with a tremendous recoil of the rifle barrel into the turret area. Each turret was a four-floor silo that had incredibly thick steel walls. This meant that if an enemy shell was dropped on the top of the turret and there was an explosion, the top and bottom would blow out. Because the entrances to the turrets were secured, the ship itself would not be in danger in such a case.

My colleague Manuel Morales, the physiologist, could find a research project almost anywhere. We collaborated and analyzed the sick-bay records of the battleship and discovered that the most frequent complaints were skin and foot problems. Occasionally a seaman would drink hair tonic or some other lotion with a high alcohol content, which would have serious side effects requiring medical care.

One custom aboard ship that stuck out in my mind was that quite a few of the men had an earring in one ear. I was told this was the privilege of men who had gone down with a ship. One could clearly see the number of experienced men on board this ship who had previously gone down with another navy ship. The significance of the single male earring has been lost in its transition from marking survival of a near-fatal event to a contemporary decorative style.

I discovered that in large research organizations one tends to develop research projects and publish with one's professional neighbors, even though they come from different fields. In addition to the dentist, I have published with ophthalmologists, biochemists, psychiatrists, exercise physiologists, and internists. There seems to be a common objective in scientific pursuits regardless of the field of specialization. I also observed that people who need to cooperate and gain mutual understanding are able to do so. My period in the navy gave me the skill to get along with people with widely different backgrounds in approaching research on shared problems.

At the end of the war, the staff at the Naval Medical Research Institute soon began to vanish as people went back to universities. Universities were expanding rapidly with the growth of returning veterans who received GI educational benefits. I had about a year left on my Ph.D. work at Northwestern University and obtained a predoctoral fellowship from the National Institutes of Health (NIH). I remember mailing the fellowship application in Washington, D.C., while Betty and I were walking with Angus and Jean Campbell. It was an odd feeling to put my future into the mailbox. I was pleasantly surprised by receiving the award of the fellowship and also an invitation to meet with the director of the NIH. Today the NIH could not afford such personal contact between the director and fellowship trainees, who now number into the thousands per year. The director and I fell into a conversation about our Midwest backgrounds—he had gone to a college in Minnesota. He was a little surprised that I used the term "experimental psychology" in my curriculum vitae. He said they did not use the term *experimental* in other fields: "We assumed that all sciences can be experimental." He quizzed me about why I had put that adjective in front of psychology, but I do not remember my reply.

In 1946 Betty and I returned to Northwestern for the fall semester, and I took my qualifying exams from a new faculty. It was strange coming back to the university campus after having spent a period of three years working in a highly technical facility with great support staff. The new chairman of the psychology department was my professor, Robert Seashore. The faculty allowed me to use my investigations of motion sickness as a data source for my dissertation. Because the dissertation involved a bit more physiological reasoning and Seashore was busy with the department, he shared the supervisory role with the physiological psychologist Donald Linsley, who had just arrived from Brown University.

Prior to receiving my degree, I had agreed to take a position in Baltimore with Nathan Shock, whom I had met during the war. He had been a colleague of Harold Blum's at Berkeley and of others I knew at the Naval Medical Research Institute. He liked my broad experience with difference kinds of measures because he himself had been a joint doctoral student of Baird Hastings and Louis Thurstone, a biochemist and a psychologist. Perhaps he saw in me a kind of young hybrid that reflected his background.

Nathan Shock was recruited from Berkeley to organize a gerontology research center under the auspices of the National Institutes of Health. It was to be located at the Baltimore City Hospitals, and Shock came to Baltimore on December 7, Pearl Harbor day, 1941, to get ready for his new position. Immediately he had to change and begin to do work of war relevance, for instance, relating to muscle fatigue. At the end of the war in 1945 he returned to the original intent of the center, which was to develop gerontological research.

At the Baltimore center at that time there were physicians who owed two years of government service because their medical education had been paid for under the wartime emergency. As before, I found that I began to do research with my neighbors. In particular, in 1948, Dr. David Solomon came from Harvard University to do research as an endocrinologist. He began to do work on aging and the stress response of the endocrine system. At that time I served as a young control subject for him while I did my own research in psychology. From colleagues I learned the language of new techniques such as balistocardiology, metabolic control studies, renal clearance capacity, and concepts that someone in psychology would not usually be exposed to. Clearly, from some of these I borrowed ideas.

The Baltimore Period (1947–1950)

One of my clear borrowings of a concept was from the physiologists who were working on age changes in renal clearance capacity. I found it intriguing that they could characterize the clearance capacity of the kidney by appropriate measurements. By analogy, I thought about processing the capacity of the human brain and began to think about suitable measurements. At the same time, I was concerned with interpretation of data that indicated that older people were slower in their reaction times. To me, this was a diminished capacity not unlike reduced kidney clearance capacity. How much can your kidneys clear per unit time, or in the case of the nervous system, how much information can it process per unit time? It turned out that the concept was clearer than the related research findings because the central nervous system does not keep the same unit fixed over time. Unlike the kidney, which recognizes the molecules it must clear, the nervous system keeps regrouping, and what was a bit of information at one point can become grouped or clumped into a larger unit. Specifically, the analytical unit keeps changing since, unlike the kidney, the nervous system heavily organizes many of its functions on the basis of experience. The behavioral "bit" does not remain fixed. I did however manage to contribute to the issue of the interpretation of slowness of behavior with age, which is a major career story.

Career: The Early Years

In a sense, the early years of my career encompassed the three years I spent at the Naval Medical Research Institute, from June 1943 to June 1946, and from 1947 to 1950 at the gerontology center. I did much on-the-job research learning and continued to be exposed to a wide range of scientists. I came to respect the work of others rather than to emphasize the uniqueness of psychology and its differences with other sciences. It placed a stamp on my career that subsequent experience and positions have not dampened but amplified. I cannot take a simple partisan view of human behavior as a sole province of psychology. The understanding of development and aging of behavior is a scientific venture in which many disciplines have roles and contributions to make.

I suppose my early years, as a pre-engineering student and later in the navy, were destined to have a formative effect on my view of the organism as having more or less efficiency to perform different tasks. If there was a reduction in efficiency, I had to seek out the mechanisms or causes. The word *mechanism* itself is a shaping kind of metaphor or an orienting term. In recent years a visiting professor gave me a present at the end of a year-long seminar. He presented me with an electrically driven simulator of perpetual motion. He labeled it the *mechanism* in playful recognition of my frequent use of the term in the seminar. I had assimilated the word from a tradition in which the term "mechanism" was used to express the linkage between cause and effect or the pathways through which cause and effect are related.

My desire for explanation was focused in 1947 at the Gerontology Center of the Public Health Service in Baltimore, Maryland. When I joined the staff of Nathan Shock, I picked as one of my research topics the slowing of behavior with age and the "mechanisms" that lie behind the slowing. In reading the early literature of Edward Thorndike and subsequently Irving Lorge and others, I felt they were minimizing the significance of slowing as an important factor in psychological abilities. In particular, I was impressed that the literature on the use of timed and untimed tests never settled the issue of which type of test was valid for what purpose. At that stage of the development of the subject matter it was assumed that intellectual power could not be fully expressed by older persons because the response processes slowed down. It became customary to attribute the slowness of behavior to either the slowness of response processes or to loss of acuity of sensory and perceptual input. Little attention was given to the speed of mediation between stimulus and response. In 1947 most intellectual tests were derived as hand-me-ups from evaluation of children in a school context. Basically, tests of intelligence were attempting to predict school success on the basis of being measures of intrinsic ability. When one patterned tests for adults after those given in childhood, they were assumed to have carry-over validity as measures of intelligence.

Sidney Pressey disputed the cause of the lower intellectual test scores of adults, and he argued primarily on the basis of content. He thought changing the content of questions posed to older adults was justified on the grounds that test questions tended to be oriented to children and youth and were not "user-friendly" for an adult population. He believed that adults' total scores would move up if we asked more age-appropriate questions in intelligence tests. However, no criteria of validity for such item selection were proposed.

Another approach was to compare timed and untimed tests in relation to age. This was followed by a period of time when psychologists often became apologists for the lower test performance of older adults; that is, the intellectual power of the older nervous system was presumably not much affected by age and that lower scores were somehow artifacts. Not much discussion was given to validity criteria that might support these judgments. It was thought that the brain could not demonstrate its full capacity or power because of sluggish or impaired sensory input and output functions. Thus, timed tests became arbitrarily viewed as penalizing the older person. I initiated a period of about six years of research in which I attempted to find out the basis for slowing with age within the organism. I focused not only on the speed of input and output mechanisms but also on slowness that might be attributed to the mediating nervous system itself.

One of the early studies consisted of age differences in the speed of doing simple addition problems (Birren & Botwinick, 1951; Birren, Allen & Landau, 1954). I reasoned that if I lengthened the series of digits to be added from two to twenty-five, the longer digit lists would have a smaller proportion of time involved in writing the answer. It follows that the correlation between a speed-of-writing test and the speed of doing addition problems should decline to zero for long problems if the slowness of writing the answers was the only relevant factor. The results showed that for young adults the correlation between speed of writing and speed of addition did decline, but it leveled off after about four digits and explained only 10 percent of the common variance thereafter. In contrast, the correlation in older adults declined but remained high, explaining almost 50 percent of the variance for long problems (Birren & Botwinick, 1951). This instance clearly showed that the limiting factor lay not solely in writing or in the response process but largely in the central processing that shared a common variance with writing speed. If one were to partial out the speed factor as expressed in writing time related to age in such tests, one would be throwing out changes that were particularly characteristic of the central nervous system. This gave rise to the idea that the biggest portion of variance in slowing of behavior with age can be attributed to the central nervous system itself and less to peripheral sensory factors and motor response processes. This seemed to be a fairly revolutionary thought at the time since it was reversing the customary pattern of causal attribution of the origin of slowness in older subjects.

Related research involved comparing reaction times using difference response modes of the jaw, finger, and foot. Surprisingly, the age differences were approximately constant across the three modes. This suggested that there was little increase with age in nerve conduction velocity, because if there were, there would be an increase in response slowness as a function of path length; for instance, foot responses would be disproportionately slow compared with jaw responses (Birren & Botwinick, 1955a).

From 1951 to 1953 I was assigned to the University of Chicago by the National Institutes of Health while new facilities were built in Bethesda, Maryland. In 1951 I had the opportunity of working with neurophysiologist Patrick Wall when he was at the University of Chicago, Department of Anatomy. He induced me to measure directly the nerve conduction velocity of rat sciatic nerves in relation to age. I found an increase in speed of conduction velocity as the rat developed, but the sciatic nerves from old rats did not show an increasing slowness trend with age. At least for me this began to put the nail in the coffin, that although there may be some peripheral changes, they are not the large sources of slowness with age in speed of behavior. In a closely related project I measured speed of startle reaction in rats in response to mild shock applied to the paws or to a sudden white noise (Birren, 1955). Results showed that the older rats were indeed slower in their behavior; however, given the previous findings, we could not attribute that to the change in peripheral nerve conduction velocity (Birren & Wall, 1956).

I also attempted to define more clearly the role of perception in slowing of behavior with age. In these studies I varied the difficulty of the perceptual task, such as judging which of two circles was the smaller. Subjects had to say as quickly as possible which was the smaller circle, the right or the left. By varying the area of the circles, one manipulates difficulty. All people are slower when you get down to a 1 or 2 percent difference in circle size. What I was doing was attempting to describe the role of age differences in the speed of perceptual judgments while varying the task difficulty. Presumably, if perceptual discrimination is the only variable, then as one made the task progressively easy, older people's performance should approximate that of the young. In these studies, as in others, there is residual difference in the speed of behavior between old and young adults after the issue of perceptual difficulty is eliminated by experimental manipulation (Birren & Botwinick, 1955b; also, Birren, Riegel & Morrison, 1962). That is, there is a residual slowness in speed of perceptual judgment with age that is not explained by sensory or perceptual acuity.

These and other experiments of the period convinced me that the major fact that we were facing was that with age there was a slowness of mediation of the central nervous system of all processes. Stated in other words, the speed of processing by the central nervous system itself slows with age. Later, this concept was expressed in terms of information processing. This has come to be known as the strong hypothesis about aging and slowing; for instance, that everything the nervous system does is slower with advancing age. The other hypothesis is that there are subfactors that account for the slowing. By analogy to the concept of general intelligence, I suggest that there is a general speed factor of central nervous system mediation that slows with age, in addition to which there are specialized processes of slowing in subsystems of the brain. This is not unlike the idea that there is a brain mass function as well as localized functions of the nervous system.

While at the University of Chicago, I had academic contacts that resulted in two scientific principles that I adopted. The first of these was from the psychologist Louis Thurstone, with whom I spent a quarter in residence. His influence on my thinking about age and intelligence is seen in a 1961 article (Birren & Morrison). In his conversations he told me that if you have only one method of measurement with which to answer a question or issue, you are probably in a weak position. He might have added that, particularly in psychology, you should measure the same concept by different methods. Perhaps this might be stated in terms of convergent validity, that two or more measures of the same concept should be used to establish the validity of a concept.

The other contact was with Ralph Gerard, a neurophysiologist. He told me that after years of putting electrodes into nerves, he still had no idea about how the nervous system was organized or integrated. This leads to the statement of principle that you have to use a methodology appropriate to the level of question that you are asking. Perhaps this might be rephrased to, "If you are trying to catch an elephant, tweezers will not do, and if you are trying to catch a bullfrog in a pond, don't use a bulldozer." This leads to the view of my career that I have subordinated method to question. My predilection is to go for the power of the question and then find one or more techniques that will attempt to answer it.

The next level of research that I undertook with colleagues was a joint evaluation of behavioral measures in concert with assessment of cerebral circulation and metabolism, psychiatric symptomatology, social functioning, and assessment of subclinical disease. The joint project was undertaken by a multidisciplinary team at the National Institute of Mental Health (NIMH). Measurements were made on a group of forty-seven men over the age of sixty-five, each of whom volunteered to be a resident in the institution for a two-week period (Birren, Butler, Greenhouse, Sokoloff & Yarrow, 1963).

Out of that massive collection of data, we ascertained that the brain circulation and brain metabolic values in healthy older men were equivalent to those earlier reported for young adults. There was thus no necessary reduction with age in general metabolic activity of the brain or circulation. At the same time there were observed reductions in speed of reaction time and higher than expected measurements obtained on global verbal information. This leads to the expression of the principle that a healthy older adult continues to acquire information and store it but processes it more slowly. By contrast, if one measures an older adult whose verbal information level is only equal to young adults, one suspects that there has been a loss of verbal information accompanying a reduced integrity of the central nervous system.

Subsequent research indicates that slowness is exacerbated by the presence of disease, particularly cardiovascular or cerebrovascular disease, but even in the healthiest older adults one observes a tendency to slowness. The foregoing suggests that there is a characteristic trend toward slowness of behavior with age, although modulated by conditions of health and physical fitness. It appears that this is an intrinsic change that might be regarded as a species characteristic; that is, all things being equal, older adults will tend to slow their behavior with advancing age. The slowness, which may be due to an intrinsic quality of the central nervous system, will have consequences for cognitive functioning and, ultimately, reasoning. That is, if one does not enter data quickly enough into the nervous system and process it, the nervous system can dissipate the information and reduces the likelihood of task completion and number of elements that can be combined in a complex task. An older subject may be slow in doing a task not because it is difficult, but rather the task is difficult because of the slowing.

The foregoing is opposite to the paradigm found in children who are learning to read. They are slow and process each element separately. Later, they combine words into phrases and read rapidly orally or silently. Thus, familiarity improves the speed of reading. Later in life it is suggested that the slowness is not related solely to practice but to an intrinsic change in speed of processing that slows the overall reading or cognitive performance. This line of reasoning has been very difficult for developmental psychologists to accept, because learning is usually studied as a function of the number of trials or amount of experience, and differences in performance are explained by differential practice and exposure. Attempts to explain differences in performance solely based on the implicit model of lack of practice or disuse is a legacy of studies of early development.

Another principle that emerged in midcareer was that the performance of healthy older adults is much more like that of young adults than it is like unhealthy older adults. Earlier we apparently had in our research samples an undifferentiated mixture of persons showing both disease and aging. One of the more general principles I have evolved is that aging is a multilayered process. Although there are patterns characteristic of us as a species, for instance slowing, there are subpatterns that are more related to age-associated diseases. Future research will no doubt establish subpatterns by comparing psychological performance with longevity or remaining years of life, or with differences in mortality and morbidity in relation to behavior. For example, it is widely noted that women live longer than men. If there is an intrinsic pattern of aging and an intrinsic relationship between the length of life and behavior, then the performance of women in the later years should be better or change more slowly than that of men. How long we live and our adult diseases can also be examined in relation to early life-behavior samples. These questions devolve into matters of whether there are behavioral markers of aging, like genetic markers, that will forecast the length of life. Somehow, behavioral markers of aging have not been as widely sought after as, for example, have genetic markers. Yet behavior is a sample of the integrity of the central nervous system, and it should provide the basis for developing markers of aging.

It is provocative for me to consider whether there are exemplar behaviors that become markers of aging in the sense that they are differentially predictive of longer or shorter lives. This line of thought led Laurel Fisher and me to propose a number of criteria that a behavioral marker would have to meet in order to qualify as a marker of aging (Birren & Fisher, 1992). Such markers could be put in a matrix along with biological and social markers that might differentially predict resilient, fully capacitated, long-lived persons from more vulnerable, disabled, and shorter-lived persons. Given my multidisciplinary-orientation background, I suspect that there are deferential patterns of aging and that the next round of research, perhaps derived from longitudinal studies, will be revealing differential patterns of aging, some of which might be linked with particular syndromes and diseases. Perhaps another pattern might be a disuse pattern that will come to be distinguishable from the effects of disease in the active person. What follows are criteria proposed for evaluating markers of aging. Here they are stated in terms of validating slowness of behavior as a marker of aging. However, they can be stated in the general sense of criteria to judge the validity of any proposed markers of aging—biological, behavioral, or social.

1. It should be related to length of life; that is, quicker behavior should be associated with a longer life.
2. Adjacent phylogenetic species should also show slowness of behavior with increasing age; slowness should be shown to have a shared genetic basis.
3. Since females have a longer life span than males, greater changes in speed of behavior should be seen in older males than in older females.
4. It should be correlated with physiological and anatomical indications of aging, such as lung vital capacity, skin elasticity, bone mass, muscular strength, maximum heart rate, hearing threshold, glucose tolerance, measures of brain excitability, and brain metabolism.
5. It should be correlated with other behavioral processes, such as attention, perception, memory, problem solving, and reasoning.
6. It should be reduced but not eliminated by exercise, proper diet, not smoking, and moderate use of alcohol.
7. It should be exacerbated by the presence of age-associated conditions, such as coronary artery disease, cerebrovascular disease, diabetes, and Alzheimer's disease. However, the absence of detectable disease should not eliminate the slowing entirely.

One of the relatively unexplored areas is that of *terminal decline,* in which an individual may undergo a rapid disorganization of physiological and behavioral functions shortly before death. The relation of terminal decline to markers of aging probably remains to be explored in longitudinal studies in which one has frequent measurements. The task is to determine if the patterns of terminal decline are predictable or if, like storms of weather, they emerge as paradoxical changes.

Career: The Later Years

I left the National Institutes of Health in 1965. At that time I was responsible for the research program on aging, both intramural and extramural, within the National Institute of Child Health and Human Development. Robert Aldrich, then the director, was a pediatrician deeply interested in the carry-forward effects of childhood health and experience into adult life. After organizing the National Institute of Child Health and Human Development, but unfortunately for me, he left to return to his professorship in pediatrics at the University of Washington.

The institute was in a growth phase and so was my career, and they took different directions. The University of Southern California (USC) had received a major pledge of money to create an institute for the study of retirement and aging. The president of USC had been an assistant surgeon general in the public health service and a biomedical scientist, and he had a strong interest in the subject matter of adult change and aging. The university invited me to become the director of the institute at USC in 1965. Within the university I moved very quickly to establish a program of graduate education, since one of the big deficiencies in the country at that time was the lack of traineeships and scholarships to encourage graduate students in various disciplines to pursue the study of adult development and aging.

The family transition to California was not an easy one. My family had to establish roots in a new community. We had lived in Maryland for a long time and had not expected to leave. Our three children had been students in the school system there. But we did move, and I think eventually we all grew as a result. I am reminded from time to time of the paraphrased statement attributed to Ernest Hemingway, "Life breaks us all but some are stronger in the broken places." Our son Jeff had a particularly difficult time the first year in transition but became thoroughly rooted in California. The difficulty of families adjusting to moving at that period was not very well considered, because the tradition of America was one of supporting career movement, and the rest had to fall in line. I am much more sympathetic today to young careerists who have to move a family lock, stock, and barrel to a new community.

At USC I was initially startled by the lack of facilities. I was thoroughly used to the large structure and support mechanisms of the National Institutes of Health, and I was ill prepared for the lack of microstructure and facilities at USC. One strength was very apparent, though: I was only one telephone number away from a decisionmaker. It was a slim and efficient bureaucracy and it could move limited resources quickly. An associate dean of a nearby large and distinguished public university said that I could do things within one year at USC that would take three or four years to bring about at the public university with its large bureaucracy.

A negative aspect of one of the issues of subject-matter inertia is the fact that developmental psychology still has not widely embraced the study of adult life and aging. There are, I think, both turf issues and some diffuse psycho-emotional subject-matter attachments. The turf issue consists of child psychologists not wanting to expand a faculty with someone interested in reseach on adult development and aging. One would have thought there would have been more encouragement of the subject matter of adult change by child psychologists in order to see the adult outcomes of early behavior patterns. Another issue concerns the fact that the model child continues to expand, grow, and rise in competence. Adult life is marked by increasing probabilities of negative instances and declines in capacities as well as increments. This requires a more complex outlook on research than the psychologically expansive products of child development. I often think that some longitudinal studies of the future will begin with the conditions of uterine life and experience and follow through the expression of the human genome in the context of environmental effects. For example, what are the consequences of a stressful pregnancy and a low birth-weight child for adult development and aging and predisposition to disabilities in late life?

Perhaps I was thoroughly sensitized to the power of longitudinal studies by my colleague K. W. Schaie, whom we attracted to USC to be the director of research for the Andrus Gerontology Center. His insistence on the analysis of the compartments of variance of: A) time of measurement, C) cohort effects, and D) ontogenetic change remain with me now as almost a ritual or mantra of interpretation. There are obvious and large cohort drifts in the population of older persons since we began studying psychology in the latter part of the nineteenth century.

Another intellectual influence on me at USC was my colleague James Henry, a physiologist. He showed that the necessary and sufficient condition for producing cardiovascular disease in mice was the social environment in which the animals lived. Clearly, genetic potential varies the magnitude of the effect, but nevertheless, inbred strains of mice will or will not show a rise in blood pressure with age and other phenomena as a consequence of the social environment. This gave rise to my current conviction about the psychophysiology of aging, that the current major contributors to health and the diseases of adult life are factors of social class, education, and environmental exposure. Not only does our heredity contribute, but our psychosocial losses and powerlessness also have disease outcomes in adult life. In such bidirectional relationships or ecological relationships we have had a bias or a favoring of biological determinism and do not encourage as strongly the study of social determinism. Some scholars in the field have said that we have medicalized aging, that there has been an engulfing character of the medical enterprise and distribution of health services that has favored a limited perspective on the factors that influence the health and well-being of the population. In the analysis of patterns of aging, I believe an ecological orientation is essential.

An earlier example of paradigm inertia was one that I experienced at the National Institute of Mental Health. In 1960, Robert M. Butler and I proposed that we establish a laboratory within the NIMH to study the issues of adult development and aging. At that particular time there was a dominant view that the organization of behavior was laid down early in the life of the child and that the basic pattern was lived out or expressed in the daily events of life. The thought that interactions and new factors could arise during adult life seemed far-fetched, and the senior administrators turned down the proposal. Subsequently, social and scientific pressures built that led to the creation of the National Institutes of Health. Ironically, I was offered the opportunity of heading the new institute, but I was well anchored at USC. Fortunately, Robert Butler was able to become the first director of the National Institute on Aging (NIA) in 1975.

In the same period that the NIA was created, I was approached by several other opportunities for new positions. One was to become the academic vice president of USC, and the other was to head a major retirement organization. Both of these I declined, following the advice of an academic vice president I respected. He suggested I might have a better career by staying close to my discipline and avoiding the politicization of general administrative positions.

When I came to USC in 1965 I was forty-seven years old and had not been heavily involved in teaching. I was not bored with student interactions and volunteered to teach courses in psychology. I discovered that there was a pattern of burnout and disenchantment in midcareer faculty who had been teaching throughout their careers, in contrast to my midcareer enthusiasm and energy. Also, I was not competing for and with the graduate students, as were the younger faculty members who were asserting their intellectual dominance, nor was I trying to minimize my interactions with students. Since my career was already established, I could be more openhanded in supporting the students in their steps toward creating careers. I welcomed the interactions with the graduate students, and I used to say openly that the students had the obligation of teaching me new things. For me, it was a wonderful period of growth at USC from 1965 to 1989, and we tackled many complex and new topics in research and teaching in the psychology of adult life and aging as well as more broadly in gerontology.

In 1989, when I was seventy-one years of age, I became emeritus at USC, and there was an uncomfortable atmosphere surrounding the question of what to do with me, the professor who had been the founding dean of the Andrus Gerontology Center. At the same time, David Solomon at UCLA was looking for a director to organize the Borun Center for Gerontological Research. He recruited me, and I enjoyed the transition and taking on another opportunity for guiding the growth of a research program.

What have my most recent experiences at UCLA taught me about the principles of academic life and developmental psychology? I came to recognize again the great inertia that is built around existing subject matters and the complex rationales that surround academic decisions. One large factor in the picture is, of course, the availability of money to support new ventures. As a relatively new topic within the sciences and arts, the issues of adult change and aging are still not accepted on a par of importance with more traditional topics. Apparently it will take roughly a generation for organizational changes to occur that will support scholarship, research, and teaching about the course of adult life. Being convinced of the scientific importance as well as the practical implications of studying adult development and aging, I am impatient with systems and individuals that appear blind to the significance of the subject matter.

Perhaps one of the most convincing statements of this character was made to me by Phillip Handler, a distinguished biochemist at Duke University and later president of the National Academy of Science. He said that he had taught and done research in biochemistry during its building-block stage. His biochemistry book, used by medical students, described the components of the metabolic cycles of organic systems. He said that this was the biochemistry of the past and present, but that the biochemistry of the future was going to be the *biochemistry of differentiation and aging*. That is, the building blocks of the systems have to be placed in a dynamic context.

By analogy, I think that it is now time to say that the psychology of the future will be the psychology of development and aging. Already we are seeing the ending chapters of introductory psychology textbooks emphasizing development and aging. This trend will continue, I believe, and one will see the "building-block topics" of psychology placed in a dynamic context of how they differentiate, develop, and age. The essential point here is that research on elemental behavioral processes studied by psychology do not, in and of themselves, explain phenomena of development and aging or the dynamics of change. Studies of sensation, perception, learning, memory, intelligence, and so on, do not produce knowledge that contradicts development and aging, but they do not explain the dynamic processes. In this regard, I believe that in the future there will be a stronger organismic orientation, and we will take seriously that the organism is a self-regulating system and, to a considerable degree, a self-structuring system providing its own energy for change. With the growth of research, psychology will undoubtedly come to recognize patterns of adult change related to different outcomes and develop interventions to maximize productivity and the quality of life.

References

Birren, J. E. (1955). Age differences in startle reaction time of the rat to noise and electric shock. *Journal of Gerontology, 10,* 437–440.

Birren, J. E., Allen, W. R. & Landau, H. G. (1954). The relation of problem length in simple addition to time required, probability of success and age. *Journal of Gerontology, 9,* 150–161.

Birren, J. E. & Botwinick, J. (1951). Rate of addition as a function of difficulty and age. *Psychometrika, 16,* 219–232.

Birren, J. E. & Botwinick, J. (1955a). Age difference in finger, jaw, and foot reaction time in auditory stimuli. *Journal of Gerontology, 10,* 429–432.

Birren, J. E. & Botwinick, J. (1955b). Speed of responses as a function of perceptual difficulty and age. *Journal of Gerontology, 10,* 433–436.

Birren, J. E., Butler, R. N., Greenhouse, S. W., Sokoloff, L. & Yarrow, M. (Eds.). (1963). *Human aging.* Washington, D.C.: U.S. Government Printing Office, Public Health Publication.

Birren, J, E. & Fisher, L. M. (1992). Aging and the slowing of behavior: Consequences for cognition and survival. In J. J. Berman & T. B. Sonderegger (Eds.), *Psychology and Aging: Nebraska Symposium on Motivation, 39* (pp. 1–37). Lincoln: University of Nebraska Press.

Birren, J. E. & Morrison, D. F. (1961). Analysis of the WAIS subtests in relation to age and education. *Journal of Gerontology, 16,* 95–96.

Birren, J. E., Riegel, K. F. & Morrison, D. F. (1962). Age differences in response speed as a function of controlled variations of stimulus conditions. Evidence of a general speed factor. *Gerontologia, 6,* 1–8.

Birren, J. E. & Wall, P. D. (1956). Age changes in conductive velocity, refractory period, number of fibers, connective tissue space and blood vessels in sciatic nerves of rats. *Journal of Comparative Neurology, 104,* 1–16.

Schlack, C. & Birren, J. E. (1946). Influences on dental defects in naval personnel. *Science, 104,* 259–263.

3

Marie Skodak Crissey

How does it happen that an individual becomes a psychologist—rather than an engineer or an artist? Can the precursor events and choices be identified? And what is the role of chance, or of social or economic pressures and opportunities? Can, perhaps, some glimpses of a long career and the self-selection of autobiographies shed some light on this?

Ohio

I was born in 1910 in Lorain, Ohio. It was then a modest Lake Erie port town in the Western Reserve. This was an area where New England families who lost property through fire or battle during the Revolution had been resettled. The peaceful fishing and ship-building community changed abruptly at the beginning of the 1900s, when coal from West Virginia and iron ore from Minnesota met in the newly established steel mills. To supply the muscle and run the machines that converted the raw material to shiny rolls of steel, men from central, eastern, and southern Europe came to the promised land. Few spoke English; most were accustomed to minimal housing. Ethnic and religious customs encouraged enclaves with familiar sounds, smells, and foods, which eased homesickness. The "old Americans" entrenched in "the North End" viewed the newcomers in "South Lorain" with mistrust. For some fifty years, the only high school was in the North End. Many South Lorain teenagers had an hour ride each way on the streetcar to make the 8:00 A.M. to 4:00 P.M. class schedule. It was only after the 1920s and 1930s that the Polish, Hungarian, and Italian surnamed athletes were welcomed. To this day there is no high school in South Lorain, even though the power of the community is no longer vested in the North End.

It was to this community that my parents came from Hungary. Both were educated as teachers and came from the petit bourgeois level of society. Relatives included small landholders, small shopkeepers, mid- and lower level administrators, and noncommissioned officers in the military. A number of the more ambitious entered religious orders, which offered a chance for advancement to leadership positions.

Since most of their compatriots in Lorain were uneducated peasants and the property in the North End was viewed as too expensive, my parents settled in the "West Side," between the two clearly identified subcommunities. My mother spoke no English when she came to Lorain, and I do not recall when she learned it, but both my parents were fluent speakers in the teacher conferences by my grade-school years. However, family conversations were in Hungarian so that we would remember the ancestral tongue. Conversation on Sunday was usually in German so that we could learn it naturally. When my parents wanted to discuss private matters, they conversed in Slovak, so my sister and I absorbed a good bit of that language as well. In the neighborhood there were similarly upwardly mobile Polish and Italian families, so some of their words were absorbed also. Four years of high school Latin gave many clues to the Romance languages and no doubt ultimately helped me pass the Ph.D. requirement French exams.

This was the family setting. Memories of early childhood are hazy. I was regarded as independent and headstrong. Was much of that the result of what would now be regarded as experience bordering on early trauma? When I was two and a half, to assuage her bitter homesickness my mother took my one-year-old sister and returned to Hungary for several months. I supposedly had a nanny, but from all accounts spent much of the time locked alone in a bare room, or as a better alternative, in a barricaded storeroom in my father's office. At any rate, a photo taken on my mother's return shows a thin, sad-faced, unhappy child.

Did that episode make a difference? Probably. In contrast to my cheerfully outgoing sister—who had been the cherished baby visiting among the relatives—I was an independent, self-motivated miniadult. I didn't need others for companionship or to suggest games or to give me praise or support. I didn't fight or argue, I just went about my own way. I watched what adults did, then taught myself. Thus, by the time kindergarten was near, I learned to read and write in Hungarian. I could do simple crocheting and sewing, could build a boat that floated using hammer, screwdriver, and saw, and could prepare a simple breakfast. I probably had more than the normal load of self-assurance, and if I was regarded as overbearing, that would not be a surprise.

When the time came to enter school, we were still living in a largely immigrant part of town. My mother's English was still marginal, so my father enrolled me. The kindergarten group was large and mixed. After the initial circle of all the chairs with the introductory teacher talk, finger plays, and songs, the teacher designated who would go to the red table and who would go to the blue one. After a few days I became aware that the red table had books with pictures and generally did more interesting things. So the next morning I simply joined the red table and occupied myself as the others did. I recall the teacher coming to me and trying to get me to move to the blue table. "I stay here" was my response. It was her first realization that I spoke some English, unlike the children at the blue table. The following day I brought a book and read from it in fluent Hungarian, which of course she didn't understand, but she got the point. I then got to read the English books and began my lifelong romance with the printed page.

My elementary school years were perhaps a bit more eventful than they are for most children. World War I raged in Europe. The United States joined shortly. The flu epidemic came in 1917 and again in 1918. Since my father spoke a number of eastern European and Balkan languages, he volunteered as a translator who accompanied physicians ministering to the ill steel workers in the crowded boardinghouses. On more than one occasion he took me along. I would wait in the boardinghouse parlor and read my book. At home, I did some of the cooking, going upstairs to my mother's sickbed (she had also contracted the flu) to write down the dictated recipes, then down to the kitchen to make them up. I vividly remember Armistice night. We bundled my ailing mother and sister in shawls to watch the excitement in the streets, convinced that with the end of the war, the flu, too, would disappear.

Although the war was over, it was 1922 before we were able to reestablish contact with relatives in Europe. My mother, still homesick for Hungary, took my sister and me there with the implication that she would purchase property and we would stay. The excitement of travel over the ocean and through strange lands overshadowed any worry about leaving our home in the United States. It was an interesting experience. A storm at sea slid the plates around on the table. The trains ran through still-ruined Belgium and Germany. Autos were rare; the horse-drawn fiacres were fun. The bread was hard and often sour. The meals were often skimpy, though obviously special for guests. My mother was sadly disappointed, and as September came we returned to a relieved father and a new principal in the old grade school.

My sister and I were several weeks late for the opening of school. Not only had new friendships been established, but we returned with jeweled rings in newly pierced ears. Without them in Hungary we had been strangers from a foreign land. Now, back in the United States, we were the ones with "Hunky peasant" earrings at a time when no self-respecting American girl was so adorned. It was predictable that I would become entangled with someone who spoke words of derision and was a few sizes larger and some years older, but less agile, than I. The principal soon appeared, separated us, and sent *me* to the office to await judgment. It took her a while to repair the damage to my opponent. Meanwhile, I remembered the legends about the lady's skill with the paddle and the ingenuity of her punishments.

When she returned, she invited me into the inner office, generally reserved for parent conferences and major offenders. Graciously she invited me to sit in the big chair by her desk and inquired about my summer experiences. She already knew about my double promotion the previous year just before we left for Europe and that for several reasons I was having to establish new friendships. Then came a brief lecture, the nub of which has remained with me a lifetime: Those who have talents and capabilities beyond the average have a special responsibility not only to use them but to understand and be patient with their fellows not as well endowed. Thus it follows that one tries to understand the motivation of others, overlooks their inadequacies, and applies the concept of noblesse oblige.

Her skillful handling of an unhappy child did not immediately transform me into a paragon, but there were no more conflicts, and I did leave my earrings at home. In the school years to come I was fortunate to have some excellent teachers who challenged my interests in literature, history, and the sciences.

The high school years came. The walk of fifteen long city blocks took nearly an hour each way. The classic precollege course of four years of Latin, four of English, and maximum science and math allowed few extras. As an honor roll student I could add some nonrequired courses. One was agriculture with a handsome novice teacher who was blushingly aware of why there were so many girls in his classes.

Since the manual arts classes were not open to girls, I took home economics and made the obligatory cooking apron and white sauce but whittled and sawed my craft projects at home. Among the youngest and certainly the least athletic, I had no talent for group teams. I shared my mother's total inability to sing on key or manage a musical instrument. I lacked time for the school paper. I was a lackadaisical member of many clubs, officer of some, and fairly active but not memorable on the debate team. My social life was minimal. I lived too far from the North End friends I preferred. Encouraged by my parents, I devoted hours to homework.

In retrospect, I see my lifelong practice of a multitrack life began in the high school years. At first mostly on Saturdays, then, in the upper grades, quite regularly after school as well as on weekends, I worked in my father's office. It was a kind of paralegal, real estate, insurance, travel agency office with a varied clientele. He was not a good businessman. It was not an elegant office. I hated the cleaning and sweeping. I didn't mind the two-fingered typing. I learned to be pleasant to all kinds of people. I empathized with the frustrations of common workmen coping with the bureaucracy of governments, corporations, and the minutiae of city living. The teacher and physician parents of my friends seemed to have much neater, better organized lives. I looked to high school graduation as the gateway to a more enjoyable existence.

I graduated second in a class of some 170 and won the memorial cup in chemistry as well as the usual recognitions customary for good students. There were no scholarships, grants, or subsidies in those days, nor was there the kind of help that would have been invaluable for someone whose parents were unfamiliar with American college and enrollment procedures. Even with counseling I might have ended up at Ohio State University, as I did in fact. As a late enrollee, I found myself in the most expensive and socially sophisticated dormitory. My father assured me that money was no problem, that some rental property income was dedicated to my education.

Ohio State University

First terms at college are notoriously trying, even for well-prepared newcomers. For me, it was a disaster. I had as roommate a transfer from a finishing school in the South who was courted by the leading sororities. I had not even heard about sororities and could not understand why my dorm mates were so involved with something called "rushing." I was not accustomed to dressing for dinner. Indeed, most of my clothes closet space was given over to my roommate's elegant wardrobe. I found myself in a remedial English class, a blow after honors and A pluses in high school. The compulsory gym class was designed for those now labeled "physically challenged." Chemistry, my planned major, was in an enormous barn of a laboratory, a contrast to my cozy lab and lecture arrangements in high school.

In midterm came the news. The house—my financial security—was lost; the Depression had hit Lorain, and my father, early. My meager savings would be enough only for tuition for the two remaining terms of the freshman year. There might be some help from my parents—surely the business recession was temporary. To add to my miseries—and expenses—I developed a skin problem. The dermatologist said briefly "reaction to stress," and the ointment didn't help either. In spite of the disappointments and unhappiness, it did not even occur to me to leave, to go home. I looked at the hundreds—no, thousands—of fellow students. Many were not better dressed. They didn't look all that much happier. Many were smarter, but many were no more capable than I. If they could figure out a way to the future, it must be possible for me.

The remedial English teacher (decades later he became president of one of the Big Ten universities) decided to plumb the depths of his students' inadequacies. To see whether we could use commas or construct a grammatically correct sentence, he assigned an essay, "What I Think of My University Experience," to be written in the one-hour class period. What a chance to vent my feelings! I wrote and wrote. Gradually the others finished and left. I wrote on. Finally, drained and exhausted, the last to finish, I turned in my masterpiece. It fleetingly occurred to me that it might be my last assignment. But he said he wanted to know, and I told him.

The next week he returned the essays (except mine) and illustrated a proper sentence. At the end of class he asked me to come to his office. He explained that he had done a little detective work and determined that I had been confused with a student with a similar surname and should have been in an accelerated class (this was in the days before computers). Since it was too late to make the change, he would exempt me from class attendance, assign readings in the classics, require reviews and critiques of these, and periodically discuss them with me. I could hardly believe my good fortune. They were delightful sessions. I learned a lot.

Shortly after this my elegant roommate pledged a sorority and left for more congenial quarters. Soon too, I sensed that the gym instructor disliked the class almost as much as I did (she was into soccer and hockey), and if I complained of periodic pains I could happily miss class. She never checked the calendar, and time went fast. I did sometimes wonder how my alter ego made out in accelerated English and fast-paced gym.

The first term was ending. Somehow I found the dean of women's office with its housing lists. The new term found me settled in a brick house presided over by a little old lady whose contact with the seven or eight coeds in the "approved house" was limited to the collection of rent and locking the door at curfew. My relations with most of the girls were not much closer except for the one graduate student, who seemed much older. Our relationship has endured for some sixty-six years, and the seven-year difference in our ages seems unimportant. Barbara had taught science in a high school and was back getting her masters in biology, working on an obscure anatomical problem in frogs. Her budget was, if anything, more limited than mine, her wardrobe more modest. From her I learned how to make an acceptable meal out of day-old bread, milk, an egg, and spices.

We settled the world's problems over the one-burner gas stove in the basement and the improvised dining corner. I learned from her that the philosophy of life that my life and family influences had initiated was not only applicable in this new, university setting but was amenable to expansion. For example, that problems—of any kind—could be solved, or at least modified, and perhaps tolerated until improvements could be made. Solutions to problems were in one's own hands, one could not really rely on other people. Others had their own agendas and concerns. To rely on others would be to set oneself up for disappointment. To feel hurt as a result of disappointment was futile, and it was useless to waste energy on emotion or regrets or hurt feelings. And so it went.

I supplemented my savings with occasional housework and babysitting, often in the homes of professors. This gave me a peek into varied social and cultural lives. Much as I valued the thirty-five-cent-an-hour standard fee, this experience's greater value was in dusting away reverence and awe of the professionally eminent.

In the meantime, I did well in the history, botany, and biology classes. But chemistry required more precision and mathematics than I possessed. A change of majors was in order. Whatever I elected had to eventuate in employment. So, with the self-assurance gained in cleaning the homes of professors, I made the rounds of deans and registrars. Liberal arts was unwilling to approve extra hours so that I could graduate sooner. For extra work, I intended to get compensatory credit. The home economics school seemed interested in me, but some contacts with their students found few who were congenial. The School of Education was willing to let me take as many hours as I could pass to major in history plus anything else (its dean also eventually became president of a large Big Ten university).

That summer I went home for vacation. Not only I, but my family, and even the people of the town, had changed, or so it seemed to my sophomore eyes. The grim shadow of the Depression was darker. Family finances were even less secure. My sister was in her senior year in high school with college to think about. So I began the second year enrolled in the School of Education with a history major and general science minor but with no great enthusiasm for the career of a junior high school teacher. I returned to the "approved house," this time to a tiny single room. Instead of the uncertain income from housework, I began a "real job"—as a waitress at the Faculty Club. Basically this required fourteen hours weekly at thirty-five cents an hour and discounted meals, with occasional extra hours on weekends or for special functions. The luncheon and dinner hours could be managed with shrewd scheduling of classes. I remained there for the three years until graduation with increasing responsibilities, becoming a substitute dining room manager on occasion.

After a brief but intensive training on proper table setting, service, and appropriate behavior, novice waitresses were assigned our base tables. All the waitresses and busboys were students. Those with seniority had a choice of tables. There was no tipping, but some departments (faculty tended to gravitate to accustomed tables) were much more pleasant than others. As a newcomer I had little choice; I soon learned that I had the military (ROTC) table, and that it was well to keep a distance from some of the officers.

I was assigned two other smaller tables. The guests looked professional. The occasional women who joined them were "different." They seemed more casual in dress and behavior. As I became more proficient and at ease in my serving, I could catch comments and discussions that were intriguing. These people were psychologists! I had no idea what psychology was or how it might be useful, so I became particularly attentive to half-filled coffee cups and water glasses. The more I heard, the more interesting the content of the discussions became.

As education already required credit in psychology, I enrolled the next term. Dr. Sophie Rogers, with a joint appointment in liberal arts and at the medical school, brought the clinical/people emphasis to the class, which balanced the rat/laboratory bias of the textbook. Witty, fair to both men and women, she represented the "women who made it in a man's world" without belligerence or unpleasantness.

From that class on, there was no hesitation. I would become a psychologist working primarily with children who needed special help. The new profession of school psychology offered an avenue understandable to my parents and open to women, where my combined teacher training, science background, and clinical preparation would be appropriate. By careful scheduling I was able to take nearly every course offered in the psychology department at that time, including several in industrial and test development. I did avoid the rat-lab- and statistical-research-oriented classes. To round out my preparation I took a minor in social work and the related sociology courses.

By ingenious scheduling, overloaded programs, and two summer school sessions, within four college years I completed a teacher certificate, a B.S. in education degree, and an M.A. with a psychology major and social work minor. In addition, I had work experience in a private girls' school, an institution for the mentally retarded, a juvenile court, and a settlement house. Along the way I made

Phi Beta Kappa and three other societies honoring superior students. I continued my income-producing waitress job, changing it slightly the last year to be head waitress in a two hundred–room dormitory. The price for all this was a barely visible social life. I went home by train only between quarters. Occasionally I spent a few hours with graduate-student friends, but mostly there was no choice. I needed the money and I wanted the good grades and the qualifying experiences. I was not, however, a total isolate, and many of the friendships survived for years of Christmas correspondence.

In the late 1920s the word "psychology" was not generally known, as it is now. Course offerings were in the upper classes, or more often at the graduate level. The students who enrolled were generally more mature, with aspirations for college professorships. Among my classmates I was not only by far the youngest but much the most naive. Rumors of parties in which I did not participate did not bother me. I would have felt out of place, and in any case I was too busy to spare the time. I was in awe of advanced students and departmental assistants like Ernie Newland and Frank Stanton, who were about to win the Ph.D. and enter prestige jobs. The young instructors and about-to-become professors like Luella Cole, Al Kurtz, Sidney Pressey, and Harold Edgerton, who were enthusiastic about their own interests, gathered their own special groups. Emily Stogdill and Mervin Durea worked to develop counseling skills among students often more interested in the statistics of Herbert Toops and the industrial concerns of Harold Burt.

My own special mentors were Henry Goddard and Francis Maxfield. Their particular interest was in mental development—retardation, giftedness, and intellectual and learning deviations of all kinds. This seemed to me to offer the most practical application of psychology in "real life." Quite unlike each other in many respects, Goddard and Maxfield showed a kindliness and warmth toward children, parents, and teachers that contributed to their skills as clinicians. Their New England and Quaker backgrounds seemed to give them an approach that was both objective and empathic. Their skill in evoking and interpreting juvenile responses to test items set models for novice examiners.

My graduation in 1931 with the B.A. in June and the M.A. in August was in the nadir of the Depression. Many teachers and others were paid in scrip, redeemable in local stores for necessities. Educational frills, like school psychologists, were among the first to be sacrificed. Classmates with doctorates were grateful for modest postdoctoral appointments. At twenty-one, with no jobs available, I thought it appeared to be a good time to take a kind of sabbatical to indulge in a year abroad, the wander year of the medieval scholar. Our family had kept their European contacts. My father located the resources of the International Education Association. I was accepted for tuition-free status at the Peter Pazmany University in Budapest. The stipend for room and board was supplied by the Rockefeller Public Health Institute. Travel and personal expenses were my responsibility. I had no illusions that the central European psychology would add much to my employable competence, but I was more than ready for a change of scene, and hopefully for a more relaxed life.

Budapest

The 1931–1932 years were difficult in Europe as well as in the United States. The university closed for a "coal holiday" of two months in December and January. There were rumblings of discontent in Germany, where there was a delay of some six to eight years between graduation from teachers colleges and appointments to the classrooms. A young man named Hitler was becoming active organizing the discontented. At one point, when Japan invaded China, the American embassy contacted the dozen or so American students in Budapest and alerted us to the possibility that we might have to return home on short notice.

The psychology in the liberal arts faculty, the medical school, and the teacher-training institute where I enrolled was an odd mix. I was exposed to more Rorschach, psychoanalysis, graphology, and hereditary effects than was generally known in the United States at that time. My sharing of individual tests of intelligence and achievement were regarded as futile in the central European school systems. So I enjoyed the student opera and concert tickets, the "penny trains" to all parts of Hungary, the pleasures of contact with cousins and uncles and aunts (we had no relatives in the United States). I had a monthly allowance of ten dollars from my mother, who carefully saved that amount nickle by nickle.

The impecunious but pressure-free life could not go on forever, so in early spring I wrote innumerable letters and resumes to schools, institutions—wherever a job might exist. There were two responses that were perfect for my needs. The first, from the State School at Rome, New York, offered a three-month summer internship for maintenance and a modest stipend of, as I recall it, one hundred dollars for the three months. The other was a letter from Dr. Goddard's secretary at Ohio State University notifying me that I had been appointed assistant in the psychology department clinic. The duties involved supervision of testing by students, counseling, history taking, report writing, and general clinic scheduling and supervision. This half-time position would enable me to continue to work for a Ph.D., and with a stipend of fifteen hundred dollars I felt I could help with my sister's law school expenses. And so I collected the illegible autographs of my Budapest professors, whose statements were supposedly to the effect that I had been a satisfactory student during their lectures. In scrawled Hungarian and German they were testimonials to a year that made me a year older and hopefully a bit wiser.

Rome, New York

I don't remember how I got to the small town of Rome in upper New York State, or out to the institution. It was at that time one of the largest and most progressive of facilities for the mentally retarded. Dr. Charles Bernstein had developed a program of "colonies" detached from the impressive, fortresslike main building.

The colony was generally a Victorian-type residence in the small towns or farms some five to fifteen miles from the central offices. Generally eight to twelve wards lived there with a mature couple and occasionally additional aides. Each colony was unique, depending on the needs of the residents and the capability and imagination of the houseparents. My assignment was to give individual mental tests to the colony residents, who were to be evaluated annually until the age of ten, biannually between ten and twenty, and at least every three to five years as adults. The results of the tests were reviewed by the staff psychologists in conjunction with observations of the houseparents and social workers. Placements in appropriate vocational programs, colony assignments, or releases to parents or community were decided with Dr. Bernstein's advice.

Generally I spent about a week in each colony living in the guest room but spending time with the residents. The childrens' colonies included a classroom that served for the testing in the summertime. Scheduled tests were coordinated with the boys' or girls' chores, such as weeding in the vegetable gardens, berry picking, and so on. Older residents worked on the farm, in the dairy, or in local industries. Some of the residents in the female colonies had employment as maids, day workers, and garment and glove stitchers. Social activities were provided either in the communities or at the institution. Part of my assignment was at the institution, where generally the residents were more handicapped, had medical or behavior problems, or were awaiting placement in the colonies. It was expected that I would participate with residents, especially in the colonies, and the Wednesday night movies, Saturday dances, and Sunday ball games were not only my main social opportunities to meet other staff members but an unbeatable education in knowing, understanding, and dealing with individuals with limitations.

The fairly routine but responsible work experience at Rome provided a transition between the relatively low-key and culturally different life in Budapest and the more stressful but familiar demands at Ohio State. When I returned to OSU, I became clinic assistant, a quasi staff position. Many of my former friends and associates had graduated. There were fewer assistants, the financial pressures had increased, personal rivalries and friction between faculty members and subdepartments were more evident. In the course of the year budgets and stipends were cut substantially. I enjoyed the work in the clinic. I developed some skills in counseling students, conducting "how to study" programs. The few classes I could take (having exhausted the "interesting" ones while a student) explored areas I found remote from "real life."

Then suddenly a notice appeared on the bulletin board inviting applications for a three-month summer job in Iowa. It was the summer of 1933. Jobs were still very scarce. My assistantship was for the normal school year. Iowa offered fifty dollars a month and maintenance in the institution. While not particularly appealing as a permanent job, this suited my needs of the moment. My application was accepted and I was on the bus to Iowa City the day after my sister graduated from Ohio State's law school.

Although familiar with central Europe and some of Germany and Austria, I had never been west of Toledo. The broad fields of corn and wheat, the widely spaced farmhouses with peeling paint in those dust bowl years, were a bit forbidding. At the student union I was met by a graduate student, Orlo Crissey, who was responsible for coordinating the schedules of the three summer "brain testers." Two other recent M.A. graduates had resumes similar to mine. Marjorie Page from Minnesota and Emalyn Weiss from Pennsylvania, also prepared to be school psychologists, were similarly available for the summer and were interested in additional experience.

The positions had been invented by Harold Skeels, then a research professor at the State University of Iowa's Child Welfare Research Station (ICWRS). One of his responsibilities was the development of research opportunities for graduate students who were interested in various psychological, social, physical, and educational aspects of child development. The six state institutions housing hundreds of children from infants to adolescents seemed to offer many interesting problems. On his visit to the orphanage, originally built to house the children of Civil War veterans, he contracted chicken pox. Skeels used the convalescence period to develop the interest of the orphanage superintendent in participating in university-funded research. The only cost was to be the occasional housing and feeding of graduate students. The general atmosphere of the political bureaucracy that prevailed is reflected in the fact that the superintendent's preparation for his job had been in his experience as a small-town editor. He called the official register of the children "the herdbook."

Although the state governing board had mandated intelligence tests of the children to assure that "normal" and "retarded" were appropriately placed, most had never been examined. Later in the summer, when we reviewed records at the Glenwood State School for mentally retarded, we discovered that Henry Goddard had been there and had administered the initial 1911 and 1916 revisions of the Binet to a number of the residents who were still there in 1933. It was probably his suggestion that resulted in the policy of universal testing of residents. So it was our task to evaluate the some 700 children in the orphanage, the 200 children in the facility for "difficult children," the approximately 1,500 residents at the Woodward State School, and some 2,000 residents at Glenwood. If all went well, we were also to give tests to the 150 delinquent girls at Mitchelville and the 300 to 400 delinquent boys at Eldora.

The purpose of the testing was to establish baselines for later research in which various groups could be matched and experiences compared. The Kuhlmann infant series was used with children under three, the 1916 Stanford-Binet for all others. The wide-range reading and arithmetic tests gave a rapid estimate of school achievement. The figure-drawing test was often used as an introduction, although usually the children were so delighted with the attention from the "brain sisters" that cooperation was no problem.

It was an interesting summer. There were few young resident staffers, especially in the evenings when we might have had free time. The three of us could rarely be housed simultaneously, so we rotated in teams of one and two. The duo would have the state car, which made escape to the nearest town possible. The housing was clean but spartan. The meals were substantial, with plenty of mashed potatoes, ripe tomatoes, and corn on the cob. The weather was even hotter than most Iowa summers. It was the time of dust storms. Open windows provided the only air conditioning. We learned about institutional living, the qualities and differences among staff and administration, but most of all we learned about children. We played with them, were aware of their loneliness, and worried about the superficiality of our brief friendships with them.

The summer ended. We made our reports and went our separate ways. Marjorie Page went to the Child Welfare Research Station to earn her Ph.D., Emalyn Weiss to the special education program in Pennsylvania's Lancaster County, and I back to Ohio State. Perhaps it was the warm friendliness of Iowans that made me more aware of the tensions and interdepartmental hostilities at OSU, which had escalated. Stipends and faculty salaries had been cut—again. Jobs were even more rare. Graduate students, who would have been employed in some niche in normal times, struggled with further education as a better alternative to selling apples. Qualifying exams had devastating failure rates. Rumor had it that the experimental psych examiners deliberately failed clinicians, and vice versa. Morale was abysmal for many reasons, not the least because of finances.

Then came a letter that was my salvation. It was from Harold Skeels on official state of Iowa stationery. He now had a joint appointment with the Board of Control (which managed the children's institutions) and the Iowa Child Welfare Research Station as research professor. He was offering me a position as assistant state psychologist. Essentially I would continue the work done the previous summer with some additions and statewide responsibilities. The salary would be one hundred dollars per month, with maintenance at the institutions.

No job offer could have been more welcome. My father's business had failed, and the stress had damaged his health. My lawyer sister had a city job as a welfare social worker. The maintenance clause enabled me to help my family, but most of all I was able to leave the disappointing university situation. So in January of 1934 I went to Iowa free of academic pressures and problems, well prepared for a job that offered everything I enjoyed.

Iowa

The Depression in 1934 still had not "turned the corner." As a way of sharing costs, the salary and expenses for the new psychological services in the children's institutions and the state department of child welfare were spread over as many entities as possible. Since Skeels, as head of the service, was also a half-time appointee at the University Child Welfare Research Station, the headquarters was designated in Iowa City. It was there that secretarial-service, record-keeping, and planning functions were located. Records relating to individual residents of the various institutions were of course kept in those places. In retrospect it all seems complicated, but with goodwill and understanding and efficient secretarial help to keep records, reports, and travel itineraries flowing, the backlog of work was kept manageable.

Periodic contacts with ICWRS kept me in touch with the staff and students there. The general atmosphere of research, intellectual curiosity, awareness of new directions, and specific researches in mental, social, and physical development were of special interest. Perhaps the most significant part of my responsibility was the evaluation of children before the completion of adoption. Since the basic concepts and practices in adoption have markedly changed in the past fifty years, a brief description may be interesting.

When I went to Iowa in 1934, that state was regarded as about average in sophisticated social consciousness and public policy. The concerns about social problems that largely affected the cities had extended to Iowa as well. The ICWRS had been established in part to help parents become more skillful. Family service and children's agencies were available in the larger communities. Educational opportunities were universal. Adult literacy was among the highest in the nation. Crime was comparatively infrequent. Iowa had problems, mostly financial and as the result of the dust bowl years, but traditional family values were widely accepted and followed. The people were kind, friendly, and hard working.

What then was to be the role of the state psychologist? The administration and integration of intelligence test results of the children and residents of the six institutions was of research interest mainly to the university. The immediate purpose, however, was to assist in planning for the individuals. The basic concepts, based on contributions from Goddard, Terman, and others, were that intelligence was a sine qua non for effective education or vocational placement. Since the measurement of intelligence was possible, knowledge of a child's mental level would help develop appropriate plans for the individual.

A specific application of this concept was in adoption. It was assumed that the more closely the child could match the adopting family in potential, the greater the likelihood of successful outcome. The instances of legal suits by families whose adopted child, placed in infancy, proved to be retarded at school age was a powerful inducement to try anything that would avert such a situation.

In pre–World War II Iowa, as in most of the United States at that time, out-of-wedlock births supplied most of the infants available for adoption. Illegitimacy, even in families in which it was not uncommon, was regarded as a shame, a disgrace to be concealed. There are no reliable data on abortions, but it is generally believed they were rare. Information about birth control procedures, in-utero development, and sexual matters in general was not widely available. Early marriages legitimatized some children. Private placements or children's agency placements were believed to be responsible for children from "better families." Less competent or affluent families found themselves channeled to the county and state agencies and eventually to the state child care resources. At that time there was no Aid to Dependent Children. Except for widows, single mothers were virtually unknown. Information about family medical or social history was sparse and unreliable. Mothers who gave birth at the university hospital were fairly often given intelligence tests shortly after delivery. Contact between mother and child ended with her signed release for adoption. Contact with the natural father was rarely established, and information about him was unreliable.

Families interested in adoption have understandably preferred to adopt infants. Although the adoption procedure was similar in the private, public, and state agencies, the following descriptions refer to the state facility with which I worked. The adopting family would contact the state placement agent in their geographic area, have a preliminary interview, and arrange for the necessary letters of recommendation from family physicians, religious leaders, and various community references. The state placement agent was generally an intelligent woman, occasionally with some education beyond high school, but not at that time a trained social worker. Usually a political appointee, she kept in touch with her headquarters at the state child welfare department as well as the childrens' institutions. In reality she had no contact with the institutions for the retarded or the delinquent, since foster placements from these were rare. Her evaluation of the potential adopting family was shared with the state office and the superintendents of the orphanages. Originally the placement decisions were made by the superintendent and head nurse, representing the child, and the state placement agent, representing the petitioning family. By 1935 there were monthly meetings that included psychologists and teachers when older children were involved.

Even after the inclusion of a psychologist on the placement committee, the evaluation and selective process remained essentially the same. The available petitioning-family folders were reviewed for age, education, occupation, coloring and appearance, gender or age preferences, and any details that illuminated personalities, possible contributions, or limitations. There were usually more applicants than available infants. Then the folders of the available infants or children were reviewed for gender, age, coloring and appearance, religion of family, health, and any special details to be considered. Usually there was little useful social or medical history about the maternal side, and still less about the paternal side. Comments such as "She never knew his name because he kept his hat on" were not uncommon.

Matching was based on the gender preference of the petitioning family and on their religion. Jewish, Catholic, and Lutheran children were placed in similar families; otherwise, Protestants were regarded as one group. Prior to 1934 other details were usually ignored. After that time there was some attention to maternal IQ, educational level, and occupational status. However, there were few instances that would have deviated from the generally lower socioeconomic status of the majority. Infants were placed as early as the legal and medical process could be completed. It was not uncommon, in the days before antibiotics, for the place-ment to be delayed or cancelled by a baby's illness. Usually the state agent took the children to the adoptive home, where the long-awaited infants were joyfully and uncritically welcomed.

The state agent left a few instructions regarding care and feeding and usually made a follow-up visit in several months. At the end of twelve months the family could apply for final legal adoption. The state agent had usually made one to four visits during this period and, assuming there had been no problems, would rec-ommend the adoption. In the rare cases in which health or adjustment problems had emerged, adoption could be delayed. In the Depression period, delays for fi-nancial reasons were frequent, and during these delays the state agent might or might not continue periodic visits.

At the beginning of 1934 an additional step was interposed. With the availabil-ity of a psychologist, a mental test was to be given before the final adoption to as-sure that the child was normal in intelligence. This was not a simple decision in-tended merely to avoid lawsuits for misrepresentation. Theoretically, all children in the orphanages were "normal," the "retarded" ones having been placed in ap-propriate institutions. The available information on biological family histories was replete with comments about intellectual and social inadequacies. Available IQs and educational status of natural mothers showed substantial numbers to be retarded, with the median in the slow average (80 to 90 IQ) level, and few with IQs above 95. It should be recalled that between 1920 and 1940 it was generally accepted by psychologists as well as the general public that intelligence was a ge-netic trait, reasonably consistent through a lifetime and predictable from parent to child. Skeels's undergraduate background had been in dairy, that is, bovine, heredity and its effect on milk production. I was influenced by H. H. Goddard and quite familiar with the family studies of the Jukes and the Kallikaks. These had "proved conclusively" that deficiencies "ran in families." It is understandable that prior to going to the adoptive homes we not only reviewed any relevant in-formation with special care but were prepared to negotiate the return of a child deemed unsuitable for that home and family.

For various reasons, including anticipated changes in final adoption proce-dures, there was an accumulation of petitions for final legal adoption in 1934. The procedure included the preadoption psychological evaluation of the child after at least twelve months in the adoptive home. Since the rather sketchy histories of the children's natural families suggested there was a high risk of developmental de-lays, and possibly of jeopardy in the adoption, both Harold Skeels and I felt a spe-cial responsibility in these examinations. By the end of that year some two hun-dred children under the age of five years had been seen. None were retarded. All were at least average, with IQs well above the 90 to 100 range. Clearly, this sig-naled a need for further research, and since most were "my children," the project became my Ph.D. dissertation and lifelong research interest.

Briefly, children who had been placed under six months of age, first examined at about two and a half years had a mean Kuhlmann IQ of 116. When reexamined at four years, they had a mean 1916 Binet IQ of 112. Subsequently, there were follow-up examinations at approximately seven years of age and again at about fourteen years in 1946, when it was anticipated that no further tests would be given. At a later date when the one hundred subjects who had been seen at all four examinations were in their middle thirties in age, a follow-up assessment was again possible. The results confirmed that all subjects continued to be normal and above average in intelligence. Education and vocational placement was consistent with their respective test results. Neither the subjects nor their children were retarded. None were on welfare.

There were a number of other studies of children who experienced adoption at different ages, or whose life experiences were unique in various ways. Probably the most spectacular study was one conducted by Skeels and myself. Briefly, twelve children who as infants showed marked retardation in development without identifiable physiological problems were moved from the orphanage for normal children and placed as "guests" on adult "high grade moron" wards in institutions. From a situation where each had been the least appealing of a large group, the subjects became the favorite singleton in a group of adults—staff members and residents. Each received copious attention and stimulation, in a relatively short time attained intellectual normalcy, and was placed in an adoptive home. As adults these subjects became self-supporting, with high school educations plus additional schooling and eventual skilled, office, or professional vocations.

A contrasting group of twelve had as individuals been identified as normal in infancy and eligible for adoptive placement. Various impediments of health, legal complications, and mischances kept them in the orphanage. Repeated psychological testing showed progressive reduction in IQ, eventually resulting in transfer to institutions for the mentally retarded, where, no longer infants, they became like the typical residents. As adults they have remained retarded and unable to live independently. A twenty-fifth individual, although initially identified with this second cohort, received special attention at critical periods in his childhood and as an adult is self-supporting and engaged in a skilled trade.

The studies showed that it is possible to maintain researcher-subject relationships over a lifetime, through changes in residence, occupation, and family situations. The cooperation of the adopting parents and the adoptees was delightful. Examinations were conducted in the homes. Parents, and when appropriate the children, were given an interpretation of the tests and the results. There was always ample time for discussion of the implications of the results, suggestions for help with education or behavior issues, and for adolescents considerable discussion of vocational planning.

These studies constituted part of a stream of research reports under the guidance of George D. Stoddard, Beth Wellman, Harold Skeels, and others at the

ICWRS. The findings indicated that IQ was not constant over a lifetime, that it was closely related to environmental stimulation and educational opportunity, that extreme changes for individuals could occur as a result of life experiences, and that a child's mental development was more dependent on his home stimulation than on his parental genetic endowment. The debates regarding these propositions about the role of nature versus nurture enlivened research- and professional-organization meetings for many years. The Iowa studies, and others that followed, constituted the theoretical underpinning for changes in adoption practices as well as for the development of Headstart and Homestart programs and some aspects of special education.

Michigan

As important as this research was, it was not the whole of my life. I left the state job in 1936 to become a research assistant at ICWRS and completed my Ph.D. in 1939. Research and university positions were still in short supply, and I was pleased to become assistant director of the Guidance Center in Flint, Michigan. The director, Orlo Crissey, whom I had met in Iowa, undertook the development of a major guidance and counseling program in the high schools under the joint administration of the University of Michigan and the Guidance Center. I had responsibility for the staff of social workers and psychologists who provided clinical service to agencies, schools, and individuals in the community. The Iowa research was continued on a spare-time and vacation-period basis for some years. As a major contributor to the Iowa concepts of the modifiability of intelligence and the influence of environment on mental development, I was involved in the debates and discussions on both a local and national level. But the supervision of staff and participation in community and agency roles was how I earned my living.

In the meantime, Germany invaded Poland in 1939 and the Depression gradually ended as industries became involved in war production. Priorities changed abruptly with the bombing of Pearl Harbor in 1941. By 1942 the guidance project ended. Orlo Crissey moved into industrial psychology and the war effort. I became director of the Guidance Center and, as head of a community agency, increasingly involved in consultation with family services and child-placement, delinquency-prevention, and youth programs—a far cry from person-to-person or research interests. I became involved with establishing Big Brother programs, child care facilities for mothers newly employed in war work, and other community activities. On a volunteer basis the Guidance Center staff and I assisted in the selection of skilled workers for the war effort.

Eventually World War II also ended. Jobs opened up and psychologists newly released from the services were available to fill them as well as to attend or teach the university graduate programs. Administration of the Guidance Center was transferred from local to state funding. I entered private practice, one of two psychologists in private practice in the state and the only woman.

Beginning in about 1942, I taught classes for the University of Michigan extension service and the on-campus summer school. The courses were related to counseling of high school students, child and adolescent development, vocational guidance, tests related to guidance, and interest and aptitude assessment. At the graduate level, most of the enrollees were teachers or social workers interested in master's degrees. Since I was then currently involved in the application of what I was teaching and the students had in most cases immediate need for the material covered, general interest was high and the discussions lively. I continued teaching two or three courses a term for fifteen years. Although some courses were on the Ann Arbor campus, others were at evening extension centers one hundred to two hundred miles distant. Finally the extensive traveling and the late-night hours persuaded me that it was time to change.

Among the consultant tasks in my practice was my evaluation of infants for adoptive or foster placement for several public and private children's agencies in Michigan and Iowa. For a number of years I evaluated the interests and capabilities of juniors in the school for the blind. Similarly, I dealt with clients for the vocational rehabilitation office. The continuing contacts with schools, pediatricians, and community leaders brought private referrals for learning disabilities, vocational and educational guidance, behavior problems, and other situations with a need for assessment and counseling.

Following the end of World War II, in the late 1940s, there was an upsurge of concern about education and particularly the needs of schoolchildren beyond traditional academics. Although special classes for mentally retarded children had a history dating back to the 1890s, it was in the 1940s that funds became available for the expansion of other programs. The development of associations for children with special needs, such as the Association for Retarded Children, brought additional pressures. In Michigan, as in many other states, psychological and social service programs were developed to assist both students and teachers in coping with behavior, adjustment, social, and learning problems. In Michigan the program was initially designated the "visiting teacher" service to avoid what was regarded as a possible stigma attached to "social work" from the welfare programs of the Depression.

At the inception of any new program there are some technicalities to be considered. For example, schools at that time had only two classes of employees—certified teachers, including administrators (who had been teachers), and noncertified employees like secretaries and janitors. There were few psychologists or social workers who had teaching certificates, and still fewer teachers who could qualify as social workers or psychologists. To assist in the cross-certification of persons in any of these groups, the major universities offered special courses in social work, psychology, and education. It was in these areas that my academic background and my work history became useful. I taught the courses for crossover aspirants for a number of years at the University of Michigan.

In 1949, the new, young, and forward-looking superintendent of the Dearborn Schools was reorganizing the administrative structure of the system. In the process he had acquired two temporarily certified "visiting teachers." For various reasons he wanted to have a strong unit of special services and asked me to join the central staff. I was not anxious to leave the interestingly varied challenges of private practice but agreed to go on a half-time basis for two years. As happens with many part-time arrangements, the half became larger and larger, so that in a few years I agreed to a full-time appointment. This made for a tidier fiscal arrangement, which pleased the business office.

Dearborn

Dearborn, a middle- and working-class suburb adjacent to Detroit, at that time was a rapidly growing community. It had been the home of Henry Ford, and major auto factories were still located there. It had some notoriety as a "pure white" city. The ethnic background of the working-class area was largely Polish and Italian. The upper-middle-class area was largely populated by college-educated engineers and professionals from the nearby auto companies. In the fifty years since then, Dearborn has changed, as have many of the Rust Belt suburbs. It now has the largest Muslim and Middle Eastern immigrant population in the United States. Many professionals have moved still farther from the urban center.

The school system was recognized as above average in the caliber of its faculty and the achievements of the students. Salaries were above the average of the state. A program for mentally handicapped children had been initiated in the early 1930s but had aged along with the teachers who had initiated it. There was a good counseling program in the high schools. The two visiting teachers had begun the social work courses that would qualify them as school social workers. Former elementary school teachers—one of science, the other of social studies—they possessed not only abundant energy and tireless interest in their schools, teachers, and families but were also interested in applying new approaches and ideas.

I was given a great deal of freedom to organize the program. Discussions with principals, administrative staff, and the two visiting teachers, as well as input from the informal grapevine that exists in every school, eventually resulted in arrangements that worked well for the twenty years I was in Dearborn. The unit had several changes of title over the years—Psychological Services, Special Services, and the like. Its purpose remained the same: to serve children and staff with diagnostic psychological evaluations and with remedial and counseling help emphasizing prevention of more serious maladjustments or disturbances. The program began with the two visiting teachers, who served the elementary and middle school buildings and a population of some twenty thousand students. The social work staff was increased whenever financially possible, reaching twelve staff memebers after twenty years.

Parochial and private schools had been added in the meantime, and financial problems did not always permit a full staff. As some of the middle school students entered high school, services followed them there. Some social workers were particularly skilled in helping adolescents, others in helping families and younger children. As far as possible, assignments to buildings or areas were made to accommodate skills and preferences. Early in the program, contacts were made with the universities most active in training school social workers (University of Michigan, Wayne State), and in the course of time interns or trainees were assigned to work with the best-qualified Dearborn staff. In the early years seminars and workshops were arranged, bringing experienced social workers, psychologists, and psychiatrists to provide inspiration and practical suggestions. Although arranged and funded by Dearborn, these programs were open to other school professionals in neighboring school districts. Eventually these workshops were taken over by the universities and by the professional organizations.

It also became apparent that my time was more effectively spent with teachers, principals, and various groups rather than in the individual assessment of students. However, the group tests, classroom-teacher observations, and my own brief reviews still needed the clinical studies of certain students. These discussions with teachers, parents, school social workers, and others were seen as most effective when carried out by the psychologist who had worked with the child. At that time, the University of Michigan in its clinical psychology program had an abundance of graduate students seeking practicum experience—some in schools rather than in clinics. Modest stipends provided internships over several years until it was possible to employ psychologists for the school system. By 1969 there were six members with master's degrees or ABDs on the psychology staff in addition to myself.

Since one of the mandated responsibilities of a school psychologist was the identification of candidates for special education for the mentally retarded, the supervision of these special classes was included in my purview. For local reasons, special classes for the physically disabled, visually or hearing handicapped, and homebound remained in a separate category. Although special classes for the mentally retarded had existed in Dearborn for many years, the lack of a qualified psychologist and absence of leadership had resulted in stagnation. Children remained in a program with the same teacher for years. Regular classroom teachers were reluctant to nominate students, and by agreement simply lifted them year by year until they could leave school or be excluded. In some respects handicapped students were "mainstreamed" then, but the classroom teacher had no help with the students who could not keep up.

The entire program came under review. The students were reevaluated, some for the first time in years. Friendly pressure for revisions and program updating encouraged some teachers to elect the retirement for which they were overdue. Close contacts with the special education training departments of Wayne State University and other schools made possible the recruitment of a young, energetic, and creative staff. The program was formulated, covering the early elementary through high school years. The staff was encouraged to focus on real-life skills and academics to provide the reading and math useful in daily needs. The high school program was integrated with the mainstream as far as possible—special students with acceptable skills were included, for example, in shop, art, crafts, and music classes. The special classes ran the popcorn machine and sales at high school athletic events. Part-time work placements were arranged for most during the last two years of school, with supervision by the special education teacher. Students were included in the regular commencement exercises.

Partly as a result of my statewide contacts with parents of severely handicapped students, I was aware of the needs of those excluded from school altogether. The process of initiating a program for the so-called uneducable retarded was long, even devious, in the 1940s through the 1960s. Eventually the parents were organized and reassured that the schools were indeed interested in their children (previous rejections and exclusions had convinced them to the contrary). Precious space was found in the school system, which was coping with continually increasing enrollment in all the grade levels. The parents in the area where the classes were to meet were reassured that no harm would come to their "normal" children as a result of meeting the observably handicapped. So in the late 1950s the first Michigan public school classes for children previously excluded from them were begun in the Dearborn schools, a pioneer among public schools in the country in including severely handicapped children.

There were other projects responding to needs identified by the staff of social workers and psychologists. There was an experimental group of dyslexic, attention-deficit-disordered elementary children taught by an experienced remedial-reading and physical-development-oriented teacher. Though the initial group was small, the experiment proved that grouping such children (as advocated by some educators), was counterproductive.

Because increasing numbers of attention-deficit- and behavior-disordered children were being identified, close relationships were developed with pediatric neurologists and a clinic whose staff developed an interest in these problems. Various medications, notably Ritalin, were utilized and results assessed.

When federal funds became available in the 1960s, a major project was formulated in the school with a heavy population of the children of immigrants from the Middle East. It also had the lowest family income, and the largest failure rate, and student turnover. The objective was to study the efficacy of early identification and remediation of potential health and learning problems. Along with this, the most vulnerable and "at risk" children were to enter a kindergarten program designed to remedy the language, motor skills, and cognitive deficits that separated them from adequately prepared kindergarten enrollees. They were to receive supplementary meals, the full-time services of a school social worker, and medical care when needed.

In addition to these, there were other projects that, unhappily, as anyone who works in a public school milieu can attest, failed to meet the criteria of meaningful research. The results were rarely written up for publication. Once the answers and suggestions were evident, the programs were either modified for practical use or discontinued. More often, the demands of the job, the exigencies of finances, and lack of time prevented the details and safeguards and write-ups that "real research" would have required.

Psychology as a science has its origins in academia. Its extension into applied fields was supported by the universities and by the American Psychological Association (APA) through major conferences in which basic principles and related training needs were defined. Among the conferences in which I participated were the 1951 Conference on Counseling Psychology held at Northwestern University, the 1958 Conference on Graduate Education in Psychology in Miami, Florida, and the 1954 Thayer Conference on School Psychology at West Point. I have been a member of APA since 1938–39 and was president of the Division of Consulting and the Division on Mental Retardation, as well as a member of many boards and committees.

While busy at the Dearborn schools, I continued my private practice in Flint on weekends and school vacations. The lack of the blocks of time, which seemed essential for the completion of reports of the research projects, which in themselves lacked academic standards of purity and rigor, led to the accumulation of boxes of data to await my eventual analysis. They are still waiting.

Retirement

In the meantime, my private life had changed. I married Orlo Crissey in 1966 and acquired three adult children and their spouses. In the course of time there have been added nine grandchildren, ten great-grandchildren and one great-great-grandchild.

I retired from the Dearborn schools in 1969. Orlo retired from General Motors in 1970. Although we continued some professional obligations for several years, the active involvement in psychology tapered off. Unlike many retirees, we declined consulting opportunities. The vacation trips that had been usurped by our jobs and responsibilities to our profession we now enjoyed with freedom. We traveled extensively, enjoyed our home and garden, and observed the changes in our respective fields. We marveled at the speed of change, the departure of colleagues, the mind-boggling contributions of technology. We had each thoroughly enjoyed our working years. We felt we had made some contributions to society and to our professions. We had certainly received recognition for our efforts.[1]

A review of a long and active life is a humbling experience. The choices made sometimes seemed inevitable at the time—or heartrendingly difficult. In retrospect it is tempting to speculate on where another choice might have led. In one segment of my life it seemed almost inevitable that I would become an academic, devoted to research, publication, and teaching. In some diluted way this has remained in my life through the years as a minor theme—but incomplete, fragmented, haunting. The boxes of data, the sheets of incomplete evaluations, continue to induce guilt and determination to get at the unfinished business. In actuality, I have spent most of my working life in service activities. Helping children, adolescents, and their families, is what probably the majority of psychologists in APA really do in one form or another.

At times an even larger portion of my time was devoted to administration, to making it possible for others—psychologists, social workers, teachers, parents, other administrators—to carry out their responsibilities more effectively. This might be done through chairing case conferences or programs or crafting new programs of education or social service. It required the understanding and adroit education of community groups and political entities to lead to the acceptance and cooperative development of new programs in schools, in agencies, in public services.

Nor were any of the results attributable solely to my efforts. The ideas and influence of all the people I encountered—Henry Goddard, George Stoddard, Beth Wellman, Harold Skeels, to name only the best known, and the many associates in Iowa, Ohio, and Michigan—shaped my thinking, my behavior, my goals. Human beings—like the forty-year-old severely handicapped man brought to the Rome State School in a basket by his aged parents—influenced my concepts about social responsibility. The changes in attitudes and behavior that seemed to sweep like tides over society as a whole influenced me as well. At the beginning of my career there was no question that "nature" was dominant, that human beings could not change what heredity had ordained. The studies with which I was involved were not the only ones to contradict this and shift the emphasis to "nurture." But the adoption studies and the follow-up over the years were the most persuasive and understandable.

Probably every generation thinks that the social changes in its lifetime surpass those of any other period. Only those interested in history are apt to know that previous generations of professionals had to cope with different problems, were surrounded by different attitudes, operated with different givens, had different social objectives. The task of delineating the differences in psychology, education, and child development between 1930 and 1990 must be left to more discerning viewers—and another book. But a few of the differences may be noted. In 1930, out-of-wedlock pregnancies were socially disapproved of and concealed, the child was placed for adoption, and there was almost always no further contact between mother and child. In 1990, out-of-wedlock pregnancies have increased in frequency, are accepted by society, and the child is kept by the mother, who joins the growing number of single parents. In the 1930s, adoption records were sealed. Adoptee searches for natural parents were discouraged. In the 1990s, open adoption is increasingly frequent, with varying degrees of mutuality between natural parents and adopting parents.

In 1930, special education of mentally handicapped children was moving in the direction of separate classes and specialized training from the previous direction of exclusion or regular class placement. In 1990, "mainstreaming" and community placement and inclusion in all activities is usual. In 1930, concepts of human heredity were based largely on Mendelian and Darwinian theories and gross family studies and class descriptions. In 1990, more sophisticated microscopic studies of brain/neurology structure and human psychology suggest there is an organic/structural basis for behavior. In 1930, environmental influences were measured only by very gross classifications (for instance, occupational title or educational level). In 1990, environmental influences are described by the nature of adult or peer relations with the subject.

Did I enjoy my life as psychologist/educator? Yes, very much. Would I choose it again? If these were the 1930s—yes. If the choice is for the 1990s, I am not so sure. It would be tempting to opt for research in either the neurological/psychological basis of behavior or in the details of environmental impact that result in behavior.

What were the influences that guided my career? Chance, opportunity, or choice? I leave it to the reader to identify them.

Notes

1. Among the many honors received from professional colleagues and community groups, perhaps the most cherished was the Joseph P. Kennedy Award for Research in Mental Retardation, shared with Harold Skeels.

Representative Publications

Crissey, M. (1984). Prevention in retrospect: Adoption follow up. In J. Joffe, M. Albee, W. George & L. Kelly (Eds.), *Readings in primary prevention of psychopathology: Basic concepts* (pp. 348–363). Hanover, N.H.: University Press of New England.

Crissey, M. & Rosen, M. (Eds.). (1986). *Institutions for the mentally retarded: A changing role in changing times.* Austin, Tex.: Pro. Ed.

Cutts, N. (with Newland, E. & Skodak, M.). (1955). *School psychologists at mid century.* Washington, D.C.: American Psychological Association.

Roe, A. (with Gustad, J. W., Moore, B., Sherman, R. & Skodak, M.). (1959). *Graduate education in psychology.* Washington, D.C.: American Psychological Assciation.

Scholl, G., Bauman, M. & Skodak-Crissey, M. (1969). *A study of the vocational success of groups of the visually handicapped.* Ann Arbor: University of Michigan School of Education.

Skeels, H. & Skodak, M. (1965). Techniques for a high yield follow-up study in the field. *Public Health Reports, 80,* 249–257.

Skodak, M. (1939). Children in foster homes: A study of mental development. *University of Iowa, Studies in Child Welfare, 16,* no. 1.

Skodak, M. (1967). Adult status of individuals who experienced early intervention. In B. W. Richards (Ed.), *Proceedings of the First Congress of the International Association for the Scientific Study of Mental Deficiency* (pp. 11–18). Surrey, England: Jackson Publishing Company.

Skodak, M. (1967). *A follow up and comparison of graduates form two types of high school programs for the mentally handicapped.* (Final report of Office of Education, Project No. 6–8680). Dearborn, Mich.: Dearborn Public Schools Press.

Skodak, M. & Skeels, H. (1945). A follow-up study of children in adoptive homes. *Journal of Genetic Psychology, 66,* 21–58.

Skodak, M. & Skeels, H. (1949). A final follow up of one hundred adopted children. *Journal of Genetic Psychology, 75,* 85–125.

Skodak Crissey, M. (1975). Mental retardation past, present and future. *American Psychologist, 30,* 800–808.

Wellman, B., Skeels, H. & Skodak, M. (1940). Review of McNemar's critical examination of Iowa studies. *Psychological Bulletin, 37,* 93–111.

4

David Elkind

Birth, Family Background, Early Years

As a grown man traveling to my father's funeral with a couple of my uncles, I heard for the first time that my conception was an unwanted pregnancy. Indeed, some years later my older brothers told me that my mother had tried, unsuccessfully, to abort me by riding on a roller coaster. However unwanted, I made my entrance into the world on March 11, 1931, just as the Depression was descending on the country. I was the sixth, and last, child of Peter and Bessie Elkind, who as adolescents had immigrated to the United States to escape the pogroms against Jews in Russia. My father was a machinist and moved to Detroit, where the growing auto industry provided him the best job opportunities.

In Russia my grandfather had owned a tobacco factory, and my father learned his trade working in this factory. Although he had less than a high school education, he was an avid reader and in his younger years was active in the labor movement. My mother was the daughter of a shamus, the caretaker of the shtetl synagogue. Her own mother died when she was quite young, and she took on the responsibility for rearing her younger siblings and thus had little formal schooling. As a child I remember trying to teach my mother to read to prepare her to take the examination required to get her citizenship papers. By then I had become, if not the favorite, at least not the scapegoat or the focus of resentment.

Perhaps because of their own backgrounds, my parents did not venerate education in the way that many Jewish parents did. My father always worked with his hands, and he believed that was the only honorable occupation for a man. Nonetheless, my oldest sister did go to college and got a degree in education. She taught in an early childhood setting for a number of years. Later she went to law school and after graduation edited a prestigious law journal. My two oldest brothers, however, followed in my father's footsteps, and one opened his own machine shop while the other started his own printing business. My younger sister worked as a secretary until her marriage. The brother closest to me did not attend college either but worked as a production manager in an advertising firm before starting his own highly successful packaging and shipping company.

It was not, therefore, an intellectual family, and I never felt any pressure to achieve academically. From my earliest years, however, I was a voracious reader. There were only a limited number of books in our small three-bedroom apartment (we had to eat in shifts), and I quickly went through them. Then I discovered the public library. After one of my older brothers generously bought me a bicycle, the library became my favorite place. If I found an author I liked, I read every book that he or she had written. I recall reading all of the Edgar Rice Burroughs *Tarzan* novels and all of the *Dr. Doolittle* stories. The practice of reading all of an author's works is one I still subscribe to, but my tastes have changed.

It is always dangerous, of course, to rely on reconstructive memory to give a true account of determining factors in one's life. With that caveat, several events stand out, on reflection, as giving me some indication of where I was headed. First there was the radio program *One Man's Family,* which we listened to weekly. One of the characters, Paul, was a kind, sympathetic person who listened to everyone's problems and gave sound and wise counsel. I identified with Paul and always wanted to be like him. It may be one of the influences that turned me toward clinical psychology. Second, I began writing poetry and stories in elementary school and even had one of my poems published in the school paper. The compulsion to write has stayed with me all these years. For most people writing is anxiety provoking, but for true writers this relationship has a different valence. We become anxious if we are not writing and, in effect, scribble to reduce our anxiety.

Finally, I owe a great deal to my father. As a machinist he worked in small machine shops that did custom work. He would often come home frustrated because the blueprints he was given to work from, drawn by college-trained engineers, were impossible to machine. He had to redraw and redesign the product so that he could turn the pieces out on the lathe or milling machine. Although my father effectively reinvented many of the machines he built, he never got any credit for his contribution—which often made the company a lot of money. That is one reason, perhaps, that he had a job throughout the Depression. My father thus sensitized me to the importance and complexities of translating theory into practice. Later, combined with my writing avocation, I extended this awareness to a concern for translating complex theories into language that nonprofessionals can understand.

After World War II, we moved to California. We had aunts there, and one of my brothers had spent some time in San Diego in preparation for going overseas to fight in the Pacific. In addition, my father had emphysema (contracted in Russia when his father's factory burned and he had tried to save some equipment), and the cold winters were becoming more difficult for him as he got older. After attending elementary and junior high school in Detroit, I went to high school in Los Angeles. I was always a rather indifferent student, getting Bs and Cs and an occasional A. In retrospect I realize that I was bored and frustrated and simply got by with the minimum of work.

Fortunately, or unfortunately, in high school I became friends with a group of boys who came from more traditional Jewish homes and who had high (or what seemed to me as high) educational aspirations. They were also athletic, which I was not, and played a lot of cards, particularly during lunch. I was not an experienced card player and was always making stupid mistakes, like not counting suits, when we played hearts. At such times they would tease me by chanting, "Oh Elkind, so dumb."

It got to me, I guess. So I decided to see whether I was so dumb after all and really applied myself during my senior year. I still recall how one day, in our business law course, I gave both the defending and opposing arguments of a difficult case after my friends had been called on but were unprepared. For that year I got all As with the exception of a B in Spanish. Since I had done so well I decided to apply to UCLA, where all my friends were also applying. At the time I was working after school for a small clothing manufacturer and was learning all facets of the business. When I applied to UCLA, I chose apparel merchandising as a major and thought that would be my lifelong occupation. Thanks to my good grades during my senior year in high school, I made the grade-point cutoff and was admitted to the university.

College and Graduate Education

Perhaps because my family life had not prepared me for college, I was terrified at being there and was sure that I was going to fail and would again be the butt of my friends' derision. Thanks to my anxiety, I studied diligently all semester long. To my amazement I got all As that semester, with the exception of a B in art history, the course that was required for majors in apparel merchandising. That poor showing in my alleged major, and my early fascination with helping people, reinforced by taking the introductory psychology course taught by social psychologist Richard Centers, helped me to decide to become a psychologist. My grades won me a university scholarship, and during my sophomore year I changed my major to psychology.

Over the next three years I never lost my anxiety about failure and put all my energies into course work. I continued to get all As and to win state scholarships. I made Phi Beta Kappa in my junior year and graduated with highest honors. The psychology faculty encouraged me to apply to graduate school, and I did so when I learned that there were no jobs available for someone with a mere B.A. in psychology. At that time the Veterans Administration (VA) had set up the Clinical Psychology Training Program to recruit psychologists to work for the VA after graduation. The program paid not only tuition but also what at that time was a generous living stipend in return for twenty hours of work each week. Fortunately, I was accepted into the program. Without it, I would never have been able to afford graduate school.

Although the faculty at UCLA was excellent, there was nonetheless a schizophrenic character to the department, which I ingested and which contributed to the repeated upsets in the course of my professional life. Those professors who worked in the traditional psychology subject-matter areas—learning, social, physiological, and so on—were deeply invested in positivistic, experimental science. The clinical faculty, on the other hand, was heavily committed to Freudian theory and projective testing. This led to some unsettling experiences. To illustrate, one morning I attended an experimental course and learned that the Rorschach was unscientific and that one might as well use tarot cards. That same afternoon I participated in a Rorschach seminar and observed Bruno Klopfer use the Rorschach test to diagnose a brain tumor before it appeared on any neurophysiological test.

When it came time to do my dissertation (I finished in three years and attained my doctorate just after turning twenty-four), I was in a quandary. Although I wanted to do something clinical, I also wanted to do something scientifically rigorous. I decided to do a learning study, but one that would test the theories of both Hull and Freud. My idea was that according to both these theories, learning would be most efficacious if it was done under the motivation of two drives rather than one alone. Accordingly, I ran rats who were hungry but not thirsty, rats who were thirsty but not hungry, and rats who were both hungry and thirsty. As predicted, the rats who were both hungry and thirsty ran faster to reduce their drives than did animals deprived of either food or water alone.

I finished my degree before I finished my clinical training and spent a year after receiving my doctorate in the VA Mental Hygiene Clinic in downtown Los Angeles. At that time my father was working in a food-packing-machine company not far from the clinic, and we drove back and forth to work together. Although he was proud of my academic accomplishments, he still could never understand how I could earn a living by just talking to people. In my father's view, if you did not work with your hands, you really did not work.

Throughout my training I was blessed with good teachers. My thesis supervisor was John Seward, an exceptionally fine teacher and researcher. I studied the history of psychology with Carolyn Fisher, my first exposure to a woman academic. Her scholarship, her erudition, and her wonderful lectures helped inoculate me against a gender bias that was all too common among academics during that period. My clinical supervisors included Ruth Tolman, Edwin Schneidman, and Norman Fareberow. When I finished my VA training I planned to get a job in a VA hospital, but my supervisors encouraged me to apply for a postdoctoral fellowship at the Austen Riggs Center in Stockbridge, Massachusetts. David Rappaport, a renowned Freudian scholar whom I knew from his book on diagnostic testing, was looking for a research assistant. I applied for the position, flew to Austen Riggs for an interview, and was accepted. I moved to Stockbridge in 1956.

Career: The Early Years

Rappaport and others from the Menninger Clinic had recently moved to Austen Riggs to transform it into a residential treatment center for adolescents and young adults. Erik Erikson, who had just published *Childhood and Society,* was also on the staff. David Shapiro, who later wrote *Neurotic Styles,* was the chief psychologist. There were many other notables on the staff, and the patients included the actress Margaret Sullivan and the playwright William Inge. Tennessee Williams came for an interview but was afraid analysis would destroy his creativity and moved on. Norman Rockwell's studio was across the street from our main building, and he often came by and shouted hello to everyone. The case conferences at Riggs were some of the most intellectually exciting and challenging I ever attended.

While I was completing my VA stint, and before moving to Stockbridge, I began receiving books from David Rappaport. Inasmuch as Rappaport was a leading Freudian scholar, I assumed that these books would be by, or about, Freud. To my surprise, the books were not by Freud but rather by a Swiss psychologist who had been obliquely mentioned in my child psychology text as a quaint fellow who interviewed children on the banks of Lake Geneva. So, a year after receiving my doctorate I had my first serious introduction to the works of Jean Piaget. It was the major turning point in my career.

When I first read Piaget, I was rather put out. At UCLA I had been steeped in experimental methodology, and designing experiments was my forte. In reading the Piagetian studies I was appalled at his failure to standardize his procedures, his lack of attention to routine rules of sampling, and his total failure to offer any sort of quantification of his results. Rappaport and I had been systematically reading Piaget's *The Child's Conception of Number,* and I decided to test his findings with a tight, carefully controlled experiment that would put his findings to a rigorous test. I had every expectation of showing that his findings could not be supported with experimental and quantitative methods.

The research design required the testing of children aged four to six or seven whom I was able to recruit from the nursery school at Austen Riggs and the local public schools. I standardized Piaget's materials and interview procedures and assigned numbers to children's responses. To my surprise, as I began testing the children, they responded much as Piaget had said they would. When I subjected the data to an analysis of variance, the age differences were easily statistically significant. From a doubter and a skeptic I became an ardent convert. I realized that Piaget could help me to resolve the schizophrenia of wanting to be a clinician concerned with meaningful content yet also being eager to be a hard-nosed researcher dedicated to scientific rigor. Piaget, unlike most researchers at the time, dealt with relevant meaningful material: how children conceptualized the world, how they understood causality, how they progressed in their moral judgments. At the same time, I found that these studies could be done in a scientifically acceptable way. The meaningful, relevant content satisfied my clinical inclinations while the ability to study these contents using demanding methods satisfied my scientific conscience.

The introduction to Piaget changed my life course in still other ways. I had gone to Austen Riggs with the aim of extending my theoretical understanding of Freudian theory and to sharpen my clinical skills. After conducting my first Piagetian investigation, however, I discovered that I liked working with children and decided that I would prefer to do clinical work with young people rather than with adults. Inasmuch as my clinical training had been entirely with VA patients, I knew that I had to do further postdoctoral work to get clinical experience with children. Rappaport was instrumental in getting me a position in the child psychiatry department at the Beth Israel Hospital in Boston, where I moved after I left Riggs in 1957.

At Riggs, I also taught a course on child development combining Piaget and Erikson. The course was quite successful and helped me to recognize that I enjoyed teaching and had a bit of a flair for it. When I moved to Boston and began working at the Beth Israel, I also took on a night teaching position at the then Rhode Island College of Education. I also did part-time clinical work at the Cambridge Child Guidance Center. In addition, I became serious about writing and established a pattern of getting up every morning at six and writing for two or three hours. I wrote and rewrote paragraphs, beginnings and endings, and so on. For a time I wrote children's stories and had two of them published. One summer I even attended the Breadloaf Writers Conference in Vermont. But I finally realized that I was not a fiction writer but rather an essayist and, in addition to writing up my research, I began writing pieces for a number of different journals, a practice I maintain today.

After two years at the Beth Israel and a part-time position working for the State of Massachusetts evaluating special-needs children, I wanted more opportunities to teach and more time to pursue my Piagetian research than a clinical position would allow. I applied for and was hired as an assistant professor at Wheaton College in Norton, Massachusetts, a private women's college. At Wheaton, I taught introductory psychology and child development. The college also had a nursery school, so I was able to continue my Piaget replication studies. Although replication studies were not, and are not, in fashion in psychology, they served an important purpose for me. First of all, they allowed me to train myself to do the Piagetian semiclinical interview. Second, although it was not clinical work, at least I was working directly with children. And finally, I believed the replication would give credence to Piaget's work and make it more acceptable to American researchers. I began publishing these studies in the *Journal of Genetic Psychology*.

While teaching at Wheaton I continued to live in Boston and commuted to Norton on the days I was to teach. Now that I had finished my education I could allow distractions and began to date. I met Sally Malinsky, an English teacher, and after a brief courtship, we married in 1960.

After two years at Wheaton College, I heard from a friend at UCLA that there was an opening in the neuropsychiatric department. Although I enjoyed teaching at Wheaton, I wanted to get back to clinical work. It seemed to me that the position at UCLA would provide opportunities for teaching, clinical work, and research. The job was also appealing because I had wanted to return to Los Angeles to be closer to my family. Inasmuch as Sally's parents were in Tucson, this would bring her closer to her family as well. I was accepted for the position, and we moved to Los Angeles. My hopes for the position, however, went unrealized.

There was little interaction between the clinical faculty and the psychology department and even less interest in my teaching a course in developmental psychology. Although the clinical work was interesting and allowed me to pursue a new direction in research, the development of perception, I was not happy.

In 1962 I learned of a position at the University of Denver. Kenneth Little, who had trained with my clinical supervisors and who had been at the National Institute of Mental Health (NIMH) for a number of years, had taken over the chairmanship of the psychology department and was looking for a director for the Child Study Center, a clinic associated with the department. It seemed made to order for me, a chance to combine my teaching, clinical, and research interests as an associate professor in a university psychology department. There was also an opportunity to hire faculty, because Ken wanted me to start a child clinical training program. So in 1962 we moved to Denver.

The Child Study Center was in an old Quonset hut left over from World War II, when it was used for student housing. Nonetheless, we refurbished it, set up a nursery school in one section, and I went about finding child clinical faculty and writing a clinical psychology training grant. The grant was awarded, and we had one of the first child clinical training programs in the country. I had learned through my experiences at Austen Riggs and at the Beth Israel that training as an adult clinician was in no way preparation for dealing with children and youth. Whether we were talking about diagnostic testing or therapy, child clinical work was not just a-size-smaller adult work, it was qualitatively different and required different training.

While at Denver, I continued my Piagetian investigations but was taking some new directions. To see whether Piaget's theory would hold in domains he had not explored, I had studied children's conceptions of their religious denomination and found that these followed the Piagetian stages. At Denver we did a study of the development of children's prayer with similar results. I also continued to pursue my studies of perceptual development that I had begun at Wheaton. Piaget had explored perceptual development primarily with illusions; I wanted to see whether similar age-related trends could be obtained using meaningful materials. We explored age changes in children's responses to ambiguous pictures, to part/whole pictures, disordered and ordered figures, separated figures, and figures that were transformed from one animal to another. In all cases we found that children's perception of the world quite literally changes with age. I was later asked to review this research for an article in the *American Scientist* (Elkind, 1975). In addition to my research, teaching, and clinical work at the Child Study Center, I also spent a day a week as psychologist for the Arapaho County Court, where I evaluated adolescents who had gotten into trouble with the law.

When I began publishing my Piagetian research, at Rappaport's suggestion I routinely sent Piaget reprints when they came out. One day in the spring of 1963 I received a square blue overseas envelope from the University of Geneva. It was a letter from Piaget inviting me to come to Geneva for a year as a member of his

Centre d'Epistemologie Genetique. He could offer a small stipend and travel expenses. I was shaken—it was an invitation I had never dreamed of and an unbelievable opportunity to study with someone whose work I had been following for years.

By this time, however, we had our first son, Paul, and the stipend Piaget offered could not cover our living expenses. I applied for, and received, a National Science Foundation Senior Postdoctoral Fellowship that made it possible for us to live overseas for a year. With son and miniature dachshund we traveled to Geneva in the summer of 1964. I first met Piaget personally at a reception for the new Centre participants. My French was not very good at the time, and we only exchanged greetings. Fortunately, I picked up spoken French quite quickly (I had been reading it for years, and that probably helped). When I was finally able to talk with Piaget at length, he explained that he had meant to go to England in 1914 or 1915 to learn English. But the war broke out and he never made the trip. Although he did understand English quite well, he really never spoke it other than to say "Hello" and "How are you?"

My year in Geneva was an exciting one. In addition to attending the weekly Centre seminar, I also audited Piaget's classes in developmental psychology and carried out several research investigations. In addition to the regular Centre members, Howard Gruber was there for part of the year, as was the British psychologist Peter Bryant. I also found time to do a little clinical work, and I led a weekly adolescent discussion group associated with the American Church in Geneva. It was through that connection that I met Henry P. David, and we did a small study together on the adaptation of families overseas.

My major purpose of coming to Geneva, however, was to study with Piaget. He had a very well run research organization. Each year, Piaget, his students, and Centre participants would set a problem for the year and everyone would design problems associated with that issue. The year I was there, the issue was causality. I tried to design a perceptual study that would relate to causality, and I investigated children's ability to conserve across illusory transformations such as the Mueller-Lyer. Although the results were as predicted and the study was published, Piaget did not see it as relevant to his causality issues and did not accept it for publication in the book that eventually resulted from that year's research projects.

I must say that Piaget was most supportive of what I was doing; my study was just not in keeping with the year's theme. It was one example of Piaget's enormous capacity for concentration and focus. His life was literally his work. He had seen about four movies in his lifetime and read novels such as *Remembrance of Things Past* as much for their psychological interest as for their literary qualities. He was enormously well read in the sciences, and I have been told, although I never observed it myself, that he was quite knowledgeable about classical music.

Not surprisingly, it was difficult to make small talk with Piaget, and he was not the easiest of dinner companions. Yet he had a fine sense of humor and a strong sense of loyalty to those he befriended. In subsequent years when we met at conferences or when I returned to Geneva, he always welcomed me most warmly and we often took walks together. Once I called him from Israel to say that I would like to come and see him on my way home. He declined, and I admit feeling a bit rejected. Later I received a very cordial letter from Piaget explaining that he had not understood my name on the phone. When he later realized who had called him he wrote to say that he would have been happy to see me if he had only gotten my name straight. It was a small gesture, but it meant a lot to me.

After returning to Denver in 1965 I talked with Ken about starting a child-development program that would nicely complement our clinical training program. At that time Ken was married to Yvonne Brackbill, a noted experimental child psychologist. She wanted to start an experimental training program that would have no place for the soft developmentalists. This was my first encounter with the schism in our discipline represented by the journals *Child Development and Developmental Psychology* on the one hand, and the journal *Experimental Child Psychology* on the other. My schizophrenia was reasserting itself, and I wanted to be where developmental psychology as well as child clinical was welcome.

Several years earlier, John Flavell had published his classic *The Developmental Psychology of Jean Piaget*. He was then at the University of Rochester, but the book in combination with his innovative research on role-taking made him very much in demand at other prestigious universities. He took a position at the University of Minnesota. This left open his professorship at Rochester. The Rochester faculty wanted to start a developmental training program of the sort that I had wanted to organize at Denver. They also had an excellent clinical training program that, although not a child program, was nonetheless of the highest quality. I was offered Flavell's position and took it.

And so in 1966 we moved to Rochester. We now had a second son, Robert, who was born soon after we came back from Switzerland. At Rochester I went about building the child-development training program and was fortunate enough to recruit Arnold Sameroff, Michael Chandler, and Michael Davidson to become members of the faculty. We applied for and received a National Institute of Child Health and Development (NICHD) child developmental training grant and began training developmentalists. I still did not give up my clinical work and did evaluations and consulting for the Rochester Child Guidance Clinic. As part of my work for that clinic I did court assessments of juvenile delinquents, much as I had done in Denver.

Soon after I arrived at the University of Rochester I published a paper that has been the most reprinted and most cited piece of work that I have done (Elkind, 1967). It is still generating a lot of research work. It was an attempt to conceptualize some of what I had been observing in my work with delinquents, but it was also an attempt to use my Piagetian knowledge in a clinical setting. I introduced the concepts of the "Imaginary Audience" and the "Personal Fable" that grew out of the young adolescent's newly emerging formal operations. Later we introduced a scale to measure the imaginary audience, and that scale is still generating a lot of research.

At Rochester I found a home. There was not only a supportive place to conduct research, teach, and do clinical work, there was also a strong interdisciplinary ethos that fit well with my interests in education and psychiatry as well as psychology. After a few years I had joint appointments in education and in psychiatry and taught courses and trained students in the Department of Pediatrics. Robert Haggerty was the chairperson of pediatrics and was one of the founders of the "Behavioral Pediatric" movement within pediatrics. In education I worked with Irene Athey, and we applied for and got a Triple T training grant that allowed us to build a program to train trainers of early childhood educators.

In the meantime, my perceptual work was taking me in the direction of education. I wanted to see how our perceptual tests related to reading potential and ability. We found that they did and studied children who read early. We found that these children were not only advanced perceptually and cognitively but also had a mentor in the form of an aunt, grandparent, or older sibling who reinforced their reading interests. To test out the efficacy of the perceptual abilities in fostering reading, I arranged to teach a second-grade inner-city class for a semester using perceptual training procedures I had developed. The procedures did work, but I never disseminated them after seeing how easily they could be misused.

My work with the inner-city class convinced me that many of the children who were reading poorly were being taught in the wrong way. This was before the concept of learning styles had become current. All I knew was that some young people needed the kind of perceptual training I had offered, others needed more hands-on experience, like sandpaper letters, and so on. I called these children, who were of average intellectual ability, "Curriculum Disabled." In 1972 we opened the Mt. Hope School in an old stone mansion that had been donated to the university. We took curriculum disabled children from the public schools and kept them for a year at our school, where they were tutored one-on-one by undergraduates who had signed up for the course. Most of the children were able to return to school, working at grade level after a year at Mt. Hope. As a result of that work I published *Child Development and Education* (1976).

In addition to providing a program for curriculum disabled children, the school also afforded us a laboratory for giving students a hands-on experience with children. I believe that it is just as important for students studying child development to observe and work with children as it is for, say, physics or chemistry students to have a laboratory experience. Unfortunately, after several years I lost some of the funding for the school and I was not able to get other grant monies immediately. The university, which had undergone a change of presidents, was no longer in favor of the school and would not support it during the interim while I sought new funds.

Although I liked Rochester and the university, I felt so strongly about the need for students to have laboratory experience with children that I decided to leave. The Child Study Department at Tufts University in Boston was looking for a new chairperson at the time (1977), and I applied for and was appointed professor and chair in 1978. What attracted me to The Eliot Pearson Department of Child Study was that it combined education and child development and, most importantly, had a nursery school and curriculum lab as part of its facilities. Although there were no clinical facilities, I was always able to find clinical work outside the university, so this did not bother me, and the chance to return to Boston was also attractive. In 1978 our family, which now included a third son, Rick, moved to Boston.

Career: The Later Years

The Child Study Department needed some rebuilding and reshaping. Accordingly, during my first few years there we redid the course structure and hired new faculty, including Donald Wertleib, Fred Rothbaum, Kathleen Camara, and Mary Anne Wolf. We also wrote and received university permission to begin a Ph.D program in applied child psychology. In addition, we were reapproved by the State of Massachusetts to train and certify teachers. Again I had found a place where I could further my interdisciplinary interests. What I really like about Eliot Pearson is that our students major in child study and have hands-on experience with children in almost every course they take. In addition, our graduates may go into teaching, medicine, publishing, law, and so on, but always with a strong child-development base.

As chairman of the department, I found it a little difficult to carry on the level of research that I had maintained up until that time. In addition, I was becoming more and more concerned with what I saw happening to children in the schools and in the larger society. In 1979 I wrote an article for *Psychology Today* describing what I called "hurried children," who were being pressured to grow up too fast too soon and who were experiencing stress as a result. An editor at Addison Wesley, Doe Coover, saw the article and asked me to write a book on the topic. Although I had written a number of books for an academic audience, I had never written a trade book. Nonetheless, I had written for popular audiences, most notably a series of biographical sketches of major psychologists and psychiatrists for the *New York Times Magazine*. After a number of false starts, I wrote *The Hurried Child* in the summer of 1980 (Elkind, 1981). The book was an instant success, and I suddenly found myself on the major TV shows and in demand for lectures around the country and the world.

Thus began a whole new phase in my career, that of author-lecturer. Partly as a result of the new demands brought about by the book and partly for political reasons, I resigned the Child Study Department chairmanship in 1983 and took an appointment as Senior Resident Scholar at the Lincoln Filene Center at Tufts, which allowed me to devote full time to my new role as child advocate. In *The*

Hurried Child I followed the example of the sociologist Erving Goffman and the historian Philippe Ariès in using materials from everyday life, newspaper and magazine clippings, music, novels, movies, and television programs as supportive evidence for my arguments. It was far different from the rigorous experimental methods that I had been taught and practiced but seemed appropriate for the issues I was addressing.

The Hurried Child was followed by *All Grown Up and No Place to Go: Teenagers in Crisis* (Elkind, 1984) and *Miseducation: Preschoolers at Risk* (Elkind, 1987). In each of these books I used material gathered while traveling and lecturing. Most of my lectures were to parents, educators, and health professionals. On these trips I also had opportunity to learn what was happening in the local area, to visit schools and clinics, and, occasionally, to meet with groups of children and teenagers. This was a new, different kind of research. It was also a new sort of professional life. In 1985 I was made president-elect of the National Association for the Education of Young Children and served as president from 1986 to 1988. I also began writing a monthly column for *Parents Magazine* in 1987 and continued that column until 1993.

Although I published several books after *Miseducation* (*Grandparenting, Perspectives on Early Childhood Education, Parenting Your Teenager in the Nineties, Images of the Young Child,* and a third revision of *A Sympathetic Understanding of the Child*), I was working on a more ambitious project. For the past five years I have been trying to understand the pressures on children and youth from a broader, social historical perspective that has been labeled postmodern. The results of that work appear in *Ties That Stress: A New Family Imbalance* (Elkind, 1994), published by Harvard University Press.

After a hiatus of more than ten years, I have returned to more traditional research. We are presently gathering data on a new instrument, the *Personal Fable Scale,* which will assess young people's sense of speciality, their sense of invulnerability, and their propensity for risk taking. We hope to use this new scale in a variety of investigations. I am also planning some new studies on perception and relating them to the current interest in Vygotsky and his views on the relation of perception to language. But I am also working on a new book on education from a postmodern perspective.

My work on postmodernism helped me to realize that in many ways I have been somewhat postmodern all along, and that may have contributed to my unease in many different academic settings. What has become increasingly obvious to me, and what I wrote about without fully realizing it, was that social science in general and psychology in particular is not and cannot be objective in the same way that physical science is. As Foucault has made clear, in the physical sciences there is a clean separation between subject and object. In the social sciences, however, this separation no longer obtains. The social scientist is both subject and object and can never fully separate himself or herself from this dual position. Accordingly, the social sciences' claim to objectivity cannot be supported.

This is important. It does not mean that we have to abandon social science. It does mean that we have to be aware of our dual position and to make every effort to ensure that our personal biases and attitudes do not affect our data collection or interpretations. We also have to think about the social repercussions of our work. We have too many examples of personal biases reported as objective scientific findings, with long-term negative consequences as a result. Finally, it troubles me greatly that my own discipline seems so little concerned with the deteriorating condition of children and youth in our society. I believe that we as social scientists must have a moral as well as a scientific conscience. If we do not care about the children and youth we study, then our results will never attain true significance, statistical or otherwise.

References

Elkind, D. (1967). Egocentrism in adolescents. *Child Development, 38,* 1025–1034.

Elkind, D. (1975). Perceptual development in children. *American Scientist, 63,* 535–541.

Elkind, D. (1976). *Child development and education.* New York: Oxford University Press.

Elkind, D. (1981). *The hurried child.* Reading, Mass.: Addison Wesley.

Elkind, D. (1984). *All grown up and no place to go: Teenagers in crisis.* Reading, Mass.: Addison Wesley.

Elkind, D. (1987). *Miseducation: Preschoolers at risk.* New York: Knopf.

Elkind, D. (1994). *Ties that stress: A new family imbalance.* Cambridge: Harvard University Press.

Representative Publications

Elkind, D. (1961). The development of the additive composition of classes in the child. *Journal of Genetic Psychology, 99,* 51–57.

Elkind, D. (1961). The child's conception of right and left. *Journal of Genetic Psychology, 99,* 269–276.

Elkind, D. (1961). The child's conception of his religious denomination: The Jewish child. *Journal of Genetic Psychology, 99,* 209–223.

Elkind, D. (1968, May 26). Jean Piaget: Giant in the nursery. *The New York Times Magazine, 6,* 27–32.

Elkind, D. (1970, April 5). Erik H. Erikson: Eight stages of man. *New York Times Magazine, 6,* 23–32.

Elkind, D. (1986). Early education and formal education: A necessary difference. *Phi Delta Kappan, 67,* 631–636.

Elkind, D., Koegler, R. R. & Go, E. (1962). Effects of perceptual training at three age levels. *Science, 137,* 383–386.

5

Dale B. Harris

Memoir has been described as the "invention of truth" (Zinsser, 1987). Gordon Allport, who worked extensively with "personal documents" as data for psychology, also recognized the subjectivity of his material but, in an early anticipation of today's relativity, saw the personal account as a legitimate construction of a reality that could also be scrutinized in other ways and by other investigators. A memoir, being retrospective, allows the memoirist to superimpose a pattern not apparent in the welter of events as they occurred. Biographers may infer different patterns. The construction achieved by subjects themselves can take into account highly personal values and goals that may not readily appear to others. And the values and goals inferred by objective observers may be miles apart from those reported by the subjects. Who has the truth? Both are inventions.

The foregoing places me in a nonbehavioristic stance in our discipline, open to the charge of subjectivity. It is the purpose of this account to show something of my course from a rigorous intellectual position to a more broad, integrative, personalistic posture. Although I started from a position that allowed only observable behaviors, I was from the start dissatisfied with the idea that words were merely behavior units. Nor could I escape the conviction that intentions have an existential quality and that words could express a person's aims and perhaps motives.

The way I traversed can only be shown in general, through persons and the readings they suggested or I discovered. I shall stick to verifiable "facts" but necessarily must indicate some personal matters such as doubts and working convictions arrived at. Necessarily, also, limited space and the reader's other concerns decree that I omit many experiences that undoubtedly influenced this journey. Furthermore, this record of professional career and intellectual venture must also omit its complement—the personal side. That account would tell of a loyal and supportive partner, our varied and exciting family life with our four children, and the extended family of occasional students, from here and abroad, to whom we supplied a "scholarship" of board and room.

Early Years

I was born in the northern Indiana city of Elkhart to a family that considered it-self middle class and was middle class in manners and aspirations but submiddle class in resources and opportunities. The city was still nineteenth-century agrar-ian in outlook as a distribution center for the farming communities to the south and east, although it also possessed a number of light manufactories such as patent medicines, band instruments, and brass foundries. It now finds itself on the very eastern edge of the Chicago Rust Belt. My father was of a moody Irish-English extraction, while my mother was the unpretentious, undemonstrative, practical, down-to-earth person of her Pennsylvania Dutch heritage.

Our home was in an area where a river looped around a large tract of undevel-oped land (some five or six square city blocks) to the south, and a railroad backed a ten-square-block city cemetery to the north and east. The nearest child lived five blocks away. My brother and I and a sister (some years younger) made do with our own resources for entertainment, including imaginative dramatic play. I early became a voracious reader, which fed this play. Both my brother and I found a playground in the undeveloped area and along the river. I was fascinated by ex-ploration; he very early developed an interest in birds and nature study, which led him eventually to a research position as a biologist for the U.S. Fish and Wildlife Service.

My schooling was conventional in the elementary grades and became more challenging in the junior and senior high years. I count three teachers in grades 7 through 9 and five more in grades 10 through 12 as particularly influential in my education. All insisted on college, all gave me solid fundamentals in their subjects, and all impressed me with their confidence in my future. The Latin teacher in particular gave me a lifelong interest in words by her rigorous attention to the notebooks in which we kept words we suspected of Latin derivation and our proofs or disproofs.

My paternal grandmother (with whom we lived) had been a teacher in the clos-ing decades of the nineteenth century and never let me forget that college was a necessity, and so my every spare penny went into the "college fund." My father was not notably successful as a mechanic, but his only sib, a brother, was a scientist with Bell Labs. So another "must" was added—that of becoming a chemist! But my developing interests in high school were much more in literature and lan-guage, certainly not in chemistry (my brother and sister both redeemed them-selves by earning graduate degrees in the biological sciences).

College and Graduate Study

At the suggestion of a history teacher and the minister of our local Methodist church, I applied for and received a Rector scholarship at DePauw University in Greencastle, Indiana. This scholarship would provide tuition and fees for four years (provided I kept my grades). I had saved a small sum from summer and part-time jobs during junior high and senior high, and with careful management this might see me through one year. An opportunity as a library page occurred in the college library, and that, plus occasional cleaning jobs, saw me through the years 1931 through 1935. For two years I was delegated to supervision of the reserve-book room during the little-used dinner hour, but this allowed me intermittent reading in political science and English literature. I was able to finish DePauw with an A.B. and Phi Beta Kappa and without the interruption the Great Depression caused some of my classmates.

At DePauw I again had a number of influential teachers. All were scholars in the old-fashioned sense of knowing their fields, keeping abreast of them, and occasionally authoring a book or paper. By modern standards teaching loads were heavy, four or five courses being standard. But there was time for students, and teachers sought to relate their fields to the making of intelligent, well-informed citizens-to-be. I recall the enthusiasm and goodwill, albeit expressed with New England reserve, of a philosophy professor, two truly inspiring teachers of comparative (modern) literature, and the enthusiasm for antique culture of the professor of classical languages. There was the young and energetic sociologist working on a study of the modern New Harmony community who encouraged my trip to Indianapolis to survey several community facilities for the homeless (this was 1933, just prior to the New Deal of President Franklin Roosevelt). More significantly, there was Edward Bartlett, the professor of religious studies, who had just completed his Ph.D. at Northwestern in what was then called character education, a subject we are now beginning again to discuss. He encouraged me to acquire a major in psychology with a minor in sociology.

My introduction to psychology was via thoroughgoing Watsonian behaviorism, served up by the old Dashiell basic text (Dashiell, 1928). Professor Paul Fay was an excellent arbiter, a thorough positivist. Behavior—muscle movements—counted, not mentalisms or sloppy personality dispositions. I embraced this view, but there was in my experience an accumulating social emphasis—on purposes, interests, dispositions—to be dealt with. Sociology and education courses seemed to assume the human being had purposes giving direction to behavior!

In my junior year Professor Bartlett started me on a research project, arranging to give the new Bernreuter Personality Inventory to two groups of male students—math majors and pretheologs—to see whether we might discover a difference in group profiles. This project resulted in a jointly published paper. In my senior year he started me on a larger project.

Wanting to study two instruments he had devised for his doctorate—a test of moral knowledge and an attitudes scale—he arranged to gain access to the state training school for boys and to use the males of a local high school for a comparison group. I was given the task of selecting some additional tests to comprise a battery, and I put together additional attitude and early personality tests (the old Woodworth-Mathews psychoneurotic inventory was one). In an early visit to the "reform school" I discovered an old elementary school classmate was an inmate and reflected considerably on the "why" of the divergence of our careers since the East Elkhart school days. It occurred to me that probably there were considerable differences in play- and leisure-time expenditures, so I constructed a Play Activities Checklist. This checklist separated the two populations more sharply than any other measure. Although this finding ignored the homogeneity of the town population, it settled me into measurement as a method and became a strong motivation for work that followed.

This study and its written report gave me basic experience with the logistics of group testing and thesis preparation. The equivalent then of today's work-study programs gave Elizabeth Saltmarsh a small stipend for typing the report (we were by then quite serious about our future together, and that collaboration continues to the present!).

There were then three men in the psychology department: the businesslike Warren Middleton, the dour and offhand Paul Fay, and department head Fowler Brooks. Middleton had me do an extensive literature study of the early personality theories (including Jung's) and tests and was generous in his praise of my paper, assuring me it was of graduate-study caliber. Knowing my interest in children, Fay had me take his child psychology course, the comprehensive and thorough character of which I did not fully appreciate until I took John Anderson's basic graduate course in child development a number of years later. Brooks encouraged my application for graduate study at Duke (I had become interested in McDougall's new hormic psychology), at Yale (the recently completed May and Shuttleworth studies on character development), at Northwestern (Paul Witty had expressed interest in my Play Activities Checklist), and at Minnesota's College of Education (high in Brooks's estimation because of its dean, Melvin Haggerty, a former animal psychologist). I was accepted at all four places, but only Minnesota offered me a stipend, tuition-exempt. I selected Minnesota.

At Minnesota I was assigned to W. S. Miller (thus he became my graduate advisor) and was quickly put to work on his analogies test. Miller had been a member of the psychologist cadre that constructed Army Alpha and Beta in World War I, so I was immersed in measurement of intelligence, not personality. Miller said he was impressed with my DePauw project but that Minnesota was scarcely the place to pursue such interests. He was willing, however, to countenance my working further with the Play Activities Blank, which I proceeded to do by collecting samples of boys in schools located in high delinquency areas of Minneapolis, getting access to juvenile court records to determine legally designated cases, and matching them with nondelinquents from the same neighborhoods, often within a block or two. I cannot resist a comment on the readiness of people then to accept the integrity of a "scientific study" and its prosecutor, in contrast to current mistrust of social scientists, however justified!

Miller was a connectionist and strong hereditarian. His basic course put students through E. L. Thorndike's three volumes of basic psychology for education, with a tough comprehensive exam at the close. I learned Thorndike. Knowing my interest in various theoretical viewpoints in psychology, Miller sent me to Richard Elliott, who had taken over the basic course of Edna Heidbreder when she left Minnesota. So I took a readings course, using Heidbreder's *Seven Psychologies.* Here were a number of viewpoints trying to deal with intention and motivation, including Gestalt psychology. I then concentrated on Gestalt, reading Köhler and Koffka. I discovered Tolman's purposive behaviorism, but that didn't advance my thinking. Nor did Gestalt offer me a comprehensive handling of experience, despite its interesting observations on insight and perceptual phenomena. I had a most stimulating course with Donald Paterson in individual differences and their measurement; he remained an influential friend. By the end of that year I had strengthened my knowledge of basic statistics, had a fairly good concept of the measurement standards then in effect, and had a solid introduction to the theory and practice of group mental and performance tests.

At the end of the school year I had all my master's thesis data, had visited the state school for (delinquent) boys at Red Wing, and had come to the attention of Eugene Carstetter in the state department of education, who was looking for an educational director (principal) for the school at Red Wing. So with Miller's goodwill (he advised me to stay two years but no more) I went to Red Wing and started a program of educational achievement testing to complement the psychological testing supplied by a state psychologist, who came periodically to assess new admissions. Working closely with the vocational director (all older boys had half-time academics and half-time shop training in one of a number of maintenance shops), I attempted to meet individual needs so that all boys under eighteen could return to public education with a reasonable chance of success. I learned a great deal about education, remedial education, mental retardation, the sociopath, and the social psychology of institutional life.

These were Depression years (1936–38), and the state offices were influenced by the liberal politics of the Farmer-Labor Party, and there were some bright and committed people working on programs. At the Red Wing state school the superintendent, a former public school superintendent, was a true professional. The vocational director and the librarian were first-rate people. The teachers were all certified and competent. The shop people were skilled tradesmen first, and many had a real feeling for their charges. The institution was not the sink that these places sometimes are.

During these two years I joined the American Association for the Advancement of Science (AAAS; I am now a fellow) and submitted a brief research paper on test results with delinquent boys. This was accepted for the annual meeting in 1936. I recall gratefully at that meeting the supportive comments of Dr. Percival Symonds of Columbia University, whose book on personality measurement was a classic.

This institutional interlude cured me of "graduate-studentitis" and gave me a clearer notion of the Ph.D. as a goal. I headed back toward the university and to some part-time work on a project Alvin Eurich was completing prior to going to Stanford University. He persuaded me to join an evaluation project in the Stanford School of Education, to which he was a consultant. I quickly discovered that "test" was a dirty word and "objective appraisal" not much better. Eurich gave me some guidance in formulating a persuasive logic for evaluating the progress of schoolchildren in the language arts, but soon he left the project for administration. I was unsuccessful in getting together devices that would suit the project directors. They preferred to collect testimonials (the "best thinking" of teachers, which didn't strike me at all as proper evaluation).

By the end of the fall term I had decided this project was not for me, that I would return to Minnesota, and that I had better study with the Stanford psychologists as much as possible. So I had work with Ernest Hilgard, Paul Farnsworth, Calvin Stone, and, of course, Lewis Terman. Hilgard encouraged my interest in a more "open" psychology than Watsonian behaviorism, and Farnsworth opened for me the fascinating history of psychology, with its roots in philosophy. Stone in animal psychology exercised perhaps the most influence. He introduced me to the work of Niko Tinbergen and Konrad Lorenz and to ethological methodology, stating that he thought this a very fruitful way of conceptualizing child behavior (I had already been introduced to the related concepts of ecology by my brother's early study). Stone's course on Freud used the *Collected Writings* and a devastating question-and-answer technique of recitation for which students prepared most thoroughly! Terman was very near retirement, spent little time with students, and excoriated me for coming from a year at Minnesota without having had work with Florence Goodenough. If I was interested in child psychology (which I had affirmed), she was the best mentor in the country! Goodenough had been one of Terman's most prized students and played a central role in the follow-up studies of his gifted children and in the later revisions of the old Stanford-Binet scales. She and her students at Minnesota had conducted important studies relating to the nature-nurture controversies of the late 1920s and early 1930s.

Despite my dissatisfaction with the Stanford Language Arts Investigation, I trace one substantial intellectual influence to its emphasis on interpretation and meaning—the reading of a discussion by a psychologist and a literary critic (Ogden & and Richards, 1927). The substance of this book, and its centrality to the language arts investigation, was that "meaning" is supplied by the reader (or hearer) and not by words that have inherent import. A poem has no special meaning, and metaphor beclouds. Only words that designate objects or operations have utility. Thus I was introduced to logical positivism and to general semantics. Further reading in Jacob Kantor's behaviorism as the mechanism whereby words (and meanings) are learned fed my growing dissatisfaction with the starkness of that approach and added to my growing sense of intellectual solipsism. Obviously not all disputes ended in war; sometimes people settled them by words having conventional significance. The dictionary had a place after all! Years later I discovered Owen Barfield (Barfield, 1952), who restored metaphor to a useful place in language (while writing this account I recall with amusement the recent flap over deconstruction theory in literature!).

Minnesota's Child Welfare Institute

On my return to the University of Minnesota in 1939, I registered for courses with
John Anderson and Florence Goodenough in the Institute of Child Welfare, one
of the five original centers established by the Laura Spelman Rockefeller Fund. In
December I was appointed to a vacant instructorship in the institute and began a
nineteen-year career there. I was to write a weekly column on children and child
research and do some traveling throughout the state lecturing and teaching extension child and adolescent development courses, which were popular with teachers. This experience taught me much about teaching general and lay groups.

John Anderson *was* the institute; he was also something of a social Darwinist.
Although I had been employed to fill a slot in the parent education portion of his
program, he believed that every young professional should be stressed to prove
his or her worth. I was to attend his classes and pay close attention to his teaching
methods (which used many charts and other graphic presentations). I served a
term in the institute's nursery school, and a very useful experience it proved to be!
In the next years I was to teach every course listed in the catalog except the popular child care and training course, but in time I was to revise the eighth edition of
the text for that course. Most institute research samples were obliged to follow the
socioeconomic stratification Anderson had devised while conducting research for
the 1930 White House Conference on Children. He edited all published material
(including professional papers) that emanated from the institute. I sweated under
his blue pencil and criticism but learned from it.

Anderson was a curious combination of the rigorous, objective behavioral scientist and the practical person. Though he denigrated the role, he was a first-rate
applied psychologist. From the start he had modeled the institute on the design of
the agricultural research stations of the U.S. Department of Agriculture: The primary emphasis was on research in child development with a strong educational
program for its consumers—parents. He devised and taught the institute's contribution to the curriculum of the General College, the general education board's
experimental two-year college on the Minnesota campus. This course, entitled
Human Development and Personal Adjustment, was essentially a developmental
social psychology for youth as consumers. This became my course until I left for
military service and surely influenced all my later teaching objectives and
method. The concept of child development as a multidisciplinary field, and the
concept of the ag experiment station's close affiliation of research and application
have remained significant for me ever since.

I promptly joined the American Psychological Association (APA). Anderson
had been active on the council and was heading toward the presidency in 1943. As
a young aspiring applied professional I was an interested bystander to Anderson's
involvement in keeping members of the old American Association for Applied
Psychology in the fold. It was an uneasy marriage, but it lasted almost exactly fifty
years. Then it was the academic wing that seceded!

The annual meetings of the APA and the AAAS thereafter occupied a regular place on my calendar. This was before the days of institutional or departmental subsidization of such travel, and I still recall Dr. Goodenough's sharp rejoinder to my remark that I couldn't afford my first meeting: "You can't afford not to go!" Those early meetings gave graduate students a platform for research reports (no poster sessions; one must face an entire audience!) and an opportunity to see in person those dignitaries who had been merely impressive names—and sometimes to talk with them. A meeting then might include six or seven hundred registrants.

As an institute research project, I undertook to assemble longitudinal data for a projected revision of the Minnesota Preschool Scales, Florence Goodenough's project. Unfortunately, we were unable to locate full records on sufficient cases repeated over time and coordinated with later records of the Stanford-Binet to permit adequate determination of predictor items for mental growth.

My doctoral dissertation consisted of an early form of factor analysis of delinquent boys' responses to the Play Activities Blank to see what clusters of items might appear, a crude approach to typology. Before the days of computers this procedure involved endless machine sorting of punched cards to establish the fourfold tables yielding contingency coefficients that served as correlations. Besides a thorough grounding in biometrics, essentially descriptive statistics, I studied R. A. Fisher's approach to the estimation of parameters in experimentation. I took Richard Scammon's course in prenatal growth, taught then by Edith Boyd. This course led me to my later contact with Scammon himself, who became another significant mentor.

During this essentially graduate-student period I participated in founding the Minnesota chapter of Psi Chi and was an early president. During my presidency the chapter paid tribute to Dr. Fred Kuhlmann, a fellow student with Terman at Clark and an early but less well known translator and adapter of the Binet-Simon scales. Kuhlmann had for many years been chief psychologist for Minnesota's state institutions and had developed an index for intelligence measurement akin to a standard score, which thus avoided the general dissatisfaction with the mental age–chronological age ratio. His careful records became the basis for some of Minnesota's contributions to the early nature-nurture controversies.

At the end of 1941 I was awarded the Ph.D. degree, soon after the birth of our first child. I recall vividly the afternoon of Pearl Harbor day; I was back at the office on Sunday when an excited grad student burst in with the news he had gotten from the radio in the teaching assistants' quarters. Soon thereafter I was working part-time as a civilian psychologist examining inductees at the Fort Snelling induction center. Later I was involved part-time, with John Anderson and several faculty members from the psychology department, in Minnesota's Army Specialized Training Program for psychological specialists in classification. By early 1944 I was solicited by Major M. E. Hahn, formerly of Minnesota's General College, who was setting up a separation program for the Marine Corps. In May I was commissioned a second lieutenant and reported to Quantico for Marine Corps training.

By the fall of 1944 the Allied forces were well established in Europe, my training was completed, and Major Hahn was back in civilian life, his program having been taken over by the Veteran's Administration and combined with a plan that embraced all services. I was then assigned as an educational services officer to the naval hospital in Philadelphia, where I learned much about disabilities and their victims, edited some materials for *Psychology for the Returning Service Man* suitable for our dischargees, conducted much liaison work between Corps and Marine patients, and gave weekly lectures on progress in the Pacific and European theaters.

I was discharged and returned to Minnesota as assistant professor in May of 1946 to resume my earlier activities. Early on I was selected to present Minnesota's first TV-for-credit course; arranging demonstrations with children was fascinating and challenging. To implement my conviction of the value of interdisciplinary work, I managed some work postdoctorally in anthropology, gaining viewpoints and skill that I found useful both then and later.

I renewed acquaintance with Richard Scammon shortly before his retirement and persuaded him to repeat his lectures on the history of science. I am certain his skillful linking of abstractions to concrete images had an impact on my teaching, and his lectures on prenatal growth, replete with blackboard drawings in color as fine as any medical artist could produce, gave me, at last, a "growth model" to integrate the developmental concepts I was acquiring. In later years my emphasis on a developmental viewpoint always embraced this background and afforded a basis for respecting the growing child's inherent activity, motivation, individuality, and autonomy, which I had found quite lacking in behaviorist paradigms. My discovery at this time of Werner (1948) strengthened my espousal of an organismic position.

I pause to introject that our four children played no small role in the reconstruction of my psychological paradigm. We have often remarked how very different in temperament, motivational patterns, and interests they were as children and continue to be as adults. One could only describe some behavior as intentional very early in infancy. Even so-called random movements converged over time on success, invariably celebrated by the infant's delight! Recent research on infants appears to bear out such cognizing ability.

Following my return to Minnesota in 1946 and during the twelve years subsequently, I was involved in a number of projects. I conducted a carefully designed study of two forms of parent education, counseling, and group study together with a control group having only routine contacts with professionals. The volunteer subjects were parents coping with young retarded children. The study introduced observations and ratings of parent-child interactions. We were concerned with measuring both attitudes and knowledge, but our results were significant only for the experimental groups as contrasted with the control: There was little difference between the experimental treatments. This study served to reinforce my doubt concerning rigorous experimentation in complex matters!

I became a member of an interdisciplinary social science team interested in establishing a center involving psychologists, sociologists, and political scientists. With the assistance of the graduate school we undertook several research projects; I was involved in a minor way with a study of the social problems and attitudes of residents in a racially mixed South Minneapolis neighborhood and in a major way with a study of social responsibility in childhood—attitudes, behaviors, and reputations among peers. Both of these projects involved the creation and standardization of measuring instruments.

Meanwhile, Hull's hypothetico-deductive approach to theory building had become preeminent in psychology. Earlier, John Anderson had been directing some of us in a systematic analysis of the thought systems of early scientists such as George Romanes, William James, G. S. Hall, J. M. Baldwin, and Jean Piaget. Although Anderson by no means rejected the "natural history" observational approach of these men, he, too, was searching for more formal, systematic theory building to undergird research. The result of these cogitations was not another theory but an essay on the particular contribution of a developmental viewpoint to the generality of psychological theorizing that I presented as my presidential address to the Division on Developmental Psychology of the American Psychological Association (APA) in 1956 (Harris, 1963).

I was greatly interested still in the problem of children's misbehavior but wished to attack it from the positive side. What early experiences and behaviors characterize the childhood of individuals who build strong, positive life patterns as young adults? I planned a study and arranged the fieldwork; Anderson took charge of data analysis. We designed a countywide study, hoping to measure all children in the fourth grade and above with a battery of carefully selected inventories, questionnaires, and tests. With the help of a county and its public and parochial schools, we conducted this extensive testing and were able to follow the older youth into the community, studying those who achieved some early measure of success as young adults and contrasting their psychological profiles with those showing poor outcomes. We became involved in public education, community solidarity, and in-service work with teachers who brought behavior problems to our attention. Anderson's big project, in which I also participated, was his follow-up of the institute's early nursery school children some twenty-five years later. Tracing subjects, formulating interview procedures and guidelines, and collecting schedule responses and personal ratings proved both challenging and instructive.

A Changing Point of View

Thus I found myself moving away from normative and mental growth studies toward parental styles of child-rearing and their social and personality outcomes. I found myself leaning toward a clinical interest in children's behavior problems, toward the "dirty" and the "applied" and perhaps toward a concern with phenom-enological approaches, certainly a partial withdrawal from my earlier insistence on the precision of measurement. For it had become apparent that one could not expect the significance of good, hard, objective data to be self-evident, as we once thought, yielding definitive answers to pressing questions. Such data required interpretation, and an adequate interpretation always required some consideration of the setting! Despite the prestige of Clark Hull's hypothetico-deductive approach to theorizing in psychology, I believed it simply did not give enough attention to psychological and social contexts. It might do for laboratory experiments but could scarcely manage in broader environments.

But I did not leave measurement altogether. In 1948 Florence Goodenough retired on disability. She asked me to take over responsibility for revising and, if possible, extending her Draw-a-Man Test (Goodenough, 1926). She wished to objectify scoring standards, extend the scale upward in age, and develop an alternate form. We agreed on a drawing test made up of three figures produced separately: a man, a woman, and self. I obtained and scored preliminary samples from socially stratified age samples of children, tried out many scoring modifications, and produced age-trend graphs. I took my materials to a conference with Dr. Goodenough, who, then totally blind, found herself unable to work meaningfully with the material. She conferred with her publisher and concluded that a revision of her book was not possible, that a new book embodying the work I had put forward was desirable, and that it should be my project. The publisher and I agreed that her seminal work deserved recognition in an appropriate share of royalties.

I did all the trial scorings and most of the scoring on the standardization samples. Because this project was not in the mainstream of current psychological interest, I did not seek graduate student participation in a faculty project. I was still ensnared by the institute edict that each graduate student formulate his or her own problem. The work was published as *Children's Drawings as Measures of Intellectual Maturity* (Harris, 1963), which laid out the entire project, including the results of smaller studies seeking to inform and support the instrument (this book was in print until 1988 and in 1980 was listed as a "Citation Classic"—see Smelser, 1987). I never fully explored the projective significance of the self drawing, for I was discouraged by the findings of the growing body of research that seemed to indicate that the psychological examiner or investigator did quite as much "projecting" as the subject! In this case I was unwilling to give interpretation free rein.

John Anderson's growing health problems dictated that he reduce his load. He decided to retire as the institute's director in 1954. His retirement was observed by a university interdisciplinary conference on the concept of development. The published papers (Harris, 1957) remained in print for twenty-five years, perhaps attesting to the challenge and appeal of the concept.

The institute, founded with Rockefeller money and a small subvention from the university in 1926 had, since the expiration of the Rockefeller grant and its cushioning extension, been making presentations to the state legislature at the time of the university's biennial request for a modest but vital appropriation, which had been forthcoming. The institute had a small income from fees for its nursery school, for classes and services, and from a block of stock awarded it much earlier by *Parents Magazine.* The university administration concluded that a freestanding institute, a department in the graduate school responsible directly to the president, no longer made sense. In due time it would be my task as Anderson's successor to negotiate a transfer to an appropriate college of the university.

Some change already was in the air. We had negotiated, partly at the request of the College of Arts and Sciences, an undergraduate major in child development. Parallel with this and overlapping with it was a nursery school–kindergarten–primary certificate curriculum worked out with the College of Education. It seemed appropriate to rename the institute, substituting the term "Development" for "Welfare," and this was done officially. The growing tendency to look at development over the life span had led the institute to organize a beginning-level graduate course named Development in Maturity and Old Age, which was welcomed by curricula in social work and nursing education. It fell to me to organize and teach this course, which drew heavily on the biology of aging and the available (but growing) research on psychological changes with age. The growing postwar interest in adjustment and personality study led us to organize some course and practicum work in projective techniques to supplement our longtime concern with mental level and intelligence. We were moving with the times, or so it seemed.

We had many staff and administrative discussions. Some universities caught up in similar reorganization of child centers and programs favored their school or department of home economics, but our school was located on the St. Paul Campus, some miles away from our facilities. The College of Arts and Sciences was a possibility and would welcome us but would probably integrate us with the Department of Psychology. I had always had good personal relations with psychology, but there persisted a certain institutional coolness, and we of the institute wanted to retain an identity. The College of Education offered to retain our institute structure and functions and to relieve us of the management of the kindergarten, which would become a part of the newly organized laboratory elementary school. These changes finally seemed admirable and were instituted in the year 1958–59.

Penn State: A Growing, Aspiring University

Several factors influenced a decision to leave my post in 1959. I had accomplished a stressful and draining task of two years of meetings and discussions. I had finally concluded that I was too much a creature of the old institute, its organization, mode of independent administration, objectives, and program, to benefit a new institute and the redirection that must follow. We were soon to become recipients of a training grant from the National Institute of Mental Health. It seemed that a fresh start from outside would be very desirable for the institute. I wanted to get on with the drawing study. So I accepted an appointment at the Pennsylvania State University beginning in the school year of 1959–60 (later, I jested that I solved my midlife crisis by changing jobs rather than wives!).

Why Penn State University, the former Pennsylvania State College? In the first place it was a land grant university, established according to the 1862 Morrill Land Grant Act, and from my Minnesota experience I was thoroughly familiar and in accord with the teaching, research, and service objectives of those institutions. It offered a solid undergraduate major in general psychology and a long and excellent graduate record in clinical and industrial applications. Penn State had just been approved for university status by the Middle States Association. President Eric Walker presented a convincing picture of the prospects for growth in excellence as well as in the physical plant. Last but not least was the advice of my old teacher and friend Richard Elliott to make a career at another than one's own graduate studies home.

My former fellow graduate student at Minnesota, Arthur Brayfield, had just gone to Penn State as department head of psychology, then located in the College of Education. He offered an attractive plan for bringing a developmental psychology emphasis to the teaching of educational psychology. It has always seemed to me that, next to parents, teachers constitute the developmentalist's chief avenue of application. The dean of that college, Dr. Ralph Rackley, was a historian and professed a scholarly emphasis for his faculty, especially for those in the secondary education areas. Brayfield had long impressed me with his emphasis on academic integrity, his keen intellect, and his direct approach to difficult issues.

For two years I taught educational psychology courses with a child growth and development emphasis, considering the as-yet-unachieved portions of the growth curve as a growth potential subject to new influences rather than predestined. The courses included attention to the new "teaching machines" and programmed learning. Meanwhile, Dean Rackley at Walker's request was involved with reorganizing the university around three "core colleges": liberal arts, science, and fine arts and architecture. President Walker asked a number of us newcomers to consider, as a study group, what the university should be doing in the 1980s. This group also helped formulate plans for reorganization. We proposed that the teacher-training aspects of the College of Home Economics should become a division or department in education, and its child development program and nursery school and science-oriented programs such as nutrition should form a new College of Human Development. Psychology would transfer from education to liberal arts. In this particular way my recent experience with the basic and applied aspects of child development was employed.

The upshot of all this was that Dean Rackley became the university's first provost, and a new dean formerly in charge of visual aids instruction took over the College of Education. He was very much concerned with method, and his approach to educational psychology stressed the mechanics of teaching. Meanwhile,

Brayfield had been attracted to the American Psychological Association as its executive officer, and I became interim department head of psychology. The opportunity arose to repeat my Minnesota experience in shepherding a department in transition from one status to another. I much preferred this role to heading a traditional educational psychology department in a conventional school or college of education.

I entered a five-year term as department head. Aside from smoothing what could have been a difficult transition (including rehabilitating a reduced budget), I believe I accomplished three benefits to the department: rescuing the clinical training program and the psychological clinic, which had been headed toward neglect and extinction; recommending two major appointments, Caroline Sherif in social psychology and David Palermo in developmental psychology; and giving administrative support to John "Mike" Warren's animal behavior program. All of these areas I viewed as essential to a quality program of academic psychology (as well as relating to developmental psychology, broadly conceived!).

During this interval I developed working relations with sociology and with the Department of Individual and Family Studies of the new College of Human Development. Later, I accepted a joint appointment in this new college and conducted a graduate seminar colisted with psychology. With contemporary interest in theory building still high, we examined the writings of well-published developmentalists with respect to assumptions, axioms, postulates, and theorems. Suffice it to say that we found no well-articulated formal theory but concluded that most theory, however articulated, grows out of a body of related studies grappling with a problem or question. And such theory leads to more focused research. Several students have attested in their later years to the lasting value of this seminar, just as I had to Anderson's earlier effort.

With sociology I participated in a number of community-development projects in selected Pennsylvania towns conducted under the auspices of the continuing education program of liberal arts. Also with this program I participated in several summer institutes for groups as dissimilar as young IBM executives and ex–coal miners. As earlier in Minnesota, I found the exposition of developmental and social psychological concepts to nonacademics challenging.

More traditional activities occupied most of my time, of course. I had completed and published the Goodenough-Harris drawing test by 1963. I did a number of small studies attempting to explore possible projective aspects of drawings, those produced under the conditions of the test and some produced under free-drawing conditions. These were essentially negative when all subject information was considered. Having heard Dr. Goodenough lament the reported loss during World War II at Munich of a multicultural drawing collection made forty years earlier (Lamprecht, 1906), I had in the 1950s made a determined effort to get collections of children's drawings from developing nations. Working through the mission societies of various churches and supplying materials and shipping costs, I assembled substantial collections of human-figure drawings from some fourteen countries in Asia, Africa, and the Pacific. These collections are now part of an archive of children's drawings in the Pattee Library of the Pennsylvania State University, along with an extensive collection of Florence Goodenough's early, and my own later, U.S. children's drawings and drawings by large samples of Native North American children. Considerable use of this archive of approximately thirty thousand drawings has been made by visitors and by graduate students, especially in art education.

Another study took me to the anthropology department's field station in the high Andes, then being used for studies of human work output at high altitude. I found several groups of children in remote places who had never used paper and pencil. I was able to demonstrate stages of drawing parallel to those well documented in literate societies and to show fairly rapid improvement under several modes of practice with drawing male and female figures.

Shortly after this experience I was awarded a Fulbright teaching fellowship to Japan in 1968–69, providing an opportunity to relinquish departmental administration. A Japanese former graduate student was teaching at the Ochanomizu National University in Tokyo and became my official go-between for six months at his institution. A direct consequence was my enhanced interest in student study abroad as well as a profound awareness of the difficulties of cross-cultural translation of concepts and ideas, especially nontranslatable nonverbal valuing and affective modalities.

A preliminary report of cross-cultural study of drawing was given at the Ninth Congress of the Inter-American Society of Psychology in 1966. I presented an invited paper on drawing studies at the Seventeenth International Congress of Applied Psychology at Liège, Belgium, in 1971 and arranged a one-day symposium (nine invited participants) on psychological research and biographical methods for the Eighteenth Congress in Quebec, Canada, in 1974. I had also participated in a more modest way at the International Congress of Psychology in Tokyo, Japan, in 1972.

Teaching—the Ultimate Academic Choice

My move from departmental administration was prompted by a conviction, growing for some years, that essentially the best job in a university is that of full professor; one has maximum freedom for study, research, and work with students. I supplemented this comfortable role in the early 1970s by taking a principal responsibility in a college committee arranging a faculty study and planning conference looking to the challenge of the 1980s and the possibility of a changing clientele. Later I was offered the post as associate dean of the graduate school but concluded, finally, that I would avoid again fulfilling Laurence J. Peter's self-designated Peter Principle and remain a teacher.

Teaching seemed to be the activity I had been inexorably working toward. In addition to the regular classroom, the experiment station tilt of the Institute of Child Welfare had thrust me into teaching general audiences, and I had proved proficiency with radio and TV lecture broadcasts. For general audiences I early adopted the practice of including a relevant scientific study in each talk, explaining the necessity of controlling conditions and demonstrating the results with charts and diagrams as well as offering clear acknowledgement of the implications and limitations of the results.

With college students I could throw open windows on ideas, and sometimes doors on opportunities, I could try to show the value of a developmental (and historical?) approach to a subject—how a present state of organization was put together over time, and where the next efforts might be exerted. Despite successes in my research efforts and despite the fun of finding answers to questions, I got more satisfaction from working with students, getting them to examine their own ideas and problems constructively. More than once I have been told I have a knack, when necessary, for getting another to recognize an inadequate idea as foolish or impossible and to view that conclusion itself as a success. I am, thus, more pedagogue than scientist, pleased to grapple with ideas and to discover patterns.

I took seriously the advising of undergraduate major students, always emphasizing a broad background as good preparation for graduate study if the student was professionally oriented. In the university there is a constant temptation for the faculty adviser to treat the undergraduate major student as another graduate student, and this viewpoint I deplored. Was this an echo of my grandmother's insistent Jeffersonian view that broad liberal education was the best preparation for a good life as well as a successful professional or business career?

In my teaching, the effort to achieve an understanding of psychological phenomena in their social contexts persisted from my own undergraduate days, where that sort of orientation first attracted me. It was greatly encouraged by teaching in the experimental General College at Minnesota, which shaped in some measure the basic or introductory courses I taught. And surely it was fostered by Scammon's example. After I returned to the classroom this orientation evoked at Penn State two experimental courses: Biographical Psychology and Humanistic Psychology. The first used reference material to supply a framework for approaching a published autobiography or memoir of each student's selection. The student then attempted to fit that person's life story into one of three possible developmental frameworks and to make sense of what the subject person thought and did, especially in regard to salient issues of life.

The second course was designed somewhat on Charlotte Buhler's idea of four major life tendencies and her emphasis on life goals, which give pattern and meaning to the life story. Against this wholistic view we considered several persisting psychological problems or controversies through readings and discussions of papers by behaviorists and others. Students were encouraged in their discussions to draw on ideas and thinking stimulated in other courses as they may be related to these issues. Both of these courses explored my conviction that there was heuristic value in studying human experience as well as the scientific value of behavioral analysis. This conviction has been strengthened by the spate of psychological writing in the 1980s on the "life story."

But the role of teacher has its down side. It is so very difficult to see positive results, especially results that may resonate in years to come! Teachers, to keep going, must become very skillful in B. F. Skinner's self-reinforcing behaviors! Teaching skill and teaching success are difficult to define and judge. Consequently (but certainly not for this reason alone), the university has always valued publication. In my lifetime scholarly production has become mandatory, to the point of evaluation by counting bibliographic entries (I once knew a medical school department head who seriously proposed weighing each faculty member's yearly output of reprints in order to correct for differences in page size!).

I have always found writing difficult and performed it under duress. Consequently, my publication score is limited: ninety-five professional articles, seven technical reports, two edited volumes and sole authorship of one book, a number of popular articles, and numerous book reviews and book notes. I have edited a number of books informally for friends and served for some years as a consulting editor to a large publishing company and to several professional journals in psychology and social work. I have come truly to enjoy writing only since retirement, which has provided time and opportunity to correspond with friends and grandchildren.

I have carried my share of leadership in major professional associations and in fulfillment of the service objective of the land grant university. I served terms on the boards of the Minnesota Children's Home Society and the Minneapolis United Fund in addition to the boards of local community organizations there and in Pennsylvania. In Minnesota there was considerable work with the state chapter of the national Parent-Teacher Association through a number of leadership training institutes and later with the publications of the national organization. In both federal and state service I have served on boards and commissions having to do with education and with children and youth issues. I was a delegate and prepared materials for the 1950 and 1960 White House Conferences on Children and Youth.

I counted as close personal, as well as professional, friends Arthur Jersild (Teachers College, Columbia), Harold McCurdy (University of North Carolina), Roger Barker (University of Kansas), F. Robert Wake (Carleton University, Province of Ontario), Susan Gray (George Peabody College for Teachers), J. P. Scott (Jackson Memorial Laboratory), Harold and Mary Cover Jones (University of California, Berkeley), Leona Tyler (University of Oregon), Wilton Krogman (University of Pennsylvania), Lee Stott (the Merrill-Palmer Institute), and historian Alice Smuts (University of Michigan). These people supported and contributed to my breadth of interest. Most held a dynamic view of the developmental process. I remember challenging Dr. Jersild why, midway in the series of revisions of his very popular basic text, he shifted from a fact- and data-oriented approach to a more personalistic, what some have called a "soft-headed," position.

His answer, in a speech and in subsequent personal conversations, embraced his readings in existential philosophy, his mission to war-devastated Japan in 1946, and a family tragedy. I was considerably moved by the feeling in his recitals, which surely supported my own quasi-philosophical, phenomenological slant on human development.

A peak experience in teaching came in 1978 when I conducted the annual Liberal Arts College honors course. The seniors with the highest GPAs in the college were invited to attend a fall seminar in which each would formulate a problem for a senior thesis. In the winter term, with the help of an appropriate faculty member, she or he would write a senior thesis, and in the spring return to the seminar to report the study to the group. Our broad topic was Constructing a Reality, whether by the math and symbols of science, writing (literature), or the graphic and constructive and performing arts. Fifteen students enrolled, and fourteen completed the three-term course. As several said, this was the first time in college they had the opportunity to work on their own ideas and to try to relate their thinking to the resources available in books and professors, and in the company of bright, critical, but respectful and friendly, student colleagues! They simply took off intellectually. Their enthusiasm, even joy, was for me a fitting celebration at the point of retirement. The following year at the APA meeting I gave an invited address for Division 37, Child, Youth and Family Services, entitled "The Proper Study of Humankind . . . ," which summarized my view of a humanistic developmental psychology and the place of interpretation in psychological reasoning.

Some Reflections

What do I have to say about the field of child development? Initially, the Society for Research in Child Development (SRCD) was multidisciplinary, focusing on interdisciplinary issues. The early meetings I attended impressed me with the readiness of scientists and practitioners from various backgrounds to exchange information and ideas, and with the ease of their understanding at the level of application, if not always at the level of scientific or laboratory derivation. Some years ago I reviewed Milton Senn's taped interviews with founders of the SRCD and was impressed by their willingness to tackle social problems and their idealism and optimism. Virtually all of them, from different disciplines and different institutions, expected research to furnish the blueprints for a well-grown, healthy, and well-educated citizenry in the future. After fifty-plus years of research, we have more children in worse difficulties than ever! And politically we seem much less agreed on how to engineer conditions of sound development.

Today the society is largely made up of psychologists. I remain as persuaded of the value of a multidisciplinary approach to social problems as I was earlier (see Harris, 1953). Psychologists' research frequently exhibits a theory base rather than a problem base, and a preoccupation with the intriguing challenge of model-building. These interests certainly have their place in any science, but some question their fruitfulness in the study of the human being's social interactions, where causation is so multiple and complex. There are also those who insist on less concern with constructs we academics invent, less attention to game-playing with words, at reinventing the wheel as a "rotary device for enabling motion," and more concern with issues that distress our citizens. Would our field of study be further along if we stayed closer to the level of observed phenomena? Or does this question merely betray my "applied" leanings? For I do believe that in an era of dwindling resources and burgeoning social problems, academics must heed society's concerns if they are to retain the support experienced in the past. The developmentalist in science must do research as a human being observing humane values.

The study of human development poses a dilemma. By its very nature the growth of the person creates a history of that person. Yet in its primary commitment to the controlled experiment, much of psychology is ahistorical. In examining learning in the course of development, the time perspective becomes vastly different from that of the experimentalist. A developmental psychologist once remarked that two boys playing catch for twenty minutes engage in more trials than any learning experiment in the literature! The concept of development may imply more than change; it may involve continuing reorganization as the person contends with his life course! Implementation of concepts of time and organization is complex. One's metaphysical assumptions, all too often implicit, are important!

And can we afford to neglect our own development as a discipline? I recall a publisher's representative who advocated a new developmental text with the argument, "It's up-to-the-minute; no reference is more than five years old!" One might wonder as to the character of a developmental discipline that is so ephemeral it can neglect its own growth! No wonder we rediscover the wheel!

A summary word about my quest, acknowledging pervasive themes. Certainly I have been more generalist than particularist. My childish curiosity (which plagued my mother with incessant questions) persisted in later life as many and varied intellectual interests. An interest in books, in words, in communication, nourished in high school, led to the study of classical languages. Ultimately this interest in symbols and words applied to psychology led back into philosophy. My interest in discovering a phenomenon's origins and its ecological "fit" in context began in college. In my psychological thinking I have sought to incorporate several principal ideas—individuals exist in a transactive relationship with their habitats, the basic fact of individual differences on all measurable dimensions—and a "theory" of adjustment: children as agents, with growing knowledge and skills, transacting with their own developmental trajectories. To the psychologist's definition of understanding as encompassed by prediction and control I would add appreciation, a wholistic, esthetic-like quality recognized by many topflight scientists when examining their work and its implications. A desire to share information and ideas with others and to excite them to such understanding persisted throughout and came to fullness in the latter half of my life.

Would I do anything differently; could I repeat my odyssey? Under similar circumstances, no, not in any major way. I would probably write more "think pieces" and seek their publication. I think I would retain the balance I worked out between research and teaching. I might write a text, striving to communicate to readers the view I tried to offer in my classes: That children and their growth are fascinating subjects, that from the very beginning children are persons, individuals, with a degree of autonomy that they seek to express in many ways; that they participate as active agents in the creation of their own influential environments; that adults have much to learn by sensitive watching and listening; that appropriate parenting, guiding, and teaching roles come much more readily to those who manage such an understanding; and that for the present we must tolerate the paradox of development, that inevitable change coexists with continuity, sameness.

Were I to repeat this journey now, at the turn of the twenty-first century, I would make my way through a very different literature and in a very different intellectual climate. I surely cannot guess the shape of the outcome, but temperaments being what they are I think I would still celebrate the marvel of individual development.

The writing of this chapter has persuaded me that I probably owe much to Florence Goodenough for three ideas that appear repeatedly in this account. She insisted that psychology was properly the scientific study of behavior and experience, and for her science was an attitude and a systematic method appropriate to the problem and phenomena under study rather than any one specific method. She insisted on analysis but also on synthesis, or reassembly of the analyzed as a final step in achieving understanding. On this issue I still recall vividly her impromptu but sharp debate with Lester Sontag (of the Fels Institute) on the floor of an SRCD meeting. She often stated that important understanding could be gained from a study of personal documents, especially diaries and memoirs. It strikes me now that serious attention to biographical method in psychology might help us maintain humanistic sympathies and sensitivities in a manipulative, variable-oriented discipline. It might inject into our research and practice an appreciation of the resilience and essential buoyancy of human personality and a fundamental respect for the integrity of the person in all her or his efforts to sort out the self.

In my lifetime developmental psychology has expanded to include aging as a process coextensive with growth and therefore as a phase of the life cycle. Medical science tends to regard old age as a disease to be cured; similarly, public policy considers aging as a social problem to be solved. Might developmental psychology moderate this discontinuity by borrowing concepts from the humanities and from the less positivistic aspects of social science? As an aged educator-psychologist I raise this final question.

References

Barfield, O. (1952). *Poetic diction*. London: Faber and Faber.

Dashiell, J. F. (1928). *Fundamentals of objective psychology*. New York: Houghton Mifflin.

Goodenough, F. L. (1926). *Measurement of intelligence by drawings.* New York: World Book Co. (Reissued by Harcourt Brace and World, 1954).

Harris, D. B. (1953). Why an interdisciplinary society for research in child development. *Child Development, 24,* 249–55.

Harris, D. B. (1963). *Children's drawings as measures of intellectual maturity.* New York: Harcourt Brace and World.

Harris, D. B. (Ed.). (1957). *The concept of development.* Minneapolis: University of Minnesota Press.

Lamprecht, K. (1906). Les dessins d'enfants comme source historique [Children's drawings as an historical source]. *Bulletin de l'Academie Royale de Belgique, Classe des Lettres, 12* (nos. 9–10), 457–469.

Ogden, C. K. & Richards, I. A. (1927). *The meaning of meaning.* New York: Harcourt Brace.

Smelser, N. J. (1987). *Contemporary classics in the social and behavioral sciences.* Philadelphia: ISI Press.

Werner, H. (1948). *Comparative psychology of mental development.* Chicago: Follett.

Zinsser, W. (Ed.). (1987). *Inventing the truth: The art and craft of memoir.* Boston: Houghton Mifflin.

6

Lois Wladis Hoffman

As a developmental psychologist who studies the influence of family experiences on socialization, it is somewhat embarrassing to approach the task of describing the factors that shaped my career development by skipping over the family influences. I see my career as shaped more by what Bandura (1982) has called "chance encounters" and "fortuitous events" and by influences at the societal level—particularly the prejudices of the times. Most of the important events that shaped my career were unplanned situations, and I chose the path of least resistance.

The Early Years

I was born in the same town in which my mother was born, Elmira, New York, a city of about forty-five thousand that is not near New York City or Buffalo or any other large city. It is in the center of farm country, of beautiful hills, near the Finger Lakes. I was the youngest child in a nonintellectual family. I had an advantage in school because I was middle class and most of my classmates were working class, and I was an honor student with little effort. I read books like the Nancy Drew and Judy Bolton series and *Sue Barton, Student Nurse*.

I wanted to go to college to get away from home—for fun and adventure. My best friend and I chose the colleges to which we would apply on our own. Neither family had any advice to offer. Her parents both worked in a factory; mine owned a clothing store where both worked. My father had gone to school through the eighth grade. My mother had attended normal school after high school, and before her first child was born she had taught school in a one-room schoolhouse.

We chose Northwestern University, which we somehow learned had a good school of journalism, because we co-edited the school newspaper and thought we might be foreign correspondents like Marguerite Higgins; and Pembroke College, the "girls" school attached to Brown, because the picture on the brochure was very attractive. We were both rejected at Northwestern because "to create spaces for the returning GIs, we are not accepting out-of-state girls."

We were both accepted at Pembroke. However, in May I returned a form to indicate roommate preference in the dormitory on which I requested a Jewish roommate because I was Jewish and wanted to meet other Jewish girls. A return letter informed me that an error had been made and that I was no longer an accepted student. Several letters were exchanged, and finally the written explanation came that Admissions had not realized I was Jewish because my name and hometown had not suggested that. Unfortunately, their Jewish quota was already filled, so I could no longer be considered within that group. The letter ended "I hope this will not thwart your attitude toward education." A letter was also sent to my friend to verify that she was not Jewish and to request a letter affirming that from her minister. It is interesting to note that I was immediately angry at the religious discrimination of Pembroke, but it was many years before I realized Northwestern had been guilty of sex discrimination.

Since it was late May, I was desperate for a college. I applied to several. Of those that accepted me at that point, all but one said there was no room in the dormitory. Since I was going to college mainly to live in a dormitory, I decided to go to that one. It was the University of Buffalo, now SUNY Buffalo, and only after I arrived there did I learn there were no dormitories. Out-of-town students rented rooms in private homes. I decided to major in sociology because a friend of my sister mentioned, when she heard where I was going, that she knew someone there and it had a good sociology department.

So, in September 1947, because of anti-Semitism, gender discrimination, and ignorance, I entered the University of Buffalo with a major selected because of a casual remark. The fact is, it really was an unusually fine sociology department. There were several exceptional young sociologists there in their first jobs. One of them was Alvin Gouldner. Because of his gift for teaching, respect for students, high expectations, and sheer brilliance, he turned my life around. My first assignment as a freshman was to read the article "Social Theory and Social Structure," by Robert Merton (1947). I didn't understand a word. I read it four times and finally enlisted the aid of an advanced student, an ex-GI, to go over it with me sentence by sentence until I understood it. To this day I remember the content of that article.

This was a very exciting time for me. I was intellectually stimulated and socially awakened. I received a fine education and firsthand research experience. Several of the young faculty actively engaged undergraduates in their research. We learned design, interviewing, coding, and analysis. Gouldner's research at that time examined the individual's experience in contact with bureaucratic institutions. One project had to do with the traditionalism of miners in conflict with the increasing rationalism of mine management; another had to do with individuals' perceptions of "red tape" in their interactions as clients with bureaucratic institutions. The work was solidly based in sociological theory influenced strongly by Max Weber, but in translating the research to testable hypotheses it cut over into social psychology.

I also carried out, under Gouldner's direction, a project on succession to leadership as a stimulus to increased bureaucracy. I watched the newspapers for announcements of persons newly appointed to high executive positions, contacted them, and arranged a series of focused interviews dealing with how they handled their problems and anxieties in the new job. The results indicated, as had been hypothesized, that the steps they took tended to increase the level of bureaucratization in the organization. This project was selected as the outstanding senior thesis at Buffalo, but I never submitted it for publication, as today's undergraduate students would. It never even occurred to me.

All of this translated easily into social psychology later in my career and might today be studied in organizational psychology. The hands-on experience was of immense value to me in subsequent work at the Institute for Social Research at the University of Michigan. It was a kind of direct, one-on-one training not available in many undergraduate programs.

The summer that followed my sophomore year I went to summer school at Cornell and finally had my dorm experience. It was fun and I could have transferred, but by then I was hooked on Buffalo. In addition to the enormous intellectual growth that extended beyond sociology to literature, music, and art, I became involved in left-of-center politics that included civil rights, civil liberties, and pro-union activities. I "sat in" at pizza parlors with mixed-race groups, campaigned for Henry Wallace, and a few years later protested McCarthyism, the Rosenberg executions, and the Vietnam War.

At the beginning of my third year in college, 1949, I decided to go to law school to become a labor lawyer to work for the unions. I was accepted at the two law schools to which I applied to enter in September of 1950, but I was told that women could not go into labor law. To become a labor lawyer, one had to serve on the National Labor Relations Board (NLRB), and the NLRB, did not take women. So I decided to finish college and go on to graduate school in industrial sociology, another shift in direction based on discrimination.

I obtained a graduate fellowship at the University of California, Berkeley for September of 1951. This time my school was well chosen since both Seymour Lipsitt and Reinhard Bendix were there. But another series of unanticipated events intervened.

In the late fall of my senior year, in 1950, I realized I had enough credits to complete my degree in January. I had hoped to get a job in Buffalo until it was time to leave for Berkeley, but my mother said that if I was not in school I was to come home (gender discrimination again). Among the many things I was prepared to do at that point in my life, returning to my family home was not one. I discussed my problem with Gouldner, who said that his friend Lou Schneider, at Purdue, had recently mentioned he had a midterm fellowship in sociology available that Gouldner was sure I could get. The plan was that I would spend the winter/spring term at Purdue and then leave for Berkeley. One of Bandura's chance encounters, however, turned me in a different direction.

Graduate School

At Purdue I enrolled in a graduate seminar in social psychology taught by a young assistant professor, Martin Hoffman. The class met at night, and after the second session he suggested we all go out for coffee. I accepted, but the others couldn't go; the coffee shop was closed, so we went instead to a nearby bar and lounge for wine. We were married in June.

I never did get to Berkeley. Instead, I completed a master's degree in sociology with Lou Schneider as chair. The research I conducted was an ambitious study of how the rural traditionalism of the workers in a Square D factory in Peru, Indiana, affected their attitudes toward wages and the union. Gouldner wanted to include my paper in his book that was about to be published, *Wildcat Strike.* He even edited it toward that end, but to my present regret I did not undertake the minor effort required to ready it for publication. At that time I was highly motivated to do good work, but I was not career oriented. Even later, during my first year in a Ph.D. program at the University of Michigan, I failed to submit a quite publishable research paper I completed as a requirement of my first-year fellowship.

In June 1953 we moved to Michigan, where my husband took a position at the Merrill-Palmer School in Detroit. He was a social psychologist, but when he accepted this new position it was to conduct research on children. He had gone to graduate school at the University of Michigan and was eager to get back to Ann Arbor and old friends. Once the move was decided, I applied to graduate school in sociology and was given a fellowship.

Sociology at Michigan was much different from my previous experiences. The department was very impersonal and formal. There was little contact between faculty and students outside the classroom. Little attention was given to the European theorists like Weber or Durkheim, and instead the emphasis was on American work, particularly demography, the Chicago "ecological" studies (not the ecology of Bronfenbrenner but the concentric circle conceptualization of Parke and others), and the current research involvements of the younger faculty. Most of the courses were dull and the teaching uninspired.

A notable exception was Guy E. Swanson, who was a stimulating teacher. His work with Dan Miller on how socioeconomic factors impact on family interaction and by that process affect child development has had a major influence on my subsequent and current work. Although I now consider myself a developmental psychologist and not a sociologist, most of my work uses a similar approach, in which influences at the societal level affect the family, which affects the child.

In September 1954, the beginning of my second year at Michigan, I joined the staff at the Institute for Social Research (ISR) as an assistant study director. It was a position specifically for graduate students enrolled at Michigan, most of whom were in psychology, but others were in political science, economics, and occasionally sociology. I thought the work there would be more consistent with my interests and previous research. At that time, ISR had three major units: the Survey Research Center, Group Dynamics, and the Economic Behavior Program. I was in the industrial psychology unit of the Survey Research Center, the only woman in the unit. I was assigned to an unfunded project, an analysis of data already collected.

Ronald Lippitt, who was in Group Dynamics, had just received funds to conduct a study of the links between the child's family life and peer relationships. He wanted a woman to work with him on the project; a study of families, he thought, should have a woman as well as a man conducting it. Shortly after I started working at ISR, he approached me to see if I would take the position. I was very reluctant. I wanted to study industry and organizations, not families; I considered family sociology an intellectually inferior area. Still, this position would have many advantages over my current assignment. I would be in on the ground floor—designing the study; and I was to be allowed to put into the study my own variables for my doctoral dissertation. I finally agreed to the switch on the condition that it was understood I was on loan and could return to the industrial research unit when the study was completed.

Career: The Beginning

But I did not return. Although I actually completed my Ph.D. in the sociology department, and although the University of Michigan did not have a program in developmental psychology until 1964, I mark that shift to Group Dynamics as the point when I changed direction and became a developmental psychologist. I remained at Group Dynamics and worked with Ron Lippitt until September of 1960, when my first child was born, and the work I did during that period set all of the themes for my subsequent work. During that period my publications dealt with the effects of maternal employment on the family and the child, gender differences in socialization, the role of the father, motivations for parenthood, and the process by which social factors affect children's development. If I were to list what I have done since then, no new topics would be added. And, at the present time, I am conducting a study remarkably similar to the one begun in 1954.

The senior staff in Group Dynamics were almost entirely the disciples of Kurt Lewin. Festinger had left by then, but Doc Cartwright, Jack French, Al Zander, and Ron Lippitt remained until their retirements. In Paul Mussen's preface to the 1970 edition of the *Manual of Child Psychology*, he noted that the 1954 edition's only theoretical chapter was concerned with Lewinian theory, which he felt had "not had a significant lasting impact on developmental psychology." Although it is true that Lewin is not often cited in developmental papers, I think he has had a profound impact. Most of the senior developmental psychologists who study the socialization process today were actually trained as social psychologists at a time when field theory and the study of group dynamics were very prominent (e.g., Eleanor Maccoby, Martin Hoffman), and many of them, like me, were trained by students of Lewin (e.g., Diana Baumrind) or worked with Lewin himself (Marion Radke-Yarrow). Alfred Baldwin was influenced by Lewin while a student at Harvard, where Lewin taught for a semester. It is quite easy to see the similarity between the work of Lewin and his students (Lewin, Lippitt, and White, 1939) on leadership styles in small groups and both Baldwin's work at the Fels Institute on democratic and authoritarian families and Baumrind's work on authoritarian, authoritative, and permissive parenting styles. The Lewin small-group work easily applied to the study of families, and as the study of small groups became less common in social psychology, the study of leadership, the expression of power, and the dynamics of interaction and influence in the family grew in developmental psychology.

Many other Lewinian ideas influenced the socialization researchers. Lewin's insistence that both the person, with all his or her characteristics and predispositions, and the *situation,* the current environment, had to be considered in predicting behavior; his view that the individual's perceptions and interpretations were important elements in prediction; his interest in the structure of the child's peer group and the child's role in it—all of these found their way into developmental psychology. And I suspect that Lewin's influence was by the route of mentoring rather than through a conscious application of Lewin's theory.

Ron Lippitt and I met regularly to talk about theoretical issues, and we were often joined by Sid Rosen, who was working on a related project. Several sessions were devoted to listing the "linking mechanisms" by which family experiences affect the child's peer relationships. These discussions were used to select the variables we wanted to operationalize in the study, and we also managed to include much of what we discussed in a chapter Ron and I wrote for Mussen's *Handbook of Research Methods in Child Development* (Hoffman & Lippitt, 1960). In the chapter, we presented a scheme for classifying concepts in family research that formed a chain of causality from parent background variables and the current social setting of the family through to the child's peer relationships and behavior at school. This scheme distinguished attitudes from behavior, the child's perceptions and interpretations from objective experience, and noted the importance of siblings in influencing both parent behavior and the child's socialization. The focus was on the linking processes with the idea that operationalizing the steps in the chain of causality was necessary for identifying the process involved.

Ron and I worked as peers during the planning stage of the study. While he was always interested, available, and enjoyed the involvement, he moved into other projects and for two years was on leave in California. Ron Lippitt not only studied democracy, he practiced it. He gave me autonomy and trust, but he was always available for support. When he was asked to write the chapter on the measurement of family variables for Paul Mussen's *Handbook,* he asked me to coauthor it, and it was published with me listed as the major author. In fact, I was the first author on all of our collaborative publications, and this was never an issue.

The research project, a study of family influences on the peer relationships of children in the third through sixth grades, involved independent measures from mothers, fathers, the children, their teachers, and their peers at school. For my doctoral dissertation, I wanted to take advantage of the rich data set but also to keep it separate from the rest of the project. I decided to look at the effects of the mother's employment on the family structure—on the division of labor and power. This was consistent with my previous interest in the occupational world and power relations and an accommodation to the nature of the project. I also examined the links from employment through the family to the child, but this was not part of the dissertation.

My own career has been most marked by the research on maternal employment that stemmed from the study, but this project was innovative in several ways. It was one of the first to examine the father's role and to use fathers as informants. It was also one of the few studies of that time to analyze the child data separately by sex of child. It was the custom either to study only boys, or to lump the boys and girls together for analyses. Lumped together, results often yielded no significant relationships because the direction was the opposite for boys and girls and they canceled each other out. Analyzed separately, two significant relationships emerged, each in the opposite direction. For example, maternal employment was associated with teacher-rated independence in daughters but with dependency in sons. Moderator variables were used throughout. For example, the relationship between the father's power in the family and the son's power in the peer group was moderated by the father-son relationship (Hoffman, 1961b); the mother's attitude toward work moderated the relationship between employment status and both child-rearing patterns and child outcomes (Hoffman, 1961a).

In several recent overviews of the research in developmental psychology, it is noted that early studies simply related a parent variable to a child outcome while modern research is concerned with process and tries to identify the intervening links. This study undertaken in the 1950s was very much a modern one in its conceptualization and design, but what was enormously different and limiting was the technology available for data analysis. During the first year of analysis the machine we relied on was a "counter-sorter." One ran IBM cards through to sort on one variable and then ran each resulting pile separately to sort on the second. The numbers indicating the distribution on the second variable had to be hand-copied from the machine and the statistics individually computed on a Monroe calculator. By the third year, there was a machine that printed cross tabulations, but the statistics were still a separate hand operation. Multivariate statistics were virtually nonexistent.

By the time my doctoral dissertation was completed I was in a publishing mode, and I submitted a write-up to *The Journal of Marriage and the Family* (then called *Marriage and Family Living*). Ivan Nye was the editor, and in his acceptance letter he invited me to join him on a symposium in Ames, Iowa, at a meeting of the National Council on Family Relations. There he suggested we edit a book on the employed mother. Ivan and I saw each other only on two subsequent occasions and both were brief. Nevertheless, we had a long and rewarding collaboration. We communicated by mail and phone. I am considered quite funny, and Ivan had a good sense of humor, and as he told me in a lovely note after our second book, that was the key that carried us through a few rough spots.

Authorship order was not a problem. My first child was born just as we were entering the final stages with our first book, *The Employed Mother in America*. I told him I didn't know who should be first, but that if he would handle the index, proofs, and final tasks, I would be happy to have him be first author. For the second book he took the initiative and said that since he had that privilege the first time, I should have it the second.

In 1959, in addition to my position as research associate in Group Dynamics, I served as a research consultant with the University of Michigan Psychological Clinic. Fred Wyatt, head of the clinic, was interested in women's motivation for pregnancy, an interest stimulated by patterns he had observed in his patients. I was interested in the topic personally. Although I was still in my twenties, I wanted very much to become a parent and was frustrated because my husband and I were having fertility problems. Always introspective, I had thought a great deal about my motivation. Fred and I met weekly to discuss the topic with an eye toward preparing a research proposal. The proposal was well under way when I learned I was to be a mother. Instead of submitting it for funding we turned it into an article that was published in the *Merrill-Palmer Quarterly* (Hoffman & Wyatt, 1960).

I intended to quit work entirely when my baby was born and had discussed this with Marty and Ron. It's ironic that I am thought of by many as the defender of mothers' employment, and in 1960 few mothers of infants worked and few men would advocate it, but I was surrounded by men who thought it was little short of outrageous that I should quit work. When the time came, Ron was sympathetic to my wishes but offered to have a research assistant report to my house so I could continue at least part-time employment from my home. Marty was really an early feminist and had always encouraged my career. In addition, as a child of the Depression he was apprehensive about having our income halved when our expenses seemed likely to double.

An additional source of pressure was Orville Brim Jr. I had met him through Ron Lippitt. We shared research interests and sociology training and had enjoyed some stimulating discussions. Hearing of my plans, he proposed that I take on the editorship of a series of volumes designed to get the results of developmental research to practitioners. The project would be funded by the Russell Sage Foundation; he was its president. With some reluctance, I eventually accepted this position after originally turning it down. The work was not to start for another year, and Marty would be an associate editor and would cover for me at points when the job was a particular interference. Work on the *Review of Child Development Research* was my only paid job between September 1960 and September 1967. For the second time, I had resisted an unsolicited job offer that turned out to be a wonderful opportunity.

Fourteen months after our first daughter was born, we had a second. Although the planning, organization, and authors were selected earlier, the actual work on the two volumes took place between 1962 and 1967 and almost all of it was done after the children were in bed. There was only one real rule in the house during that period: Bedtime was 7:30 P.M. I was a full-time mother throughout those years with hired help for routine household tasks. I do not know if my children are better for it or worse for it, but I loved it. I would not want to fill that role all my life, but for me it was a wonderful interlude. Not all parents would enjoy it, and very few would have the opportunity to combine work and parenting in that way. I was very lucky.

Marty and I edited Volumes 1 and 2 of the *Review of Child Development Research* and launched the series. We saw them as an important effort to communicate up-to-date research in developmental psychology in straight language, without scientific jargon, and with an organization that would make them useful to professionals in applied fields serving children. But equally important, we did not want to strip the research of its scientific validity by deleting the qualifying statements that are an intrinsic part of science. The target audience was not the frontline practitioners so much as it was those who trained them. The researchers who were invited to write chapters were given explicit directions so that each chapter would be an integrative review and interpretation of the up-to-date research findings, organized and written to maximize their value for the delivery of services to children. In addition, for each chapter there was one researcher who was highly competent in the topic and two persons who were sophisticated about research but closer to the application of the knowledge assigned to review the chapter. This structure and the selection of authors and reviewers was set up in consultation with a stellar advisory committee.

The bulk of my job was to read the chapters and the reviews, to integrate these and add my own suggestions for revisions, and then to sell the author on, sometimes perhaps even trick the author into, accepting the changes. To accomplish this, I rewrote many sections, and in one case almost a whole chapter; I talked and argued with authors on the phone in very long—sometimes heated—conversations. Bettye Caldwell and I had a long conversation revamping her original draft while her hands were covered with flour because I had interrupted her bread-baking; her twins were cavorting close by, and my two were napping because I was the caller. Jerry Kagan agreed to some modifications after a hearty dispute and ended the conversation with, "You're a good man, Lois." I spent a lot of time with Ed Zigler taming his chapter, though he had been selected to write the chapter originally because he was considered exciting and provocative (he was most generous in his acknowledgment to me). One author in the course of a hearty but good-natured battle called me a G—— D—— stubborn Polack. In short, the editing of these volumes was not a passive one. I put an enormous amount of effort into it, making the changes in the writing rather than just suggesting a rewrite because I think authors will accept changes more easily if they don't have to make them themselves.

The volumes turned out to be very good, at least partly, I think, because of this extra effort. If this had not been my primary professional involvement during these years, such would not have been possible. The books won an award from the Child Study Association and launched an ongoing series. Marty and I decided on the order of authorship for each volume for pragmatic reasons. Actually, he was more involved in the second volume than the first.

In 1967 the books were done, both girls were in school, and I was asked to teach a section of the undergraduate course in child development for the recently formed Developmental Area in Psychology at the University of Michigan. One of the wonderful things about my work on the *Reviews* was that not only had I not become obsolete during my homebound period, but I was very much on top of the current developmental research. I had never really taken a course in child psychology, but because of my work on the *Reviews* and the loan of a colleague's teaching notes, I moved into teaching. I became a lecturer in the psychology department.

In 1989 I was selected as an "Eminent Woman in Psychology," along with Eleanor Maccoby. We were asked to make presentations at the annual meeting of the American Psychological Association (APA) on how being a woman had shaped our careers. Our family backgrounds were very different, and Eleanor did not see gender as affecting her career line. I saw it as a major influence at each step in mine—from my rejection at Northwestern through being closed out from labor law, my going to Purdue to avoid returning home, my automatic assumption that my location would be determined by my husband's job, my inadequate motivation to prepare my early papers for publication, the move from research on industrial organizations to research on the family, and leaving that position to stay home with my daughters. Some of this was discrimination; some—like the opportunity to stay home when my daughters were young—was a special privilege; some was my own internalization of the views of the time. Much of it turned out well for me. Although discrimination and gender stereotypes led me to become a developmental psychologist, it has been an endlessly gratifying, never boring career. And even the low motivation that kept me from preparing my early research reports for publication later fueled several papers and a research project on early socialization and women's achievement motivation.

Between 1967 and 1972, however, I held the position of lecturer in psychology, and although I did not view this as discrimination at the time, I definitely do now. The position was underpaid, came with no benefits, involved no sabbatical, and was untenured. It was the standard job for psychologists who were also mothers. Though it may seem odd from the vantage of the 1990s, we were blissfully ignorant of the fact that this was exploitation and happy to have specific teaching responsibilities without additional pressures.

My home was within a mile of campus. I saw my daughters off to school in the mornings, biked to campus, taught a section of child psychology, biked home in time to greet the girls for lunch, saw them off for their afternoon sessions, biked to campus to teach another section, and was home to greet them when they returned. One of my students was Harriet McAdoo, who later told me that she would see me putting my earrings on as I entered the class—"finishing dressing."

Since she had just dropped her children off at day care to race to class, she well understood.

Marty had moved from the Merrill-Palmer School to the University of Michigan to chair the new program in developmental psychology in 1964. So in 1971 he had a sabbatical and I took a leave without pay and off we went for a year in Berkeley. During that year I wrote two of my favorite papers. One is an article called "Early Childhood Experiences and Women's Achievement Motives" (Hoffman, 1972). It is a theoretical paper and research review proposing that the early childhood experiences of girls leads to needs for affiliation that can interfere with their achievement motivation and affect their subsequent behavior. It was prepared for a special issue of the *Journal of Social Issues,* was often reprinted, and was translated into German, Dutch, and French.

The other was a chapter, "The Value of Children to Parents," written for a book edited by James Fawcett titled *Psychological Perspectives on Population* (Hoffman, L. W. & Hoffman, M. L., 1973). This assignment stemmed from the earlier publication with Fred Wyatt. James Fawcett, a social psychologist at the East-West Center in Hawaii, along with Sidney Newman of the National Institute of Child Health and Development, and others were interested in creating a new specialty in psychology that addressed population issues. The Hoffman and Wyatt paper was one of very few to address the issue of motivations for childbearing, a topic of some concern in the United States, particularly with respect to the increasing rates of teenage pregnancy and births to single women, and of great concern in the developing countries because of overpopulation. Jim Fawcett had read that paper and called me about the chapter just before we set off for California. The timing was good, the topic interesting, and I accepted.

In the chapter I presented a scheme dealing with the needs children satisfy for parents organized around nine basic needs (e.g., love, stimulation, coping with mortality, power), the alternative sources available for satisfying the needs, and the costs of children in psychological as well as economic terms. This chapter led to a major new line of research for me. Within two years I was involved in a large cross-national investigation of the value of children to parents that was based on this scheme. The study included nine countries, most of them in Asia, and I am currently launching with colleagues in China a similar study to be conducted there.

Although my colleagues in Asia and at the East-West Center have been primarily interested in this work for its significance for population problems, I have also examined the hypothesis that the needs children satisfy for parents affect child-rearing patterns (Hoffman, 1987) and, in addition, have conducted research that combines my interest in women's achievement motives and affiliative conflicts with my interest in fertility motivation (Hoffman, 1977).

The Women's Movement

As the year in Berkeley drew to a close, many things began to change for me personally and for women generally. It was the beginning of the women's movement.

The University of Michigan, like many schools, was going through difficult financial times, and many lecturers were being dismissed. With both my children in school, I had no wish to be unemployed. I requested a switch from lecturer to a "ladder" position and succeeded in getting an appointment as a nontenured associate professor. I succeeded because of two things. First, my husband went on the job market with me, and we obtained joint offers of tenured professorships at two other universities. Second, my new work on motivations for fertility was of considerable interest to the University of Michigan School of Public Health, which had a fledgling department, the Department of Population Planning. My new appointment at Michigan was in psychology and public health.

Shortly after assuming my new position, a peculiar event occurred. The Michigan psychology department maintains two folders for every faculty member—a private department file and another one available to the faculty member for keeping his or her record of productivity up to date. In going through my file for the yearly update, I found copies of two letters that had been placed there but clearly belonged in the private department file. One of the two letters was from Susan Ervin-Tripp, one of the early activists in the women's movement. The letter, addressed to the chair of the psychology department, said that as an alumna of the university it was a source of concern to her that Lois Hoffman, a well-known and highly regarded psychologist, was untenured in the department. Also in the folder was the reply from the chair. His letter indicated respect for her eminence as one of the department's outstanding graduates and assured her that my not holding tenure was not because of discrimination against women, but because I was "difficult to get along with."

I must confess that my first response to this reply was not fury and outrage but tears at reading that I was so perceived. I shared the letter with my husband and a few close colleagues, who assured me that, whatever my faults, I was not difficult to get along with. I had in fact a record of working with people who were themselves thought of as difficult. Today I would not need that reassurance—the sheer inappropriateness of the criteria and awareness of stereotyping in the evaluation of professional women would be enough—but I needed it then.

This event became a spur for me. I solicited letters from colleagues and former students. These and the two letters from my file were brought before the psychology executive committee; Elizabeth Douvan presented my case. I received a formal apology from the department chairman, whose explanation was simple: "I don't know why I said that. It isn't true." Formal tenure proceedings were undertaken shortly after that. I did obtain tenure, but for presentation to the college two steps were included: (1) my articles that were seen as dealing with "women's issues" were exempt from consideration, even though they had been published in professional journals, and (2) my husband had to attach a memo stating that I was indeed a major author on all our jointly authored publications. By this time I had four books, many journal articles, over half a million dollars in research grants, and seven years of teaching in the department. Marty and I became the first wife and husband to each hold tenure in the same department at Michigan. Within a year I was promoted to full professor.

There were two side effects. First, I became very active in the women's movement at Michigan. We achieved considerable success in having women's salaries and ranks upgraded to a level matched with male peers, in establishing norms for determining whether a department's faculty adequately reflected the gender ratio in the pool of potential faculty, and in facilitating the election and appointment of women to decisionmaking committees. Second, I became involved in establishing a women's study program at Michigan. In addition, although I cannot say the incident I described was the cause, the chairman who wrote that letter subsequently became very supportive in women's issues.

The Later Years

At the same time I achieved tenure, my appointment was switched to full time in the psychology department and there, despite some tempting lures, I have remained. There have been many changes in the ensuing years—at Michigan, in developmental psychology, and in my personal life. The Michigan psychology department has emerged as an outstanding example of gender equalitarianism and has been very successful in attracting faculty and students from ethnic minorities. The developmental program of the department has become one of the largest and most esteemed in the country, and developmental nationally has emerged as a major area of psychology.

I have become increasingly immersed in my work, and it has included teaching, research, and administration. Whereas in the midsixties it would have been very difficult for me to face a class with more than thirty students, by 1975 I taught classes with three hundred students. Through teaching at both the graduate and the undergraduate level my knowledge of developmental psychology broadened. Partly because effective teaching requires it, and partly because I am surrounded by stimulating students and colleagues, it is impossible not to keep up to date on current research and theoretical issues. Ten years ago, Scott Paris and I teamed up with Elizabeth Hall to revamp the textbook *Developmental Psychology Today*. We have completed two editions and are getting ready for a third. During the 1980s, I was involved in administration, chairing the developmental psychology program, and serving as president of the Developmental Division of the APA as well as of Division 9, the Society for the Study of Social Issues. Administration, however, cut severely into the work that had carried me to developmental psychology, so for the 1990s (in my sixties) I have returned to research.

My current research involvements are very much like my earlier work. I am examining how socioeconomic conditions and work patterns affect family interaction and children's socialization experiences, and how these impact on the child's development. It is much easier now: There are more validated measures available, an advanced technology for data processing and analysis, statistical procedures for testing complex models, and most of all, other researchers doing similar kinds of work. My work has been continuously marked by my early training in sociology in its concern with sociocultural variables and the social setting as affecting family interaction and parent-child relationships and as variables that moderate the effects on the child. Today, however, unlike in the past, most of those who study the socialization process are also attuned to the importance of these contextual variables. This means that there is now an accumulation of research and theory to tie into.

I think this shift in the field is largely because of Urie Bronfenbrenner, through his writings and the students he influenced at Cornell. But it is also because of sociopolitical changes. There is more general awareness now that the social environment in which one is reared affects how one develops. And the possibility, for example, that the discipline patterns that are most effective for producing competent children in the middle class may not be the most effective in the urban ghetto is no longer a startling idea.

Concern with process and linkages is now widespread also. It is unlikely today, for example, that a study would be published in a major journal if it simply reported a relationship between the mother's employment status and a child outcome. Some operationalizing of the mediating variables, or at least a demonstration of the conditions under which the relationship is or is not found would be required.

Increasingly also there is awareness of the complexity of the socialization process. The fact that any given outcome is a result of multiple influences is intrinsic to present-day theory, though research methods and statistics are still not adequate to permit the empirical data to demonstrate this fully. Still problematic also is the demonstration of the interactive nature of the socialization process. Even before the early work of Bell (1968), the idea that the child affects his or her environment by providing stimuli to parental reactions has been in the literature; even before Lewin, the idea that the child's interpretation is key was there (Cairns, 1983). Now, however, most developmentalists accept the idea of socialization as an interactive process and family influences as part of a system of interacting persons including siblings as well as adults, but the techniques for translating this into a research design are far from in place.

It is important, I think, as well as inevitable, that our ideas remain ahead of our empirical methods. Our field tends to deify the empirical study. It is important to sit back and think about what a given study, our own and others', actually means. How is it limited by the operational definitions, the research design, the empirical controls that were and were not exercised, the experimental setting, or the researcher's bias? To what extent has the study been stripped of its context in a way that might affect the results?

If I were to say which of my publications I have been most satisfied with, it would be my integrative reviews of the literature, because it is through the critical examination of the research on a particular issue and the pulling together of results from different studies that we see what the data really show. The single study is too limited and fragile.

In my role as teacher, I have tried to pass on to both my graduate and undergraduate students the skills for doing good research combined with the ability to critically evaluate their own work and that of others, and above all to always keep in view the whole very complicated picture. I have also encouraged my students, and most of them are women, to take more control of their careers than I did. After all, they live in a better world.

References

Bandura, A. (1982). The psychology of chance encounters and life paths. *American Psychologist, 37*, 747–755.

Bell, R. Q. (1968). A reinterpretation of the direction of effects in studies of socialization. *Psychological Review, 75*, 81–95.

Cairns, R. B. (1983). The emergence of developmental psychology. In P. Mussen (Ed.), *Handbook of child psychology* (4th ed., pp. 41–102). New York: Wiley.

Hoffman, L. W. (1961a). The father's role in the family and the child's peer group adjustment. *Merrill-Palmer Quarterly, 7*, 97–105.

Hoffman, L. W. (1961b). Effects of maternal employment on the child. *Child Development, 32*, 187–197.

Hoffman, L. W. (1972). Early childhood experiences and women's achievement motives. *Journal of Social Issues, 28*, 129–156.

Hoffman, L. W. (1977). Fear of success in 1965 and 1974, a re-interview study. *Journal of Consulting and Clinical Psychology, 45*, 310–321.

Hoffman, L. W. (1987). The value of children to parents and child rearing patterns. *Social Behavior, 2*, 1–14.

Hoffman, L. W. & Hoffman, M. L. (1973). The value of children to parents. In J. Fawcett (Ed.), *Psychological perspectives on population* (pp. 19–76). New York: Basic Books.

Hoffman, L. W. & Lippitt, R. (1960). The measurement of family life variables. In P. Mussen (Ed.), *Handbook of research methods in child development* (pp. 945–1013). New York: Wiley.

Hoffman, L. W. & Wyatt, F. (1960). Social change and motivations for having larger families: Some theoretical considerations. *Merrill-Palmer Quarterly, 6*, 235–244.

Lewin, K., Lippitt, R. & White, R. K. (1939). Patterns of aggressive behavior in experimentally created "social climates." *Journal of Social Psychology, 10*, 271–299.

Merton, R. (1947). Social theory and social structure. *American Sociological Review, 50*, 1–23.

Representative Publications

Hoffman, L. W. (1974). Effects of maternal employment on the child—a review of the research. *Developmental Psychology, 10*, 204–228.

Hoffman, L. W. (1977). Changes in family roles, socialization, and sex differences. *American Psychologist, 32*, 644–657.

Hoffman, L. W. (1984). Maternal employment and the young child. In M. Perlmutter (Ed.), *Parent-Child Interaction, Minnesota Symposium Series, Volume 17* (pp. 223–282). Hillside, N.J.: Erlbaum.

Hoffman, L. W. (1984). Work, family and the socialization of the child. In R. Parke, R. Emde, H. McAdoo & G. Sackett (Eds.), *Review of child development research, Volume 7* (pp. 223–282). Chicago: Chicago University Press.

Hoffman, L. W. (1991). The influence of the family environment on personality: Accounting for sibling differences. *Psychological Bulletin, 110,* 187–203.

Hoffman, L. W. & Hoffman, M. L. (1966). *Review of child development research, Volume 2.* New York: Russell Sage.

Hoffman, L. W. & Nye, F. I. (1974). *The working mother and the family.* San Francisco: Jossey-Bass.

Hoffman, M. L. & Hoffman, L. W. (1964). *Review of child development research, Volume 1.* New York: Russell Sage.

7

Çiğdem Kağitçibaşi

Writing this autobiographical account of how I have become involved in cross-cultural developmental psychology is an insightful process of reconstruction and a learning experience for me. Some of the basic influences that have helped shape my current views on psychology in general and cross-cultural and developmental psychology in particular can be traced to my early experiences. It is good, therefore, that I was asked by the editors to start out with my family background and early years. What I will present here will provide the reader with an international and cross-cultural perspective, given that I am Turkish and have spent most of my life in Turkey. In retrospect, I can detect some profoundly important themes in my upbringing that have served and continue to serve as guiding principles in my life. Describing my early experiences in terms of these themes may help put my personal development and current worldview and academic orientation into perspective. One of these can be called "social commitment" and the other "achievement." They reflect both the strong socialization expectations from me as well as life goals I have set (internalized) for myself.

Early Years—The Ideal of Social Commitment
I was born in 1940 as the first child of a young couple who were teachers. My parents were both from Istanbul, the modern metropolis, but as civil servants they were appointed to posts in the provincial town of Bursa, where I grew up. The early 1940s were years of hardship even though Turkey managed to stay out of the war. Civil servants, especially teachers, earned little but enjoyed high social status because they had relatively high levels of education and represented the modern elite in a traditional society.[1]

My parents were truly the products of their time; they were fully committed to the Atatürk reforms and felt that as teachers they had a mission in building up a modern secular society out of the ashes of an old one based on tradition and religion. With very limited funds they started a private kindergarten in Bursa, which slowly grew into a primary and secondary school. I was the first student of the school at the age of two and have been in schools all my life.

121

I was brought up with the ideal of doing something worthwhile for society, nourished especially by my mother. As a devoted and much-liked teacher and public servant, my mother was a role model for me. She was an innovator in a provincial town. For example, she was the first woman to drive a car and the first woman public speaker in Bursa. I could not imagine a life that was not devoted to public service just like my mother's.

In retrospect, such ideals were taken seriously by many young people in my generation, especially among the children of the educated teachers and civil servants, who carried considerable responsibility for "building a modern nation." This is also reflected in international comparative research on attitudes conducted in the post–World War II period in newly emerging nations (developing countries), which pointed to much higher "patriotism" and a great value put on "doing something good for one's family and country" among youth in these countries as compared with American youth (Gillespie & Allport, 1955).

The historical context of nation-building probably made the loyalty felt to the nation more salient in these young people's values. However, this is not the whole story, as evidenced by a great deal of subsequent cross-cultural research and current work. For example, in a comparative study of Turkish and American youth in 1966, I found the same high level of national loyalty among the Turkish sample, for whom "nation building" was not relevant. In contrast, American adolescents valued personal achievement and happiness (Kağitçibaşi, 1970).

Furthermore, in a later study with Turkish adolescents (Kağitçibaşi, 1973), I found "patriotism" (loyalty to the country) to fit into a "modern" outlook and to be associated with belief in internal control of reinforcement, optimism, and achievement motivation. It was negatively associated with a more traditional outlook characterized by religiosity, authoritarianism, and belief in external control of reinforcement.

Similar loyalties transcending the self are also found in current cross-cultural research on achievement motivation. Phalet and Claeys (1993) found Turkish adolescents in both Turkey and Belgium to combine "individual and group loyalties" (Kağitçibaşi, 1987) into a "social achievement motivation," contrasted with the individualistic achievement motivation of the Belgian youth. Similar findings of socially oriented achievement motivation are reported for the Japanese (De Vos, 1968), Indians (Agarwal & Misra, 1986; Misra & Agarwal, 1985), and Chinese (Bond, 1986, p. 36; Yang, 1986, pp. 113–114; Yu & Yang, 1994).

These examples point to the continuing pervasiveness of the expanding loyalty and commitment to entities transcending the self in the so-called collectivistic cultures. In the individualistic culture, however, "the primary loyalty is to the self—its values, autonomy, pleasure, virtue and actualization" (Kagan, 1984). Despite recent criticism of excessive individualism in the West, and particularly in the United States (Smith, 1993; Sampson, 1987; Taylor, 1989; Cushman, 1990; Bellah, et al., 1985), the difference between the individualistic and the collectivistic concerns appears to be continuing.

Thus, growing up in a collectivistic society, in addition to the other significant influences I have referred to above has set the stage for me toward a generally positive orientation to social commitment. This was further reinforced by the second main theme around which my early upbringing was shaped—an orientation toward achievement.

Responsibility and Achievement

From early on I was expected to achieve. My parents' school was the only private school in Bursa. It needed general acceptance. Examiners from other schools attended the fifth grade oral graduation examinations. When I entered the fifth grade, my class number was changed by my parents from 16 to 1 so that I would be the first student to take the oral exam, which students took in the order of their class numbers, in every subject, to make a good impression on the outside examiners. At the age of ten (the youngest in the class) I was carrying responsibility for establishing "a good name" for the school beyond that of my own! I remember feeling the weight of this responsibility, but I did not question its legitimacy.

The next year I attended the public high school for girls, as my parents' school did not contain secondary school classes at that time. Since my parents and our school were known in the educational community in Bursa, I was expected to "represent" them in this new environment also. I readily accepted as natural this even heavier responsibility and achieved. My motivation to excel was a socially oriented achievement motivation reflecting my loyalty to my family and family school. It was simply inconceivable to me not to work hard and not to achieve. My mother would tell her friends that when I grew up I would study education abroad and come back and run the school. This is what I expected of myself, too. By this time I had a younger brother; nevertheless, such high expectations continued to focus on me.

The next stage in my education was the American College for Girls (ACG) in Istanbul, an exclusive private high school (part of the Robert College, the first American educational institution abroad). When I finished the secondary school of the public high school in Bursa, I took the highly competitive entrance examinations of ACG and was accepted. This was a turning point in my educational career. This school provided me with a high level of education and an international perspective. My sense of responsibility and achievement continued in this new educational setting also. I graduated at the top of my class and was the president of the student council.

Cross-Cultural Experience

Starting with my education at ACG, I was progressively exposed to cross-cultural experiences. These have also been important in shaping my general worldview as well as my academic orientation in psychology through the years.

I was a boarding student at ACG for six years, the first two of which were spent mainly in learning English. Even though ACG was officially a high school in

Turkey, some advanced college-level courses were also offered, mainly as electives, which I took. Among these, psychology, child psychology, philosophy, and twentieth-century philosophy and the two teachers who taught them made a real impression on me. I started to think that I would probably study psychology or philosophy rather than education, to which my mother aspired for me.

My first culture-contact experiences in ACG occurred both in terms of the content of my formal education and also of living as a boarding student at an American school. They involved both simple everyday experiences and rather significant ideological influences. For example, as common everywhere in Turkey, there used to be much physical contact among girls, such as kissing on both cheeks, embracing, walking arm-in-arm in the corridors, in the courtyard, and elsewhere. This was a natural expression of interpersonal affection and warm peer relations in a collectivistic society and a "contact culture" (Hall, 1966). We used to note and get a kick out of the shocked glances of the new American teachers, mostly young women, before they got accustomed to "the ways of the natives." Some mischievous girls among us used to overdo the show of affection in the presence of the novice teachers to shock them more. After I graduated from ACG and went to the United States for further study, an important part of my self-induced preparation/orientation to living in America was to restrain myself from showing physical affection to same-sex friends.

The twentieth-century philosophy course at ACG focused on phenomenology and existentialism. Apart from scholarly work by Kierkegaard, Jaspers, Husserl, Heidegger, and Sartre, I also read some plays by Sartre. These were my earliest contacts with the pervasive individualistic perspective in Western philosophy and literary tradition. The ending words of Sartre's play *No Exit*, "Hell is other people," got stamped in my memory. This powerful statement was intriguing to me at that time; today I see it as a reflection of extreme individualism.

While a senior at ACG I applied to Wellesley College in Massachusetts and got accepted with a full scholarship. In this process Dr. Rebekah Shuey helped me. She was an education specialist and my teacher in a child psychology course; she also started a kindergarten at ACG where I did my first child-behavior observations. Afterwards she moved to Ankara and worked with the Turkish Ministry of Education in reforming the curriculum of girls' institutes in Turkey. She was my first mentor; my association with her continued through many years.

Wellesley was a challenging experience for me. As I had taken some advanced level courses at ACG, I skipped the first two years at Wellesley and started as a junior. Despite this awkward start in the middle, I did well; I also made a few friends. The course work at Wellesley was demanding; I found myself working even harder than before. I was also homesick, mostly for my family and for the closely knit human relations I was used to in Turkey. I couldn't get used to the rather rigidly structured "dating" system of mixers, proms, and so on.

Wellesley was my entry point to American culture after ACG. It was the most intensive period of culture learning for me, which was at times taxing. My main culture-learning and adjustment process revolved around interpersonal relations; I had moved from a culture of relatedness to a culture of separateness (Kağitçibaşi, 1985). For example, a simple episode has stayed vivid in my memory for more than thirty years. I had a close American friend who appeared very sad one day, and when I asked her what was wrong, she said, "It is a personal matter." This was a shattering experience for me, for she obviously did not consider me to be a close friend if she could not confide in me. What was for her a simple assertion of her privacy was for me a sign of rejection. I was encountering in my friend, without full awareness, the "independent self" with "clearly defined boundaries" and protected by "privacy" (Kağitçibaşi, 1990; Markus & Kitayama, 1991).

Similarly, the lack of neighborly visiting, even the lack of people on the streets in suburban New England were new experiences for me. Thus, these experiences, in addition to the first glimpses of culture learning at ACG, all had to do with what I consider today a basic aspect of interpersonal relations that shows cross-cultural variation, that is, interpersonal relatedness-separateness. They also have to do with the degree of boundedness or connectedness of the self. They have paved the way for some of my recent theoretical views regarding the family, human development, and the self (Kağitçibaşi, 1990, 1996).

At Wellesley I took some education and philosophy courses, but I decided on majoring in psychology, mainly because I found psychology courses more challenging than education courses and more down to earth than philosophy courses. I was first intrigued by abnormal psychology, but in my senior year my faith in Freud and the unconscious was seriously challenged by a brillant young instructor, Lise Wallach. Nevertheless, as I had already applied to Berkeley for the clinical psychology program and did not really have the preparation to replace this with anything else, I went on to study clinical psychology at the graduate level.

Whereas Wellesley provided me with learning experiences for the American culture, Berkeley provided me with rich multicultural learning. I made friends with other foreign students, mainly from European countries, in addition to developing friendships with Americans. The general international and cosmopolitan atmosphere of Berkeley and the San Francisco Bay Area was very attractive to me.

By the end of my first year at graduate school I had shifted from clinical to social psychology, mainly because I could not accept the assumptions about the unconscious processes that were not based on sound evidence. Also by this time, I had been back to Turkey twice for summer visits and had gotten in touch again with Dr. Shuey, who drove my attention to pervasive societal problems in my country, mostly educational issues, that needed to be solved. Given my continuing sense of social commitment, I felt that it was more important to help large numbers of "normal" children who, because of socioeconomic disadvantage, could not develop optimally, rather than to attend to the problems of the disturbed few.

I thought social psychology and social science would provide me with the answers I sought. I also attended some courses in the sociology department. Developmental psychology was in a separate unit, the Institute of Human Development. It was not a part of the psychology department. This is probably why I did not consider graduate work in developmental psychology at that time.

I was already asking questions regarding the relative importance of personality (psychological) and social normative (cultural) influences on human behavior. What interested me more than the lure of the experimental laboratory were the social, political, and psychological implications of the then no longer in vogue "authoritarian personality theory" (Adorno, et al., 1950). I often found myself using a cultural filter in my reading as a natural result of the sensitivity to culture I had developed by then. Thus, I realized that some of the so-called personality attributes of the authoritarian personality were social norms in Turkey. I therefore undertook to do a cross-cultural study for my dissertation research comparing Turkish and American youths' world views, in order to test the generality of the authoritarian personality theory. Indeed, I found that "authoritarianism," which was assumed to be a universally valid *personality* syndrome, was culture-bound (Kağitçibaşi, 1970).

While at Berkeley, I married Oğuz Kağitçibaşi, whom I had known in Turkey for a number of years. He came to Berkeley, and we got married there. Within a year we had a daughter, Elif. We shared child care and part-time jobs, and I continued with my graduate studies. Just as the data collection for my dissertation was being completed, my father died of a heart attack at the age of fifty-three. I learned of his death on the phone from my mother. It was very difficult for me to cope with; nevertheless, I continued to function through hard work.

My mentor at Berkeley, M. Brewster Smith, helped me greatly through my dissertation research and the laborious writing process. Because of my father's death, we had to return to Turkey abruptly before I could finish my dissertation. We settled in Bursa and started to help my mother with the school. We made arrangements with some American and British teachers who taught English at the school. We also established the high school part of the school. I was very busy running the school as the principal while writing my dissertation. I would send every chapter to Brewster, who provided me with timely valuable feedback, which I would then revise. I finished the writing within a year and received my Ph.D. from Berkeley in 1967.

Academic Career: The Early Years

Even though I enjoyed working at the school, which was after all a life-ideal set for me by my parents, I came to realize that I did not enjoy administration and really wanted an academic career. However, at that time there was no university in Bursa. While in Bursa, I applied the D–48 Test (Dominoes Test of General Ability) to the students at our school and did a validity study for this test (Kağitçibaşi, 1972). After living three years in Bursa, with the first high school graduates from our school we also moved to Ankara, where I started an academic career at the Middle East Technical University (METU) in 1969.

In 1970 we had a son, Emrah. I continued combining the different roles of mother, wife, and professional woman.

At METU, psychology was not a separate department at the time but together with sociology constituted the Department of Social Science. This was a new experience for me and a valuable one, in that I came to see events in a social context and recognized the existence of other approaches to studying human phenomena than purely psychological ones. I also became involved in the highly active and somewhat politicized community of social scientists in Ankara, including sociologists, demographers, and political scientists. This expanded perspective had a significant influence on my thinking and research in the following years. Under the supportive chairpersonship of a well-known sociologist, Mubeccel Kiray, I had a satisfying first entry into academia. I was getting interested in understanding the psychological aspects of social change and modernization and the issues of population and women's roles (Kağitçibaşi, 1973, 1974, 1975).

The year 1973 marked some important changes for me. We moved to Istanbul, and I joined the staff of the newly established Department of Social Sciences at Bogazici University. In the meantime, I was invited by James T. Fawcett of the East-West Center in Hawaii to join in a nine-country comparative study on the value of children. I was also invited by Harrison Gough, who was then the chairman of the psychology department at Berkeley, to teach there in the summer session. I combined the two activities and spent the summer of 1973 at Berkeley and Hawaii. The Value of Children (VOC) Study provided me the opportunity to study the cross-cultural context of human development, the place of the child in family and society, motivations for childbearing, and how these are affected by socioeconomic change and development. The first pilot phase of the study had been already conducted in six countries; I joined the second phase encompassing nine countries and involving nationally representative samples totaling some twenty thousand people. The countries participating in the project were mainly from East and Southeast Asia, given the area of specialization of the East-West Center, with Turkey and the United States presenting contrasting sociocultural contexts. I conducted an extensive survey with a nationally representative sample of more than 2,300 married respondents in 1975. One hundred students, whom I trained personally, carried out the interviews all over the country; it was a major task and a very special experience for me in fieldwork.[2]

The country investigators in the VOC Study were demographers and psychologists, a combination that was rather unusual and stimulating in its diverse orientations to fertility. The values attributed to children by parents and society turned out to be important in contributing to childbearing, even when socioeconomic status variables were controlled (Kağitçibaşi, 1982a, 1982b, 1983; Bulatao, 1979; Fawcett, 1983). Thus psychological analysis of motivations underlying fertility was found to be worthwhile in and of itself, something hitherto not recognized adequately by demographers and economists.

The VOC Study sensitized me to the role and the place of the child in family and society and the changes in these through socioeconomic change and development. It has affected greatly my thinking regarding the family and human development in context, leading eventually to a theory of family change and the self I have recently developed (Kağitçibaşi, 1990).

The main finding of the VOC Study was that different motivations underlie childbearing and the values attributed to children by parents. Among these, the economic (utilitarian) and the psychological values come to the fore. In low levels of socioeconomic development, children's economic value is salient. Because this value is number-based (more children providing more material benefits to the family, especially in ensuring old-age security), high fertility is the result. With urbanization and socioeconomic development, however, children stop being economic assets and become economic costs. Accordingly, their psychological values become salient. Because psychological values are not number-based (even few children provide the love, pride, and other values one needs), fertility decreases (Kağitçibaşi, 1982a; 1982b).

Here we have a complex set of interrelated variables where socioeconomic and demographic factors are mediated by psychological ones. The analysis of this complex whole requires a contextual, interactional, and functional framework, which I used in the VOC Study as well as in my subsequent work.

Academic Career: The Later Years

By the early 1980s I had completed analyzing the VOC Study findings and had written about them. At this time I was also getting more involved with social issues, in particular the problem of early deprivation of socioeconomically disadvantaged children. In the following years I found myself actualizing what I had imagined myself to be doing in the future when I was a graduate student at Berkeley—getting involved in research and action toward promoting the well-being of normal children in adverse circumstances.

I organized a team of child-development experts and psychologists and initiated a research project with the Turkish Ministry of Education to promote preschool education in Turkey. We studied the contexts in which children develop, children's literature, laws regarding children, and other topics. We also prepared books to be used by parents, preschool teachers, and others regarding child development; creative play activities for children; curriculum for preschools; cognitive exercises for children; and a parent education book. These were to be used in a widescale initiative of the ministry to establish preschool centers. However, due to changes in political priorities, this initiative could not take off.

This work sensitized me further to the importance of a contextual interactional orientation in dealing with socioeconomically disadvantaged children. This is because in order to combat disadvantage, the child's environment had to be changed, and the key caretaker, the mother, thus had to be empowered. It is with such a general outlook that I undertook to do a major research project together with my colleagues Sevda Bekman and Diane Sunar. The original research was a four-year longitudinal study carried out in the low-income areas of Istanbul, and it was succeeded six years later by a follow-up study covering a ten-year period altogether (Kağitçibaşi, Sunar & Bekman, 1988; Kağitçibaşi, 1991, 1993, 1994). This is the Turkish Early Enrichment Project.[3]

In the first year of the study, baselines were established of three- and five-year-old children's cognitive and socioemotional development, the child-rearing orientations and world views of their mothers, and their home conditions. Extensive assessment of children utilizing both psychometric and Piagetian types of measures and observations of their behavior and of mother-child interaction were carried out. Interviews were also conducted with the mothers. Then a randomly selected group of mother-child pairs were subjected to intervention (mother training) in the second and third years of the project. In the fourth year reassessments were carried out to compare the trained (experimental) and the nontrained (control) groups.

The mother training consisted of two components: a cognitive enrichment program and a mother enrichment program. For the former, we used the HIPPY (Home Instruction Program for Preschool Youngsters), developed by Avima Lombard of Hebrew University of Jerusalem (Lombard, 1981). The latter was prepared by the project team. Mother training was conducted once a week in group settings and in the home (on an alternating basis), where mothers were taught cognitive materials that they taught to their own children at home. Through group discussions they were also sensitized to the needs of their young children and to their own needs and were supported to communicate better and to cope with problems effectively.

The fourth-year results showed great gains for the experimental (mother-trained) group, compared with the control group. Significant differences were obtained in cognitive development, socioemotional development, and school adjustment and performance of the children. The effects on the trained mothers were notable both in terms of better interactions with and more responsiveness to their children, and also in terms of a more positive outlook on life and higher intrafamily status. More of these mothers were found to value autonomy in their children than did the nontrained mothers, and more than they themselves had demonstrated in the first-year interviews (pretest). It appeared that the intervention helped contribute to the well-being of the child through promoting the well-being of the mother.

Even though the fourth-year results were encouraging, the real test of an intervention lies in its long-range effects. We undertook, therefore, a follow-up study six years after the completion of the original research (seven years after the end of the mother training). Out of the 255 mother-child pairs, 217 participated in the follow-up, where extensive interviews were carried out with the adolescents (now thirteen through fifteen years of age), the mothers, and some of the fathers. Additionally, the adolescents' full school records were examined, and they were given a vocabulary test.

More of the adolescents whose mothers had been trained, compared with the nontrained group, were found to be still in school (86 percent versus 67 percent; $p = .002$). With only five years of compulsory education, in low-income areas especially, those students who are not successful drop out of school after primary school; thus, this finding is of great importance in demonstrating higher levels of schooling for the experimental group. In terms of five years of primary school performance also, the experimental group surpassed the control group. Clearly, better school performance had a great deal to do with greater school attainment. Furthermore, the mother-trained group scored higher on the WISC-R Vocabulary Test (45.6 versus 41.9; $p = .03$), reflecting higher cognitive performance.

In addition to these objective outcome measures and self-report measures from interviews with adolescents, mothers and fathers provided converging information about the positive long-terms effects of the early intervention. The trained group of adolescents manifested more positive attitudes toward school, greater autonomy and social integration, and better self-concept. They also reported more positive retrospective memories of their mothers (from childhood). Family relations of the trained group were found to be closer and more harmonious, with mothers again enjoying a higher status in the home, compared with the nontrained group. Clearly, the intervention had long-range interactive effects that appear to have changed the family culture and through which the children benefited (Kağitçibaşi, 1994).

This research has far-reaching policy implications, some of which have, in fact, materialized as public service. We revised the mother-training program and replaced the HIPPY with the cognitive enrichment program (Kağitçibaşi & Bekman, 1992). The program applications are expanding in Turkey. We established a Mother-Child Education Foundation for the purpose of spreading the program all over the country, in cooperation with two different ministries and UNICEF. There are plans for applications abroad, also. Indeed, some of my early dreams of public service have found expression in this project.[4]

Reflections on Cross-Cultural Human Development

My ideas about what directions developmental psychology should pursue derive very much from my personal and academic experiences, lifelong commitments, and research involvements that I have been describing up to now. Very briefly, I believe that developmental psychology should be more contextual and interactional in its orientation, situating human development within its socio-economic-cultural context. It should also have an involved stance, contributing to human well-being. However, this applied emphasis should be informed by culturally valid theory. I will demonstrate how this can be done by an example from my own research and conceptualization.

A main aspect of the Turkish Early Enrichment Project had to do with modifying child-rearing orientations. Specifically, an attempt was made to introduce "autonomy" in child-rearing while reinforcing "closely knit human/family ties." Both the fourth-year and the follow-up results showed that more of the trained mothers came to appreciate their children's autonomy while remaining as close to them as the control group of mothers. This is in line with a model of family change I have developed that reflects the typical family change patterns in the developing countries with "cultures of relatedness" (Kağitçibaşi, 1985, 1990).

This model of family change focuses on the (inter)dependence-independence dimension of interpersonal and intergenerational relations (Kağitçibaşi, 1990, 1996). In the "traditional" society with collectivistic (relational) cultural patterns, a human/family model of interdependence is common in both "material" and "emotional" domains. In the Western urban middle-class society, on the other hand, a pattern of independence prevails in both domains. The question is whether with socioeconomic development there will be a shift from the former to the latter model. This kind of a shift is typically assumed to take place, given the pervasive influence of the "modernization paradigm."

I believe that such a convergence toward the Western pattern is not, in fact, happening, but rather a third model of "emotional interdependence" is emerging with socioeconomic development in non-Western societies with collectivistic cultures. In this model, material interdependencies in the family weaken, with alternative old-age security resources other than adult offspring appearing and children's economic value decreasing, as I found in the Value of Children Study. However, given the closely knit human/family relations, emotional interdependencies continue (Kağitçibaşi, 1990).

In the family model of total interdependence, autonomy has no place in child-rearing, since an autonomous child would be expected to be an independent young adult who might look after his own self-interest rather than being loyal to the family. With a shift from a family model of total interdependence to emotional interdependence, however, "autonomy" can enter child-rearing. This is because with decreasing intergenerational material interdependencies, autonomy and independence of the offspring do not any longer threaten the livelihood of the family. Nevertheless, there is often culture lag, and traditions persist even if not necessary or even functional. Thus, a complete obedience orientation that leaves no room for autonomy may persist in child-rearing even though it is no longer functional in changed urban lifestyles.

It is here that a role of facilitator may be relevant for an "involved" developmental psychology, as exemplified by the Turkish Early Enrichment Project. We introduced the value of autonomy into our mother enrichment program while supporting the close-knit family bonds. The results showed that this intervention had an effect in changing parental orientations, resulting in greater autonomy of children while relatedness continued—a synthesis of autonomy and relatedness (Kağitçibaşi, 1990, 1996) appeared to have been achieved.

A second way in which a modification in child-rearing orientations was accomplished in the Turkish Early Enrichment Project was in getting mothers to be more responsive to their children and to help support their children's cognitive development to prepare them for school. First-year baseline assessments pointed to generally low levels of responsiveness to children among the mothers and low levels of environmental stimulation at home (Kağitçibaşi, Sunar & Bekman, 1988). This is in line with much research conducted in socioeconomically disadvantaged homes in the United States and other Western societies as well (see Kağitçibaşi, 1996 for a review). The project intervention aimed to improve the situation by sensitizing the mothers to the importance of early learning environments and by getting them involved directly in the early education of their children.

The results showed increased levels of mother-child interaction as well as more supportive mother teaching styles, more verbalization, and more responsiveness in general among the trained mothers compared with the control group. These positive orientations were sustained over time and were also shared by the fathers, as evidenced by the follow-up results. Such parenting had doubtless much to do with the satisfactory overall development and achievement of the children.

An issue of great importance in all societies is the optimal development of human potential; in developing countries whose main resources are human resources, this is a life-and-death issue. There are today concerted global efforts to achieve universal literacy and schooling, as demonstrated by some recent world conferences and public commitments on the part of many governments. Above and beyond the problems of access to public schooling, there is the further problem of school failure and dropout rates in many parts of the world, which entails great economic and human costs. Among the many reasons for this situation is the inadequate school readiness of children and inadequate family support of the child's student role.

Inadequate school readiness is a human developmental problem. It is currently defined in terms of a number of indicators, including the child's (1) activity level (health and nutritional status, affecting both school attendance and concentration level in class); (2) social competence and psychological preparedness, affecting adaptation to and coping with school requirements; and (3) cognitive abilities, including preliteracy and prenumeracy skills. Readiness is also reflected in the positive outlooks and expectations of the family members and the support they provide to the child (Myers, 1992, p. 216). Children growing up in poverty are often hampered in their development and may not have the chance to develop to their full potential.

There is accumulated knowledge in developmental psychology regarding these indicators of school readiness. Much research has informed us about the development of language, problem solving, and other cognitive skills; social competence; emotional development; self-help skills; and other factors in early childhood. However, all this knowledge should be put to more effective use in wide-scale intervention work in different sociocultural contexts, especially in developing countries. To ascertain retarded development and to promote optimal development, culturally valid measures are needed that would build upon both cross-cultural research in the field and also within each sociocultural context. Both commonalities and differences would need to be taken into consideration, integrating comparative standards and culture-sensitive conceptualization.

It is with these considerations that we undertook the Turkish Early Enrichment Project. Supporting the mothers to support their children's overall development and school readiness entailed using comparative school-related cognitive standards, but this was done within a culturally relevant contextual approach. Our research experience and the applications emerging from our project have reinforced my belief in the feasibility of such an integrative approach, combining comparative standards of human development with culturally sensitive endogenous conceptualizations of well-being.

Our study and its policy-relevant outcomes have also strengthened my conviction about the potential of psychology to contribute to societal well-being. Developmental psychology in particular can contribute significantly to global efforts to promote human potential development if it accepts both a scientifically and socially responsible self-definition. Human development is the core of societal development, and psychology is centrally relevant to it.

Notes

1. A short historical background may be in order here. The Turkish Republic was founded in 1923. The predecessor of the Turkish Republic was the Ottoman Empire, which lasted for six centuries and expanded outward from Anatolia (the land of modern Turkey) to the Arabic Peninsula, Egypt, and North Africa, and from the Caucasus to the Balkans north to Vienna at its height at the end of the sixteenth century. During the eighteenth and the nineteenth centuries the Ottoman Empire's reign was challenged through continuous wars leading to territory losses. The state also failed to keep up with the great ideological, economic, and industrial achievements in western Europe and fell into backwardness.

It was against this background that the Ottoman Empire entered World War I siding with Germany, mainly in response to British political activity instigating ethnic/national independence movements throughout the Ottoman Empire. When the war was lost, Istanbul and Anatolia, the central heartland of the Ottoman Empire, were occupied.

This was the starting point of the resistance movements emerging in many places in Anatolia that were successfully merged under the leadership of Mustafa Kemal Atatürk. A war of independence was fought for three years against the armies of the occupying forces all over Anatolia and against all odds was miraculously won. In the process, Ottoman rule was defied and rejected, and a national assembly was instituted.

In 1923 the republic was established, the sultanate and the caliphate were abolished (the Ottoman sultans had also been the caliphs of the Islamic world since the occupation of Egypt in the sixteenth century). Atatürk was elected the first president of the Turkish Republic, and a series of reforms was enacted during the first two decades of the republican era. These covered all spheres of civil society. Most important, they entailed secularization (replacement of the religious legal system with a civil one) and modernization (replacement of the Arabic alphabet with the Latin one, shifting to the Western calender and dress codes, opening up public education and civil service positions to women, and so on).

2. The Turkish VOC Study was supported by the International Development Research Center of Canada.

3. The Turkish Early Enrichment Project was funded by the International Development Research Center of Canada. The follow-up study was funded by the Population Council (Meawards Program).

4. I have also been involved in several other programs and activities designed to promote children's well-being both in Turkey and internationally. For example, I have been the academic advisor of the *Sesame Street* TV program in Turkey; an advisory board member of the Consultative Group on Early Childhood Care and Education; a trustee of the American Field Service International Student Exchange Program; a member of the Working Group on Women, Family & Children of the Population Council (Cairo); a consultant for UNICEF, the Turkish Ministry of Education, and The Turkish Radio and Television.

References

Adorno, T. W., Frankel-Brunswik, E., Levinson, D. & Sanford, R. (1950). *The authoritarian personality.* New York: Harper.

Agarwal, R. & Misra, G. (1986). A factor analytical study of achievement goals and means: An Indian view. *International Journal of Psychology, 21,* 717–731.

Bellah, R. N., Madsen, R., Sullivan, W. M., Swidler, A. & Tipton, S. M. (1985). *Habits of the heart: Individualism and commitment in American life.* Berkeley: University of California Press.

Bond, M. H. (1986). *The psychology of the Chinese people.* Hong Kong: Oxford University Press.

Bulatao, R. A. (1979). *On the nature of the transition in the value of children* (Publication no. 60-A). Honolulu: East-West Population Institute.

Cushman, P. (1990). Why the self is empty: Toward a historically situated psychology. *American Psychologist, 45,* 599–611.

De Vos, G. (1968). Achievement and innovation in culture and personality. In E. Norbeck, D. Price-Williams, & E. W. McCord (Eds.), *The study of personality* (pp. 348–370). New York: Holt, Rinehart & Winston.

Fawcett, J. T. (1983). Perceptions of the value of children: Satisfactions and costs. In J. T. Bulatao, R. D. Lee, P. E. Hollerbach & J. Bongaarts (Eds.), *Determinants of fertility in developing countries,* (pp. 347–369). Washington, D.C.: National Academy Press.

Gillespie, J. M. & Allport, G. W. (1955). *Youth's outlook on the future: A cross national study.* Garden City, N.Y.: Doubleday.

Hall, E. T. (1966). *The hidden dimension.* New York: Doubleday.

Kagan, J. (1984). *Nature of the child.* New York: Basic Books.

Kağıtçıbaşi, C. (1970). Social norms and authoritarianism: A Turkish-American comparison. *Journal of Personality & Social Psychology, 16,* 444–451.

Kağıtçıbaşi, C. (1972). Applications of the D48 test of general intellectual ability in Turkey. *Journal of Cross-Cultural Psychology, 3,* 169–175.

Kağitçibaşi, C. (1973). Psychological aspects of modernization in Turkey. *Journal of Cross-Cultural Psychology, 4,* 157–174.

Kağitçibaşi, C. (1974). Psychological approaches to fertility behavior in Turkey. *Boğazici University Journal, 2,* 157–174.

Kağitçibaşi, C. (1975). Modernity and the role of women in Turkey. *Boğazici University Journal, 3,* 83–90.

Kağitçibaşi, C. (1982a). *The changing value of children in Turkey* (Publication no. 60-E). Honolulu: East-West Center.

Kağitçibaşi, C. (1982b). Old-age security value of children: Cross-national socio-economic evidence. *Journal of Cross-Cultural Psychology, 13,* 29–42.

Kağitçibaşi, C. (1983). Assessment of values and attitudes in the study of fertility. In S. H. Irvine & J. W. Berry (Eds.), *Human assessment and cultural factors* (pp. 481–494). New York: Plenum.

Kağitçibaşi, C. (1985). Culture of separateness—culture of relatedness. In *1984 vision and reality: Papers in comparative studies, Volume 4* (pp. 91–99). Columbus: Ohio State University.

Kağitçibaşi, C. (1987). Individual and group loyalties. In C. Kağitçibaşi (Ed.), *Growth and progress in cross-cultural psychology.* Lisse, Holland: Swets and Zeitlinger.

Kağitçibaşi, C. (1990). Family and socialization in cross-cultural perspective: A model of change. In J. Berman (Ed.), *Cross-Cultural Perspectives: Nebraska Symposium on Motivation, 1989, 37* (pp. 135–200). University of Nebraska Press.

Kağitçibaşi, C. (1991). *The early enrichment project in Turkey: Notes comments* (Publication no. 193). Paris: UNESCO.

Kağitçibaşi, C. (1993). A model of non-formal education: The case of the Turkish early enrichment project. In L. Eldering & P. Leseman (Eds.), *Early intervention and culture: Preparation for literacy* (pp. 253–268). Netherlands: UNESCO Publishing.

Kağitçibaşi, C. (1994). Human development and societal development. In A-M Bouvy, F. J. R. v.d. Vijver, P. Boski & P. Schmitz (Eds.), *Journeys in cross-cultural psychology* (pp. 3–24). Lisse, Holland: Swets and Zeitlinger.

Kağitçibaşi, C. (1996). *Family and human development across cultures: A view from the other side.* Hillsdale, N.J.: Erlbaum.

Kağitçibaşi, C. & Bekman, S. (1992). *Cognitive training program.* Ankara: UNICEF Publications.

Kağitçibaşi, C., Sunar, D. & Bekman, S. (1988). *Comprehensive preschool education project: Final report.* Ottawa: IDRC.

Lombard, A. (1981). *Success begins at home.* Lexington, Mass.: Lexington Books, D. C. Heath and Co.

Markus, H. R. & Kitayama, S. (1991). Culture and the self: Implications for cognition, emotion and motivation. *Psychological Review, 98,* 224–253.

Misra, G. & Agarwal, R. (1985). The meaning of achievement: Implications for a cross-cultural theory of achievement motivation. In I. R. Lagunes & Ype H. Poortinga (Eds.). *From a different perspective: Studies of behavior across cultures* (pp. 250–226). Lisse, Holland: Swets and Zeitlinger.

Myers, R. (1992). *The twelve who survive.* London: Routledge.

Phalet, K. & Claeys, W. (1993). A comparative study of Turkish and Belgian youth. *Journal of Cross-Cultural Psychology, 24,* 319–343.

Sampson, E. E. (1987). Individuation and domination: undermining the social bond. In Kağitçibaşi C. (Ed.), *Growth and progress in cross-cultural psychology* (pp. 84–93). Lisse, Holland: Swets and Zeitlinger.

Smith, M. B. (1993). Selfhood at risk: Post-Modern perils and the perils of Post-Modernism. (Murray Award Address, American Psychological Association, Toronto, Ontario). (*American Psychologist, 49,* 1994, 405–411).

Taylor, C. (1989). *Sources of the self: The making of the modern identity.* Cambridge: Harvard University Press.

Yang, K-S. (1986). Chinese personality and its change. In M. H. Bond (Ed.), *The psychology of the Chinese people* (pp. 106–170). New York: Oxford University Press.

Yu, A-B. & Yang, K-S. (1994). The nature of achievement motivation in collectivistic societies. In U. Kim, H. C. Triandis, C. Kağitçibaşi, S-C. Choi & G. Yoon (Eds.), *Individualism and collectivism: Theory, method, and applications* (pp. 239–250). Newbury Park, Calif.: Sage.

8

Lewis P. Lipsitt

Prologue

I do not think I have it in me to write a chapter with a whole lot of sentences beginning with "I," but apparently I cannot help myself. Writing this piece is an experience like so many other risk-taking ventures in my life. I am approaching this task with great trepidation. I know I often do not do things quite like most others. With rather a lot of anxiety and with some anticipation of pride at the end of the arduous and onerous response chain, I have accepted this challenge, knowing full well I don't have time to do it, for I have agreed, characteristically, to do too many things at once.

If I make it to the end of my task having satisfied some aspect of my inner yearnings for self-understanding and historical veritude, as from finding some obscure truth (or even an inconsequential fact!), then I will be delighted with the accomplishment and will have a sense of fulfilling closure. That "rush" is what I often find myself working for. It charges my imagination and provides the motivational power to barge ahead, even (sometimes) in the face of danger to my personhood.

I have come to understand in recent years that in different phases of my scientific life I have been especially concerned with and have focused my attention on behavioral and developmental phenomena that have been of special concern to me in rather personal ways: (1) the effect of birth risk factors on later development; (2) the instrumental role of behavioral factors in survival, even of babies; (3) the effects of delayed reward on performance; (4) the origins and consequences of prejudicial behavior, including false accusation; (5) the hedonic origins of basic approach and avoidance behaviors; (6) the life-span consequences of the pleasures and annoyances of sensation; (7) the origins of developmental delays and debilities, particularly learning disabilities, and, do I dare say it; (8) the ontogeny of danger-seeking or risk-taking behavior.

Each of the above themes has impinged on my own life history in ways that are interesting to me and have provided some of my motivation to study them. Fear of smothering, crib death, adolescent suicide, and, more generally, the role of behavioral misadventures in human life destinies have occupied much of my intellectual and professional life as scientist and administrator. I do understand that this creates the appearance of a person walking, in some respects, on the dark side.

At the same time I am a basically happy person, given simply to highs and lows dependent upon how things are going. I realize that "how things are going" is not the richest independent variable handy to behavior analysts. So be it. There is an aspect of my personality—I like to think it a favorable attribute—that has gotten me into trouble on occasion. Being misrepresented by others or treated in a demeaning way by Machiavellian bureaucrats whose own personae depend heavily on self-congratulation is rather the bane of my existence. I have low tolerance for such people and virtually no skill in hiding this.

I believe that a symbiosis has existed from my earliest days as a psychologist between my personal integrity on the one hand, and my professional and scientific goals and ideals on the other. My personhood has been intimately interwoven with my career. On a few occasions in my career, when I have felt that my best shots at making constructive impacts on the field were thwarted, I have become deeply saddened. That I have survived reasonably intact has been a rush in itself.

Birth, Family Background, and Early Years

I was born in New Bedford, Massachusetts, in a hospital where my father's brother was the highly respected chief pediatrician. One oft-told family story was that my father and uncle, one in law school, the other attending medical school, had only one overcoat between them to use when dating on cold winter nights in Boston. (They both married late!) My father's parents were of eastern European Jewish origins, with very modest means and great dignity. My father believed strongly in the importance of education and literacy, which, he was fond of noting, do not always co-occur.

Another family story with which I was entertained from time to time was that I was born essentially unattended. My mother had been heavily medicated for her third birth in less than three years, and my father and the obstetrician were enjoying cigars in an anteroom waiting for the action. A nurse chanced to look under the sheet, and there I was!

In my adulthood, and occupied in my research career with the adverse effects sometimes occasioned by perinatal hazards such as delayed breathing, I got the opportunity to explore my own birth records and could find nothing to suggest that anybody had any concerns about my well-being. I was apparently a normal full-term baby boy who breathed and cried well and had a good set of reflexes. I have been pretty much the same ever since.

I did not become the pediatrician that my parents and my pediatrician uncle presumed I would be for the first nineteen or so years of my life. Why I was selected for that special encouragement I am not sure. As the third of the first three children of my parents, and with no other child born into the family for seven years thereafter, I was referred to by my parents and relatives, for perhaps too long, as Baby Lou. I was named after my maternal grandfather, Louis Paeff, and my name was Louis for the first two or so years of my life, when it was discovered that my name at birth was recorded by a nurse as *Lewis,* and thus the birth certificate read *Lewis*. Later, my mother recollected that she was heavily medicated for the birth and probably assented inadvertently to the nurse's spelling. Although the *Lewis* spelling was to be my name forever after, I have noted in letters my mother saved from her own siblings that I continued to be "Baby Lou" and "Lou" for years afterward. I have the impression today that as a young child I thought rather a lot about childbirth and about the phenomenon of the anesthetized mind, the nature of babyhood, and about identity. I was seven years old when the next child, a fourth son, my brother Cyrus, was born. I recall being fascinated by him and his behavior and am sure, in my memory, of having had a nurturant and watchful attitude toward him. In fact, once he was finished with breast-feeding and was no longer in a crib in my parents' bedroom, he and I shared a bedroom and, for a time, the same bed. I think all of these events may have been determinative of aspects of my career, which, after all, has had much to do with birth conditions, early development, cognitive confusion, and questions of identity, attachment, nurturance, and life-span development.

My father, Joseph Lipsitt, was a talented attorney who began his career as a newspaper reporter, then returned to school to qualify as a lawyer and set up a small and independent practice in New Bedford. He worked at this until he died at the age of eighty-one. He also dabbled in building construction and reconstruction and told his friends that he made his money in law and lost it in real estate. My father bought the Delano estate in Fairhaven, Massachusetts, where Franklin Delano Roosevelt visited often while a student at Harvard, and did rather a thorough renovation job of the estate. Actually, he didn't begin the day he bought the estate intending to make any such purchase. He was at his bank that morning when a manager there asked why he wasn't over at the auction. "What auction?" my father asked. He went and bought the place. That's the sort of exciting thing he sometimes did.

My father was a man of principle. He was concerned with social justice and with the law. (He was also an admirer of FDR, which may account in part for his impulsive acquisition of the Delano estate.) If he felt mistreated or saw someone else undeservingly abused, he got energized and would sometimes call for community notice of the situation. When he got involved as a council member of the Boy Scouts, he noticed that the town to which we had moved by then, on the Massachusetts seaboard near the Cape Cod Canal, had de facto segregation: There were two scout troops, and because one of them was located in one part of the town and the other in another part, one of the troops was largely white and the other of color. My father initiated the process that consolidated the troops.

Joe Lipsitt identified very personally with causes he was championing as a lawyer. For example, he got into an argument with the publisher of the only newspaper in New Bedford, and the newspaper henceforth would not publish his name in connection with any of their case reportage. The newspaper was the *Standard Times,* and my father referred to it, at home and probably to his friends and associates, as "The Slander Slimes." He took delight in noting that the newspaper would not print his name, for that was a clear demonstration of the paper's dishonesty and hypocrisy. Moreover, he said, anyone reading of a case and finding the name of either the plaintiff's or the defendant's lawyer absent could immediately realize that "Joe Lipsitt was the lawyer." The newspaper publisher thus unwittingly provided my father with a great deal of free notice.

An important lesson I learned from my father is that there are some things you just have to fight for because there are mean people in the world. Defeat, injury, and life crises are often not as severe as they at first seem and can on occasion become springboards to better times and favorable outcomes. It is a lesson that I have rarely had to call on but that in the past few years has meant much to me as I struggled with my greatest life crisis.

As must surely be seen by now, my father was a significant figure in my life, not merely because he was my father but because he was a special man—with personhood. Every child finds every parent's weak spot. I found my father's; all I had to do as a young child was say "you promised," and my father complied, provided it was something reasonable and that he might in any event have allowed. I feel guilty to this day for having misused the "promise privilege" as a child once or twice. But the importance of trying to keep promises, not to mention trusting others, was deeply rooted in my relationship with my father.

One other "privilege" that I misused, but only once, was on a rare occasion when my father and I were swimming at the end of the town pier. I think I was about twelve years old and was by this age a fair swimmer. Dad was standing on the dock, drying, having had his swim. I had won a contest or two during Fourth of July festivities when the town held swimming contests, and I could stay under water rather a long time. I dove in from the dock and swam around underneath the surface for a while, then swam underneath the pier and came up, quietly, for air there. I was hidden from sight. Dad called to me, and I could hear him pacing the wooden dock above, calling for me and, as I now surmise, beginning to be quite unsettled. (I never knew my father to panic.) After a little while I went under water again and under the wooden frame of the pier and surfaced next to the pier. My father was visibly relieved and said quietly: "Don't do that again. Tell me before you do it." Dad was well known for his humor and indeed his penchant for practical jokes, but I don't think he found my trick funny.

My mother, Anna Naomi Paeff, was the same age as my father when they were married, thirty-three, and was a graduate of the New England Conservatory of Music. My mother's parents were also of eastern European parentage. Some of her older siblings were born in Russia. Music and academic accomplishment were highly valued in her family. Two of her sisters were truly fine musicians: Sonia the pianist and Reba a flute player and composer as well as author of several acclaimed children's books on musicians and on African children. The sister who did not excel in music after trying the violin, Bashka Paeff, became a noted sculptor. Some of her best works include the white marble bust of Justice Brandeis at Brandeis University; the Boy and Bird Fountain in the Boston Garden; the mother and child (for which my mother posed) at the former Rosenwald estate in Ravinia, outside Chicago; the World War I memorial in Kittery, Maine (for which my father posed when he was a law student courting my mother); and bas-reliefs of Simon Flexner of the Rockefeller Institute, Martin Luther King at Boston University, and Harry Solomon of the Boston Psychopathic Hospital.

My mother's sisters all married men who became distinguished university professors. A brother, Spinoza, was a fine violist, and Sonia's son, Raphael Hillyer, was the founding violist of the famous Juilliard Quartet. In short, my mother's family provided me with aunts, uncles, and cousins who were quite exceptional and served rather as family heroes, people of accomplishment (the women as well as the men) whom my parents hoped their children would emulate.

My mother was famous among her siblings as "Anna with the children." She kept having children almost to the age of fifty! Although she did not drive, she found time to get her children to music lessons, to serve as a Cub Scout den mother for many years (until she was almost eighty years of age), to serve as the local impresario for her brother's concerts, to serve The Heart Fund for decades as a volunteer, to be an accompanist to a local singer, to give piano lessons most of her adult life, and to oversee the rental of properties that my father acquired, often against her greater caution in the realm of investments.

My mother, with a lot of promotion from my father as well, sold her kids on education, and all five of us became college graduates. We figured once that we have thirteen degrees among us. Paul is both a lawyer and clinical psychologist, Don is a psychiatrist, and both Cy and Peter are artists.

After Paul, Don, and I were born in a time span of less than three years and Cy was born after a hiatus of seven years, the last baby of the family, Peter, was born five years later. None of us knew how old our mother really was; she was reticent, to say the least, and perhaps superstitious, about revealing her age. She was almost ninety when she died in her sleep in Marion, Massachusetts, by the shore. We did not know her age until then; she claimed to be the same age as Jack Benny—thirty-nine.

Significant for an understanding of the familial cohesiveness that pervaded our upbringing, all five of the Lipsitt brothers eventually acquired summer places in our small hometown, to which my parents moved their brood, then of four sons with a fifth on the way, in 1939. Our parents were powerfully and enduringly meaningful to us. After some of us brothers traveled large distances for schooling and military service, we all came to live eventually within a forty-mile radius of our family homestead and visited our parents frequently. My brothers and I all have vivid recollections of "marker celebrations" with all the family present, many of these in association with holidays, particularly Thanksgiving. Our father prepared the very elaborate dinners that celebrated Thanksgiving as well as his and my brother Don's birthdays.

It is important also that my parents were not welcomed enthusiastically upon moving from New Bedford to Marion. We became, as far as we know, the first Jewish family to reside in that town. As youngsters, I and my brothers encountered anti-Semitic attitudes soon after our arrival there. However, each of us made friends and felt quite comfortable with our respective circles of chums. Although I was aware as a child that our presence in this town was an annoyance for some natives, I didn't learn until my late teens that my father had bought the house, which was to become the family home for the next forty-two years, using a surrogate purchaser. By prearrangement with the accomplice, the property deed was then transferred to my father's name. We would not have been able to acquire the property otherwise, and my parents wanted to live there, in a quiet New England town with excellent schooling possibilities.

After my father died it was painful but enlightening to discover just how much my parents endured in our earliest days in our new "hometown." My father had saved, in an envelope dating from 1939 and labeled in his hand, "The Local KKK," some gems of reaction by a few townspeople. In it were some worrisome anonymous messages left on our front door, and some in our mailbox at the local post office. One of them, apparently addressed to my mother, typifies the lot (spelling, punctuation, and underlining preserved): "We Don't want you. You are jews and have selected to place yourselves in a sacredly protestant colony. (It) is not worth the discomfort That awaits you all. I am in a position to know. Do not allow your husbands boldness, and he is bold, to place you in this colony. You are a sweet person. This is sane advise—Take it."

Bold indeed. As I think today about the potentially precarious conditions under which we lived, I am full of pride that my parents chose to endure whatever resistance they might encounter during those days in which the messages of Nazi Germany were encroaching on American minds. More important, my parents were able to carry this out with a minimum of obvious disruption in their everyday lives. Whatever perturbations they had over these hostile intrusions were not saliently transmitted to me or my brothers. We were taught that accomplishment, particularly in education and music, could open closed doors. We survived the initial turbulence without any great incident that I know of. I was always conscious, however, that we were Jews in a non-Jewish environment and that I might not always be welcomed into the homes of my young friends.

That there was always an anticipation and expectation of rejection in places where I might go is best represented by the fact that I never felt I could set foot on the grounds of the small local yacht club located just three houses from ours. I did not fully appreciate the extent of my assimilation of that presumed exclusion until I was a married adult, summering with my wife and children in Marion. My young daughter, Ann, wishing to learn to sail well, came home one day and said "I'd like to join the yacht club." My immediate thought was that she could not do that. Ann said that she had been enjoying sailing with several yacht club members, that she only needed three parental members of the club to endorse her candidacy, and that they would vote on accepting her, whereupon she would pay a modest fee for adolescents. She easily obtained the endorsements, I underwrote the fee, and she became a junior member of the yacht club.

Ann took me onto the grounds of the club one day. As I entered I felt a bit like one of Mary Cover Jones's children, whom she helped get over a fear of thunder and lightning by gentling them into the anxiety-inducing storm. My young daughter was unknowingly my therapist. Since then she has been a wise counselor to me on numerous occasions.

The Lipsitt family was actually accepted quite warmly by most of the towns-folk. My pianist mother organized her first three sons into a quartet with her. Paul played the cello, Don clarinet and sax, and I the violin. Mom accompanied us, and we played for various assemblages in the region. Hardly musical at all, my father nonetheless took pride in these doings and drove us where we needed to go. Mom did not drive. Dad said that he had given Mamma one and a half driving lessons before we were born.

Dad (or Dadda, as we more often called him) also organized us to carry out common tasks. He encouraged us all to become Boy Scouts (most of us became Eagle Scouts) and to qualify as camp counselors. He became active himself locally and then regionally in Scout Council. Eventually he and Mamma were honored with the prestigious Silver Beaver Award.

Shortly after moving to Marion in 1939, Dad rounded up his three oldest sons in his study, the front room of our house, which served also as his modest local law office, an extension of the practice he continued in New Bedford. We were going to publish a town newspaper, he said. There was none, so we would do it. Dad was still a newspaperman at heart. Each of us had special duties. I was the dog editor most of time, which meant that I had to find interesting stories about dogs in the community. *The Sippican Compass* was typed out on mimeo-graph stencils by Dad on a small typewriter of the 1920s. A hand-cranked mimeo-graph machine churned out the pages for stapling and delivery. We got ads, and Dad stenciled them with some skill and artistry. Don and Paul were responsible for cranking the machine, seeking the ads, and circulating the paper. I can still smell the mimeograph ink and hear the sound of the drum rolling out the copy. After a year of this, Dad took his oldest three to the New York World's Fair. The family story (not true, I'm sure) was that "the boys earned their way with their newspaper," which sold for two cents a copy. Humor was a distinct feature of the Lipsitt household.

Writing is still an important pursuit of mine. Had I not become a psychologist, I think I might have enjoyed being a journalist. I was on my high school newspa-per staff. Then I joined the staff of the *Chicago Maroon* at the University of Chicago as an undergraduate, and I am currently in my tenth year as founding editor of the *Brown University Child and Adolescent Behavior Letter*. I have been an editor of some sort continuously since the age of ten.

The prospect of becoming a career journalist competed with a part-time intent to become a pediatrician like my uncle, who wanted me to take over his New Bed-ford practice. Events conspired to turn my head in other directions, but in some ways I have had it all ways.

As I think of the variety of influences impinging on me as a youngster, I think I am indeed my parents' child. I have worked all my career with children and have been concerned with their well-being. I have been a writer. I have enjoyed scholarship and university life. And I enjoy music, although I never developed special talent as a performing musician. I think I am a devoted family person. I know I derive extraordinary pleasure from my wife, Edna, son, Mark, and daughter, Ann. And finally, I am dogged in my pursuit of personal integrity and in my expectations of others in that regard. As in the life of my father, that latter attribute has sometimes given me grief, but I have had mostly pleasure and personal fulfillment from it.

College and Graduate Education

In my last year of high school, in 1947, in Marion at Tabor Academy (a private prep school that also served as the local high school), I applied to a number of colleges but really wanted to go to Cornell University. A classmate friend had also applied there, and we talked of rooming together if we both were accepted. Although we had rather comparable academic records, he got in and I did not. Both parents of my friend were Cornell graduates, and it is no secret that universities favor the progeny of their own graduates. Universities also try to diversify geographically. Today I understand this better than I did then. At the time, however, I was crushed.

I went to my school counselor and told him of my disappointment in not getting admitted to Cornell. Not Jewish himself (there weren't any Jewish teachers at Tabor), he replied, perhaps feeling that he was being generous and not blaming me personally for my failure: "Why don't you apply to the University of Chicago? They take late applicants, and they like Jews there."

I did. They did. And I graduated with my bachelor of arts degree from the University of Chicago in 1950. When I returned to the Chicago campus in 1995 to receive a professional achievement citation forty-eight years after my experience of dismay as a high school senior and forty-five years from my University of Chicago bachelor's degree, I sat in the magnificent Rockefeller Chapel to receive the award from the university president with my devoted and supportive wife of forty-three years sitting at the front of the chapel looking on. I had difficulty keeping from weeping, so emotionally loaded and enduring was the memory of my early disappointment combined with this splendidly serendipitous outcome.

Because my Chicago experience turned out to be so right for me educationally and in so many other respects, including the acquisition of lifelong friendships, I kept asking myself how it was that I got so fortunate. That they should see fit to honor me for having been so lucky seemed excessive! This award was followed in one year by my receiving the Lifetime Mentor Award of the American Association for the Advancement of Science for my work in promoting the careers of women and minority scholars. Both citations came at a time in my life when I was seriously saddened by a professional disappointment, the psychological consequences of which are only now dissipating, several years after the crisis. Thus what I have just described were sweet experiences indeed.

In my last year of study at the University of Chicago, 1949–50, where, like all undergraduates in the marvelous Robert Hutchins Great Books curriculum, I majored simply in "liberal arts," I tried my mind on a variety of disciplines. Fortuitously, again, I had what I now regard as a critical intellectual and personal experience. I worked at the faculty club during my entire three years at Chicago as a waiter, switchboard operator, Sunday-morning cook, and in other capacities. Sometimes I had to miss extracurricular events that would otherwise have attracted me. One day I suddenly had a time period free and strolled by a bulletin board that invited students in to hear a man named Donald O. Hebb, professor of psychology at McGill University, talking on a topic that by now I have forgotten. I had gradually been coming around to thinking, partly from lectures of David Reisman on Freud, Eckhard Hess on ethology, Ernest Burgess on group processes, and Clifford Shaw on delinquency, that psychology might interest me. I had also attended some of the classes of my brother Don, then an undergraduate at New York University, who would soon go on for a master's degree in psychology. Don later went to medical school, became a psychiatrist, and has been chief of psychiatry at the Harvard-affiliated Mt. Auburn Hospital for many years.

D. O. Hebb helped to galvanize that burgeoning interest when he told the audience, merely as a prologue to his lecture, that he had been a graduate student in economics when he was struck with a crippling disease or injury that left him lame. He was now walking with a limp, he said, and everyone could plainly see this. But, he said, every time he walked down Michigan Avenue or any street with lots of plate-glass windows and caught a glimpse of himself, he was startled to rediscover that was himself, limping. This personal self-deception, he said, so fascinated him that he decided to change careers and become a psychologist.

Hebb, of course, became a giant in our field. Several decades after this experience of mine, I had the opportunity, when Professor Hebb was receiving the G. Stanley Hall Award from the American Psychological Association (APA) Division of Developmental Psychology, of which I had by then become president, to tell him of my great interest in his lecture that day. Most especially, I said, his story about how difficult it was for him to accept that he had a different appearance than the one with which he had grown up captured my fascination. He said that he remembered telling the story often after he had moved from economics to psychology, especially in his early days as a psychologist, but that he had by now grown quite accustomed to his "new" appearance. He was visibly pleased that I remembered the lecture and that it helped to draw me to psychology. (I did not tell him that I could not recall anything else in his presentation that day.)

From Chicago I went to Boston, hoping to decide what to do with the rest of my life. Paul and Don were in school there, I had friends in the area, and I was pleased to be closer to my parents' home and have a chance for more recreation and social life, which I had rather neglected while working hard at Chicago. I had for the most part worked my way through Chicago. Although tuition was only $450 a year at the University of Chicago, and although my parents supplied me with some support, I earned a little more than $450 and at least one meal a day at the Quadrangle Club, the locus of numerous important experiences for me as an undergraduate. Now I needed to wind down, I thought, and let my past experiences crystallize and perhaps push me somewhere. I did some boating and swimming in Marion, worked as night clerk and switchboard operator in a medical office building in Boston and lived with my brothers, and began to think more about what I might like to do when my school years were over. I enrolled in a few psychology courses at Boston University.

Although I became destined in Chicago to go into psychology—one kind of psychology or another—I had no major as a Chicago undergraduate except in liberal arts, in the custom of that university. With Don's encouragement, I enrolled for a semester and summer of advanced undergraduate work in psychology at Boston University, where he was working on his master's degree. I took a course in learning with Leo Reyna, one in personality with Henry Weinberg, one in abnormal psychology with William Hire, one in social psychology with Robert Chin, and one in history of psychology with Wilhelm Pinard—to realize that I was going to be, as I thought, a clinical psychologist. I was attracted to psychodynamics, and I wanted to be in a helping occupation. Although the scientific aspects of psychology seemed to me rather dry and laboratory work a bit of a drudge, I liked the idea that one could use scientific approaches to understand how people got to be the way they are and how to help them cope better. I viewed Freud as a scientist (and still do) making systematic observations, going back frequently to the drawing board, revising his ideas on the basis of new inputs, and putting newfound knowledge to work in improving people's perspectives, their sense and appreciation of themselves, and their well-being. I was a committed empiricist at my core and wanted to be a scientist-practitioner before I had ever heard the term.

Most importantly, I met Edna Duchin during this period, although I had no intention of marrying in 1952, the year in which I found the woman for my life without even searching. Moreover, I thought I might lose her if I didn't do some life arrangement very soon. I became the first of the five Lipsitt brothers to be married. Edna was a college senior studying to be an elementary school teacher. We married on the same day she got her bachelor's degree at Lesley College in 1952—the same year in which I received my master's degree in psychology from the University of Massachusetts in Amherst.

A student friend with whom I was in courses at Boston University had directed me to the graduate program at the University of Massachusetts, where as a native of Massachusetts I could matriculate for little cost. I applied and got in, enrolled in the fall of 1951, and stayed through the summer of 1952. Edna and I lived in Amherst during our first months together and ran a rooming house that Edna tended while I continued work as a research assistant to Claude Neet and Robert Feldman.

Edna has been the principal stabilizing influence on my personal life and my primary support in all aspects of my career. Whenever I have taken on a task of organizing something, she has been co-organizer, as of the meetings of the International Society for Infant Studies, held in Providence in 1978 and 1996. Edna has been gracefully involved in aspects of my career that hardly anyone would presume. She has edited my writing, ever for the better, and is the last person to see almost everything I write before it goes "to bed." Our closest friends and associates tell me they feature her in their memories as a hostess and cook without peer. In an age of transition regarding the wife's involvement in a man's career, I am pleased to say that I could not have done whatever it was I have done without Edna. She has endured taunting by misanthropic women who feel this is not the way for a modern woman to live. When I remind Edna she could have had a marvelous career of her own, for there were wonderful opportunities, she insists she *has* had a career of her own; anyone who does not appreciate that does not understand symbiosis—or love.

At Massachusetts my interests in clinical psychology as well as social psychology were intensified, the first by a clinical practicum experience at Northampton State Hospital, and the second by my master's thesis, which related to Floyd Allport's concept of generalized personality attributes, called "teleonomic trends," that played out differently in different contexts but were at the core of a person's being.

This research experience, with Theodore R. Vallance as my advisor, was intense and satisfying. The idea of putting numbers to qualitative personal attributes was appealing, as was the spirit of exploration and the testing of hypotheses about the behavior and attitudes of real persons.

This work with humans was complemented by important experiences I had working in a rat laboratory, where I ran animals on a Lashley jumping stand in studies following a paradigm created by N. R. F. Maier (1949). First the rats were given a solvable discrimination task; for instance, they must jump to the white swinging door and arrive on a platform, where they would be fed briefly before being returned for the next trial. If they went to the black door, whether on the left or right, the animal would find the door impenetrable and drop into a net below, from which it would be returned to the launching platform for the next trial.

After the rat acquired expertise in jumping always to the correct door, black or white, the second phase of the study involved a change to a task that was "unsolvable." Now the reinforcement was given in half of the trials to black and in half to white, at either the left or right windows. If the rats jumped, they would receive the opportunity to feed on only half the trials, and there was no discriminative stimulus that was correct. Under this condition, the rats became psychologically odd in a way that had a lasting impression on me. Today I tell of these studies in my teaching, some forty years later, and as I speak of them can still feel the astonishment, the wonder of it all, that I felt upon first observing the phenomenon. It was a demonstration of the very, very powerful effects of a *learning experience* on an organism when subjected to conditions in which the animal is essentially help-less to cope with an inescapably frustrating and unsolvable task.

First, the animals stopped jumping, or tried to. (The experimental procedure forced the jump through prodding.) The frustrating trials were administered de-spite the animals' attempts to decline the choice. In a few trials noticeable changes occurred in the animals' demeanor. They began to look listless, and before be-coming quite strikingly catatonic sometimes jumped off the stand away from the apparatus. After some trials, the rats became like balls of fur in one's hands. They were floppy, de-energized, noncomplaining, defeated organisms. They would jump only with prodding, as with a flick of the tail.

At this point, the original solvable task was resumed with, for example, the white door correct and the black incorrect. The animals would be forced to jump and would thus receive information about the perfect correlation between the card, white or black, and the reward. In principle, the rat could now select one of the cards consistently and win its food on every trial. However, the psychological debilitation incurred by the previous regimen of frustrative trials was persevering. The animals continued with a position fixation or continued to jump randomly to white or black, even though the problem was now solvable. Then, "therapeutic intervention" was introduced.

It became apparent that a number of different procedures could break up the animals' fixations and cure their catatonia. Seizures induced by electroshock, sim-ulating shock therapy given to humans for depression, worked. So did having the animals fall into water on trials in which an incorrect choice was made. So did "guidance" in the form of offering the opportunity to walk across a platform to the windows rather than requiring a jump.

My fascination with these systematic studies of extreme effects of unsatisfying experiences was enormous and galvanized my understanding, even insistence for the rest of my career, that (1) developmental experiences have profound effects, (2) adverse conditions can debilitate, (3) organisms can recover from terribly stressful experiences if given rehabilitative opportunities, and (4) the processes involved in these psychodynamic changes can be observed systematically, can be quantified, and are verifiable. Life destinies may be profoundly altered by chang-ing the environmental context and the expectations of the organism. I later found this work to be very relevant to an understanding of such research as that of Curt Richter and Martin Seligman on helplessness, hopelessness, and "unexplained death," especially because I joined my friend Lee Salk in some studies of crib death.

This animal research experience, coupled with clinical practicum training at Northampton State Hospital, was immensely formative. Although I could not have known just what shape my career would take following my University of Massachusetts experience, I was surely going to be some kind of scientifically ori-ented clinical psychologist, which perhaps today would be called a behavior-ana-lytic orientation.

Career: The Formative Years

By the time I received my master's degree the Korean War was just over, but the draft was not. I had enjoyed school exemptions until this time, but now my draft board was breathing down my neck. While enrolled at the University of Massachusetts I had applied to various graduate programs in clinical psychology (Massachusetts had at the time only a master's-level graduate program) and had been accepted in some. I almost became a graduate student at the University of Florida, but with strong intimations that the draft board would find me a viable candidate for service before I could begin, I quickly explored alternatives to the army infantry and decided to join the air force. I signed up for four years, went through basic training at Lackland Air Force Base in San Antonio, found my way during basic training to some opportunities for psychological work at that base, and stayed in San Antonio. I received a direct commission while serving as an enlisted airman but was never activated as an officer. After two years in the service I was discharged under a reduction in force that President Eisenhower instituted when the war threats had dissipated.

My professional career really began in the air force. With my master's degree, I was assigned to a unit doing follow-up psychological testing of airmen who had done poorly on the Air Force Qualifying Test (AFQT). Some of these individuals were destined for discharge as incompetents unless they could be shown to be better endowed with talent than the AFQT indicated, or unless they could be matched with assignments that were appropriate for their intelligence levels. The chief clinical psychologist to whom I was assigned, Colonel Milton B. Jensen, Ph.D., was attached to the psychiatric unit of Lackland Air Force Base hospital, the largest psychiatric facility of the U.S. Air Force. He was doing this project rather on the side because he had confidence in and compassion for airmen who were disenfranchised by poor test performances. Colonel Jensen eventually wrote a rather remarkable paper, groundbreaking for its time but never as far as I know published, titled "Our Undeveloped Mental Resources." In it he reported that low-testing, low-achievement individuals in our society are often cast aside as incompetent when in fact they usually have useful talents. Some, he said, may actually have remarkable areas of expertise, if these could only be cultivated and capitalized upon. Some airmen who "washed out" before Jensen effected his psychometric innovations were not unlike some students whom I now teach in college, but today they have the advantage of having been identified as dyslexic or as having some other learning disability.

In doing this group retesting work in that part of the air base that housed the Human Resources Research Center, I gained lots of experience in individual psychometric evaluation of hundreds of airmen. After a few months, Dr. Jensen took me into the psychiatric clinic to become his clinical aide. As an airman second class there, I obtained extensive supervised experience in diagnostic evaluation of a vast array of patients. In my two-year tour of air force duty I was privileged to test, study, and assist in the diagnosis of a large number of disturbed individuals, including severe depressives, flagrant psychotics, murderers, men who flew planes but had agoraphobia, pilots who suddenly had problems "bringing the plane home," and all types of character disorder.

During this period I met and worked under the direction of Major Louis J. West, M.D., director of the Lackland Air Force Base psychiatry service. He helped me crystallize my life plans. "Joly" West was broadly trained in psychology as well as psychiatry and was a better interpreter of Minnesota Multiphasic Personality Inventory protocols and psychographs than most psychologists I knew. Joly West eventually founded the first psychiatry department in the country with the words "behavioral science" in the department name, at the University of Oklahoma Medical School. He later repeated this pioneering step when he became head of the psychiatry and biobehavioral sciences department at UCLA. He held some fascinating interdisciplinary staff meetings at Lackland, and psychiatrists, psychologists, and social workers worked there together constructively and with mutual respect.

While working as a clinician, I was reinforced in my belief that a career in clinical psychology was a reasonable option for me, for I enjoyed learning about patients' problems and about the diverse treatment plans of well-trained professionals for fixing those problems. At the same time, I had a rising suspicion that my real interests, and perhaps my best talents, resided not so much in diagnosing (labeling, as I saw it) people in distress, but rather in trying to figure out what the processes were by which they came to be the way they were. I was process-oriented, and I was wary of the very speculative nature of much diagnostic work. Moreover, I saw very little being done empirically to affirm the reasonableness of the approaches used in the treatment of many patients. I was becoming increasingly mindful, moreover, that psychologists on the team were often involved in the labeling process more than in the exploration of causes and the fixing of the problems. I did not want to be a mere technical aide to psychiatrists, a role to which many psychologists of the day acquiesced. I became increasingly aware that the clinician's task was largely one of inferring from patterns of present behavior, essentially repetitive reenactments of old issues, what the underlying problems were.

During this transitional period I was becoming clearer that I wanted a career in teaching, and that the origins of, more than the culmination of, human adjustment problems were what fascinated me most. Just at that time, my friend from graduate school at the University of Massachusetts, Dave Palermo, wrote to me from the University of Iowa, where he was then studying child psychology. Dave had been headed for a career in clinical psychology but found his way instead to the newly established experimental child psychology program at Iowa, administered through the much-acclaimed Iowa Child Welfare Research Station. He wrote to me of his great pleasure with the program he was in and, as he described it I came to realize that that was what I, too, wanted to do—perhaps preparatory to a clinical psychology scientist-practitioner career later.

In 1954 I applied to the University of Iowa when I realized there was a possibility that the air force would start reducing its ranks by first discharging those airmen who held direct commissions. I was accepted at Iowa. I begged for the discharge, I got it, and Iowa got me. My Iowa period, from 1954 to 1957, when I received my Ph.D., was nothing less than a riveting experience. This is where I acquired most of the skills, and much of the philosophy of science (e.g., McCandless & Spiker, 1956; Spiker & McCandless, 1954), that have fueled my career-long enthusiasm for empirical approaches to understanding the nature and origins of human behavior. Just as important, this is where I met three professors who, as it turned out, had immensely formative effects upon my research styles, my career, and my pleasure in life. Intellectually, I carry a lot of all three of them with me to this day. Boyd McCandless, Charlie Spiker, and Alfredo Castaneda were eventually to be longtime friends of mine, and we were mutual confidants. All three, sadly, died rather young.

Edna and I headed for Iowa City in August 1954, and our first child, Mark, was born five months later at the University of Iowa Hospitals. The resident obstetrician allowed me to be in the delivery room for the birth. At that time, this was an unusual permission for a father to have. On that occasion I got to see the youngest baby I had ever seen. It was an overwhelmingly exhilarating experience. When later writings began to appear on the early bonding relationship between parent and child, I knew just what they meant.

From 1954 to 1957 I was a graduate student in experimental child psychology, working terribly hard in a rigorous program that I sometimes despaired of completing satisfactorily. The intensity of the curriculum in quantitative methods was greater than I had anticipated, but I have been very grateful for it since. My fellow graduate students, besides Dave Palermo (who was soon to graduate), during my first year in "the Station" were such remarkable colleagues as Sheldon (Shep) White, Hayne Reese, Kathy Norcross (later Kathryn N. Black), Ruth Holton (who died tragically in an automobile accident soon after her graduation), Langdon Longstreth, and Nancy Sittig Jordison, who became the first nurse with a Ph.D. in psychology I ever knew.

The faculty of the Station were an astoundingly forward-looking, very astute lot. Besides old-timers (which means that they were as old then as I am now) such as Howard Meredith, arguably the most competent and certainly the most productive developmental anthropometrist in the country, and Orvis Irwin, long famous for his groundbreaking studies of infant behavior, there was a young triumvirate led by Boyd McCandless. Boyd was an Iowa child psychology graduate himself, noted for his vast knowledge in several areas of psychology and his capacity for teaching and talking both clinical and experimental child psychology. While a professor at San Francisco State College, he had "discovered" two young scholars who would become, eventually, the cornerstone of the new experimentalism in the field of child psychology at Iowa. When Boyd became director of Iowa's child psychology institute, he simply brought in his two protégés. One of them, Alfred Castaneda, he had sent to Ohio for his Ph.D. graduate study. Boyd brought him to Iowa soon after Al completed his doctoral training. At San Francisco, Charlie Spiker had been encouraged by Boyd to do his graduate studies at Iowa. Charlie did that, and he never left the University of Iowa.

Boyd, Charlie, and Al bucked tradition in the field of child development in a way that had been anticipated by Kurt Lewin (1931) in his article that contrasted the Aristotelian and Galilean styles of science. Lewin had been a professor at Iowa, although long before I got there. (I add that because I am sometimes confused, flatteringly, with another Iowa graduate, named Ronald Lippitt, who worked with Lewin.) We had enough of labeling, said Kurt Lewin, enough of characterizing whole groups of children with inferred characteristics (like the "terrible twos"). Rather, our job was to understand the processes and mechanisms that are at work as children grow and experience—especially experience, which at Iowa meant mostly "to learn" (Spiker, 1960).

The learning connection was not an accident except in the sense that everything is an accident. Kenneth Spence was the chairman of the Iowa Department of Psychology. Students in the Station were closely affiliated with that department and enrolled in psychology department courses—with such professors, besides Spence, as Judson Brown, I. E. Farber, Harold Bechtoldt, Gustav Bergmann, and Don Lewis. One could also take a course with Arthur Benton on brain specialization, or with Wendell Johnson on causes of and cures for stuttering. These were golden years at Iowa, and I consider myself exceptionally fortunate to have found my way there. Ken Spence and Don Lewis were on my dissertation committee. I became an avid logical positivist, which I suppose I had been all along but didn't know it. I found the systematic study of behavior to be exciting—perhaps the most important field in the world! (I do rather believe that.) And I have never looked back, except to say thank you.

Career: My Thirty-nine Years At, In, and About Brown University

One morning in my last year at Iowa before graduating with the Ph.D., Boyd Mc-Candless, on the way to his usual coffee break in the East Hall lounge, walked the hallway waving a letter he had just received from Brown University. He asked as he walked by the graduate student offices: "Anyone want to go to Brown?" I replied, "Yes, please." He came into my office and showed me a letter addressed to Robert Sears, who was a director of the Station before Boyd. I was familiar with Brown because my oldest brother, Paul, had done his undergraduate work there following his service in the navy. Brown also appealed to me because it was close to where I had grown up, and I was fond of being near the ocean. (Paul later became a lawyer and was in practice with our father for several years when he decided to return to school. He received his Ph.D. at the University of Chicago and became a clinical psychologist. He has been involved in forensic psychology activities and was a founder of the American Board for Forensic Psychologists.)

The letter that Boyd McCandless had from Brown was written by Harold Schlosberg, chairman of the Department of Psychology at Brown. He wrote that the department was looking for someone in child psychology to join the Brown department; a situation had opened in which the department would collaborate with a newly formed institute on campus to hire a young person or two to work on a national collaborative perinatal project just then in planning. A recent Harvard graduate, Judy Rosenblith, and I were hired at the same time, each of us for half-time in the institute and half in the psychology department, and I without either an interview or even a prior visit to the Brown campus. When I arrived at Brown and visited Harold for the first time in his office, he asked me where I had parked my car. When I replied in my Eastern Seaboard dialect, he sat silently for a few moments puffing on his pipe and then exclaimed: "Good Lord! I thought you came from Iowa."

Brown University had a wonderful reputation in experimental psychology, and I found the psychology department ready and willing to forge ahead in the kind of experimental child psychology in which I had been trained for the previous three years. In fact, although the department was principally known for its teaching programs and research strengths in the fields of animal learning and sensory psychophysiology, there was a sort of sidebar history the department already had in genetic or developmental psychology. After all, Leonard Carmichael, the editor of the first *Manual of Child Psychology* (1954) and the author of the chapter in that manual on "The Onset and Early Development of Behavior," had been there as chair before he became president of Tufts University. Similarly, Walter S. Hunter had been chair and intellectual leader of the department just a few years before I got there, and he had done classic studies of delayed reaction and of double alternation behavior in children. While Hunter's interests were essentially in "comparative psychology," the studies he carried out with animals and children, some of it in the heyday of John B. Watson, were landmarks in the field, particularly as he called attention to the mediating, "thoughtful" processes that children would engage in as they sought to remember what they were to do next. Harold himself had been involved in some studies with J. McVicker Hunt, Elliot Stellar, and Richard Solomon of developmental aspects of hoarding behavior in the rat. While on the Brown faculty, Joe Hunt had also edited his two-volume *Personality and the Behavior Disorders* (1944), which had a heavy developmental flavor. Later, Hunt would write the much-acclaimed book *Intelligence and Experience* (1961), which, of course, was almost entirely developmental.

In our correspondence prior to my taking the job at Brown, Harold discovered that I wanted to do something that appealed to him very much—to found an infant behavior and development laboratory—and I found he had a plan that in turn was very appealing to me—to start an experimental child psychology training program at Brown. Both prospects were made possible by the fact that Brown University and the Providence Lying In Hospital had entered into a research partnership, the first between Brown and the community hospitals, to carry out Brown's participation in the National Collaborative Perinatal Project.

In my early days at Brown, while helping establish the Collaborative Project I continued with lines of research that I had begun at Iowa, much of this in the Hull-Spence tradition, using older children as subjects: effects of delayed reward on discrimination learning in children, the comparison of simultaneous and successive stimulus presentation procedures in children's discrimination learning, the interaction of habit and drive (anxiety or stress) factors in the performance of children in learning situations, and the role of verbal mediation in paired associates learning. These lines of work were very appealing to me. I enjoyed experimentalism and got much pleasure doing research with preschool and elementary school children and working with a succession of very fine undergraduate honors students as well as graduate students. I have had numerous students and trainees who have remained in the field and of whom I am proud. Edna and I have maintained lifelong friendships with many of them: Carolyn Rovee-Collier, Dan Ashmead, Vincent Lolordo, Carol Nagy Jacklin, Barbara Burns, Juarlyn Gaiter, Anna Christopoulos, Ted Bosack, Joyce Ching-Yi Wu, John McCrary, Frank Goodkin, Jack Werner, and Patrick Burke, to name a few. Steve Buka was my undergraduate honors student almost twenty years ago; today he is a professor at the Harvard School of Public Health, and we are collaborators in a follow-up study of children who were studied intensively from birth to seven years of age and who are now thirty to thirty-six years of age.

I have always liked working at the edge. The prospect of starting an entirely new line of research, on infant sensory and conditioning processes, was exciting. It was scary but energizing. There were new studies coming out of the Soviet Union and Czechoslovakia, and old studies being translated into English for the first time. The time was ripe. Especially, the tide was turning in favor of behavioral research with very young infants in this country, pressed on in part by the infusion of federal funds into studies like the Collaborative Project, which sought to understand better the perils of perinatal life, birth, and early development. We did not yet know that more infants, children, and adolescents die or become debilitated by behavioral misadventures than from all diseases combined. But some of us had our suspicions. The mentality of American society was shifted significantly when one of the first announced findings of the National Collaborative Perinatal Project was that the variable carrying most of the variance in the determination of mental retardation and other developmental debilities was socioeconomic level. The search for the correlates, causes, and consequences of poverty remains as one of the most challenging scientific tasks for developmental psychology.

At this writing I have been at Brown for almost thirty-nine years: as an instructor for one year, assistant professor for three, associate professor for five, and full professor for thirty years. I became director of training in child psychology in 1960 after making successful application to the National Institute of Mental Health for a training grant, which Brown's Department of Psychology held for twenty years, until 1980.

We had actually applied for the training grant the year before as well, in my name as director, but were turned down. The review committee conveyed to Harold Schlosberg that "Lipsitt is not yet mature and experienced enough to be director." The next year we resubmitted the application with Harold as the nominal director and were awarded the grant. Harold thereupon turned the direction of the grant and the administration of the child program over to me, saying that I was the one competent to run it, not he. It rather reminds me of how my father had purchased the family homestead in someone else's name. Harold Schlosberg, as a matter of fact, was also the first chairman under whom a Jewish professor (this being me) ever became tenured in Brown's psychology department.

When I arrived at Brown in 1957 I found a department with an exceptionally collegial atmosphere. The noontime chats over lunch, which most of us "ate in," were instructive and challenging. I couldn't have asked for a more hospitable and intellectually generous group of colleagues. On some of these days I had the impression I must be one of the luckiest young psychologists in the country, or world, as I discussed a study I was setting up at the hospital with newborn babies—with Harold Schlosberg, Lorrin Riggs, Carl Pfaffmann, Trygg Engen, Russ Church, and Jake Kling. Before one of these discussions was over, Carl was offering me from his lab a much-needed equipment item that I did not yet have sufficient funds to purchase. The next day he came to my lab at the hospital across town to help me set it up and try it out.

I am told that some of my best contributions to the field of child psychology were made in the newborn laboratory and in the classroom, the latter broadly defined to include my office, where a lot of teaching and learning has gone on—reciprocally between my students and myself. I can admit only to having had an empirical disposition, an urgency about data, and a theoretical eclecticism that is based in Thorndike's law of effect and is partial toward Skinnerian behavior analyses but owes a heavy debt to Hull, Spence, and their other followers. For my philosophy of science, my historical orientation, and my continuing respect for psychodynamic approaches, I could not have done without Gustav Bergmann and Charles Spiker at Iowa. Some readers will find some aspects of this tribute enigmatic, I am sure. Throughout my career I have maintained clinical interests while sticking close to the laboratory and basic learning processes. It is not widely known that Bergmann was the author of a classic philosophical paper on the close relationship between clinical and experimental psychology.

In 1967 I founded and became director for twenty-five years of the Child Study Center at Brown, organized principally to administer the Collaborative Project, which I had come to Brown to join in 1957. By this time the medical program at Brown had been founded, in part because of the success that the university-based Collaborative Perinatal Project had in working with local hospitals, especially the Providence Lying In Hospital, where the study babies were born.

This success, and the formation of committees to explore whether Brown was suitably situated to organize a medical school, were largely attributable to the genius of the first institute director, Glidden L. Brooks, the only physician on the Brown faculty at the time. He was a marvelously resourceful gentleman and for five years moved the university, with encouragement of the president of Brown at the time, Barnaby Keeney, toward the conclusion that a medical school at Brown was feasible. I was on the feasibility committee and also, eventually, the implementation committee. Brooks left Brown after five years and, among other things, became the founding president of the Medical School of Ohio in Toledo. The Child Study Center that I founded for the Collaborative Project was in part his legacy. I directed the Collaborative Project at Brown until it came to an end when the children reached seven years of age, in 1973. However, the Child Study Center continued as custodian of the records and participated in national studies based upon the Brown data combined with forty-six thousand additional cases from nine other institutions nationwide. The Child Study Center sponsored child-behavior research at Brown and provided support to students in the child psychology training program of the psychology department.

I am still involved in the study of the children on whom we first gathered data in 1959. These "children" are now thirty through thirty-six years of age, and with my colleagues Steven Buka of the Harvard School of Public Health and Paul Satz of UCLA, we are carrying out a study of those participants in the original study who were or could have been characterized during their early years as "learning disabled." Our aim is to document, using case studies and matched controls, the life-span outcomes of such individuals, those who have managed well and those whose lives may have been significantly at peril due to their disabilities.

The Child Study Center and the child psychology training program of the Department of Psychology, working in concert, kept infant behavior and development studies alive for many years at Brown, and a respectable number of graduates with specialties in child psychology emerged from our program. In recent years, with the ascendancy of cognitive studies at Brown in a newly formed department and diminished availability of support for traditional child behavior and development programs, the child psychology training program at Brown has diminished in numbers and visibility to the point that current faculty, including myself, are reluctant to claim we have such a program.

Reflections on Developmental Psychology

Upon consideration of the history of hominoids on this planet and the remarkable longevity of humankind, involving hundreds of thousands of years, the recent and rapid changes that have taken place in the way we live and the way we think about the way we live is truly mind-boggling. All of this, too, while there has been, as far as we know, virtually no change in our morphological, physiognomic, or physiological makeup.

The field of child development is about as old, roughly speaking, as the telephone, the automobile, the airplane, and television. The technology of behavior science, now so important for our understanding of the behavioral, cognitive, and neural mediation of human destiny, is about as old as the aforementioned advances in communications technology.

The field of child development, like behavior science generally, lags far behind the other sciences. Yet it is the science of psychological nature, its origins and consequences. With only gradual acquisition of a better understanding of the importance of behavior and its development, and its critical importance in affecting the destiny of mankind, I have became rather pessimistic. The technology of aggression and hatred far exceeds the technology of peacemaking and cooperation thus far.

Postscript

For as long as I live, or at least remember anything, I will probably have the feeling that I did not do enough. Although I blame my personal failings for this and consider myself entirely responsible for such a detriment of outlook, I attribute this nagging doubt that I may not have done or been all that I might have been to two major conditions of my life.

The first is that my parents had high aspirations for me, as for all their children, and it was clear throughout my childhood and adolescence that they were invested more in their children's eventual accomplishments than in their own comforts and pleasures. Their children's life destinies were their comfort and pleasure. Thus, the duty to perform was always with me and my brothers. The second reason for my hesitancy in feeling entirely comfortable with what I may have attained is that, when all is said and done, I have had a marvelous time of it (and am not finished with it yet). Somehow it always seemed to me that having a wonderful time should be second-order business, ranking in importance far below doing things properly and well.

This mandate, as it were, to always do my best carries with it, of course, some anxiety baggage. The baggage we carry, as Charlie Chaplin has so wonderfully demonstrated in numerous films, often is not without its humorous aspect, even while it tortures us. A dream I have had several times is of myself in front of a very large class, lecturing to an audience that, as I would have it, is ecstatic over the superb way in which I have put things. Presently, one from the right and one from the left, two men approach me from offstage, each taking one of my arms, leading me away, and whispering silently in my ears: "Professor Lipsitt, you are repeating yourself, over and over again."

I do believe that most people repeat themselves over and over. This is one reason why we are able to have a science of psychology and how it becomes possible for us to observe in others those persistent patterns of behavior and manners of thinking that would otherwise be dumbfounding.

My life has for the most part increased steadily in pleasure over time, despite the sadness I have experienced in a few tedious detours. I had wanted, for example, to cap my career with a resoundingly successful tour of duty at the headquarters of the American Psychological Association (APA), where I became science director in 1990 on a two-year leave of absence from Brown. So confident was I that I could be very useful to the APA and to psychology and that I could rely on my fellow executives of APA for common purpose and personal support, that I did not even insure that I had a properly executed contract when, after some wooing and special pleading by the chief executive officer of the association, I took the job. This oversight on my part was perhaps a matter of excessive risk taking, to which I am disposed and to which I have earlier alluded. I fell victim to false accusations after completing eighteen months of my intended two-year stay in that position. I learned painfully that personal integrity and desire for constructive change are not always golden keys to success in a large organization. I learned, more than one can by reading, about David and Goliath. I learned from personal experience that assaults on an individual's personhood are just as serious and just as debilitating as the author of the Ten Commandments warned.

Hoping to help my "parent organization" move toward a happier state in which scientists and clinicians alike would find the organization hospitable, I have run twice for the APA presidency. The outpouring of support that my candidacy attracted has been reward enough for now. I ran second among five candidates on both occasions. Although my loss of the elections in the midst of foul political publicity has formed the lowest spot of my life, these years have also provided a truly validating experience as so many friends, colleagues, and family members rose to my defense and provided much needed psychological support. Nonetheless, harassment by false accusation is no fun.

My mother lived long enough to tell me, when she was in her eighties and when I, in my fifties, was deeply immersed in my teaching and research career, "Lew, you're working too hard." My father, a literate man who spoke fine English, lived to greet me frequently with a smart smile, calling out "Hello, Perfessah!"

In my turn, I lived to please them, to enjoy my siblings and their families, to have a long-lasting love affair with Edna, to enjoy beyond description my wonderful son and daughter, to relish the estimations of highly respected scientists who think that I have contributed substantially to my field, and to have very fine, bright, scholarly, humorous friends. I have had many, many laughs. I have, finally, had a great deal of fun. Strange that I should feel I haven't done enough, but there it is. I have been very lucky.

References

Carmichael, L. (1954). *Manual of child psychology.* New York: Wiley.

Hunt, J. McV. (1961). *Intelligence and experience.* New York: Ronald Press.

Hunt, J. McV. (Ed.). (1944). *Personality and the behavior disorders: A handbook based on experimental and clinical research.* New York: Ronald Press.

Lewin, K. (1931). The conflict between Aristotelian and Galilean modes of thought in contemporary psychology. *Journal of General Psychology, 5,* 141–177.

Maier, N. R. F. (1949). *Frustration: The study of behavior without a goal.* New York: McGraw-Hill.

McCandless, B. R. & Spiker, C. C. (1956). Experimental research in child psychology. *Child Development, 27,* 78–80.

Spiker, C. C. (1960). Research methods in children's learning. In P. H. Mussen (Ed.), *Handbook of research methods in child psychology.* New York: Wiley.

Spiker, C. C. & McCandless, B. R. (1954). The concept of intelligence and the philosophy of science. *Psychological Review, 61,* 255–266.

Representative Publications

Blough, D. S. & Lipsitt, L. P. (1971). The discriminative control of behavior. In J. W. Kling & L. A. Riggs (Eds.), *Woodworth and Schlosberg's experimental psychology* (3rd ed., pp. 743–792). New York: Holt, Rinehart & Winston.

Lipsitt, L. P. (1958). A self-concept scale for children and its relationship to the Manifest Anxiety Scale. *Child Development, 29,* 463–472.

Lipsitt, L. P. (1961). Simultaneous and successive discrimination learning in children. *Child Development, 32,* 337–347.

Lipsitt, L. P. (1963). Learning in the first year of life. In L. P. Lipsitt & C. C. Spiker (Eds.), *Advances in child development and behavior, Volume 1* (pp. 147–195). New York: Academic Press.

Lipsitt, L. P. (1967). The concepts of development and learning in child behavior. In D. B. Lindsley & A. A. Lumsdaine (Eds.), *Brain function, Volume 4* (pp. 211–248). Los Angeles: University of California Press.

Lipsitt, L. P. (1977). The study of sensory and learning processes of the newborn. In J. Volpe (Ed.), *Clinics in perinatology, Volume 4* (no. 1, pp. 163–186). Philadelphia: W. B. Saunders.

Lipsitt, L. P. (1978). Sensory and learning processes of newborns: Implications for behavioral disabilities. *Allied Health and Behavioral Sciences Journal, 1,* 493–522.

Lipsitt, L. P. (1979). Critical conditions in infancy: A psychological perspective. *American Psychologist, 34,* 973–980.

Lipsitt, L. P. (1979). Infants at risk: Perinatal and neonatal factors. *International Journal of Behavioral Development, 2,* 21–42.

Lipsitt, L. P. (1983). Stress in infancy: Toward understanding the origins of coping behavior. In N. Garmezy & M. Rutter (Eds.), *Stress, coping and development in children* (pp. 161–190). New York: McGraw-Hill.

Lipsitt, L. P. & Castaneda, A. (1958). Effects of delayed reward on choice behavior and response speeds in children. *Journal of Comparative and Physiological Psychology, 51,* 65–67.

Lipsitt, L. P. & LoLordo, V. (1963). Effects of stress and difficulty on the learning of oddity discrimination. *Journal of Experimental Psychology, 66,* 210–214.

Lipsitt, L. P., Reilly, B. M., Butcher, M. J. & Greenwood, M. M. (1976). The stability and interrelationships of newborn sucking and heart rate. *Developmental Psychobiology, 9,* 305–310.

Lipsitt, L. P. & Vallance, T. R. (1955). The expression of teleonomic trends in private and in group-related problem situations. *Journal of Personality, 23,* 381–390.

Palermo, D. S. & Lipsitt, L. P. (Eds.). (1963). *Research readings in child psychology.* New York: Holt, Rinehart & Winston.

Reese, H. W. & Lipsitt, L. P. (Eds.). (1970). *Experimental child psychology.* New York: Academic Press.

Rovee-Collier, C. K. & Lipsitt, L. P. (1982). Learning, adaptation, and memory in the new-born. In P. Stratton (Ed.), *Psychobiology of the human newborn* (pp. 147–190). London: Wiley.

Wismer, B. & Lipsitt, L. P. (1964). Verbal mediation in paired associate learning. *Journal of Experimental Psychology, 68,* 441–448.

9

Paul Mussen

Inevitably we developmental psychologists ask ourselves the fundamental question of our discipline: How did we become who and what we are today? We know there are no completely satisfactory answers, but, given our training and interest, we cannot help speculating, admittedly with biases and defenses. It is easy to list some experiences that surely affected our development, but we cannot rank them in order of importance. And of course we realize that many other factors, unknown, uncomprehended, or forgotten, were (perhaps equally or more) influential. Serendipity or happenstance may have immeasurable consequences, as it did in my case.

Family Background and the Early Years

My parents, Harry and Taube Mussen, were Jews who had emigrated from eastern Europe when they were adolescents (in about 1910) and then lived in Paterson, New Jersey. My father, a prizewinning student in Poland, had to go to work to help support his impoverished family immediately after he arrived in the United States. However, he was a dedicated autodidact, mastered the English language, read prodigiously, acquired a remarkable vocabulary, and published many poems. He was an ardent socialist, and after serving in France in World War I, an outspoken pacifist.

My mother's family was of high status in the Lithuanian shtetl in which she was born and raised, and learning was greatly valued in her childhood home. Although she was already sixteen when she arrived in the United States, she entered elementary school and went to high school and business school. She and my father married in January 1921, and I was born in Paterson on March 21, 1922.

As an only child (and the oldest grandchild) for nine years, I was the main object of attention not only for my parents but also for my devoted grandparents, uncles, and aunts. My life was relatively tranquil and my success in school was a source of pride for the family.

The most vividly remembered discussions at home—between my parents, between me and my parents, or between my parents and visitors—were centered on interpersonal and moral issues; prominent topics were sensitivity to others' feelings, charity, honesty, altruism, and tolerance. For my father, ideals and principles were of paramount importance, while my mother emphasized character and "a good name."

In the Great Depression my father accepted a job as a foreman in a silk mill in Willimantic, Connecticut, and we moved there when I was nine years old, just after my only brother was born. The atmosphere and pace of the small town were appealing, the surrounding areas—hills, woods, and lakes—beautiful, and the ethnic diversity intriguing—predominantly French Canadian, with many Italians, Poles, Irish, and small contingents of Greeks, Russians, Lebanese, and Jews. My life was basically happy. School was easy and fun; I had good friends and participated in enjoyable activities such as hiking, swimming, editing the school newspaper. It was not an entirely untroubled childhood, however. In the early 1930s, anti-Semitism was prevalent, and Jews often suffered humiliation and discrimination. When I was ten, my mother underwent major surgery and (very primitive) radiation treatments for breast cancer and during a pain-filled recovery became severely depressed. Episodes of depression recurred during the rest of her life. Also, when I was in high school my father's mill was phased out, and he was soon unemployed.

I ranked fifth in my class in high school (the four who ranked higher were girls!), but my studies were not challenging and provided little training in scholarship. Intellectual or educational achievement was not high in the hierarchy of goals among most of my classmates, and the school had few good teachers, limited courses, and no student counselors. Friends in other places seemed better educated, smarter, and more concerned with higher learning than those at home.

My parents, teachers, and friends encouraged me to prepare for college, although I had not shown any special talents or deep abiding interests. I loved literature, got good grades on written reports, and vaguely thought of becoming a high school English teacher. In the last half of my senior year an English teacher assigned some books in psychology, a discipline I had been completely ignorant about. Considered in retrospect, those books were very superficial, but they fascinated me more than any of my other high school textbooks. But it must have been more than reading that engaged my interest in psychology; perhaps my early experiences helped direct me to that field—the frequent discussions at home of personalities and moral characteristics; sensitivity to individual and cultural differences, perhaps related to being Jewish; and my mother's depressions. Undoubtedly there were also other factors, more subtle or not as readily recalled, that played a part.

I yearned to go to college, but because of my family's financial situation it did not seem likely that I would. Serendipity rescued me. A neighbor, a professor of agricultural economics at the nearby state college (now the University of Connecticut), offered me a job as an assistant in a research project. I would be paid thirty-five cents an hour by the National Youth Administration (NYA), a part of Roosevelt's New Deal designed to help students. It was an offer I couldn't refuse, and strange as it seems, my earnings took care of my tuition as well as living expenses at Connecticut State College, where I enrolled in September 1938.

Colleges, the Navy, and Graduate School

I was only sixteen, had led a sheltered life, and did not know how to study effectively. My first-semester grades were average, but through observation and imitation of successful students, my grades soon improved sharply.

My interest in psychology was enhanced during my second year, but I became dissatisfied with the confined climate of the college. Serendipitously, a young psychology instructor told me about scholarships at Stanford that gave preference to students from Connecticut. His reports and *Psychology and Life,* the text of the introductory course, led me to conclude that Stanford was the world center of psychology. I applied for, and won, a scholarship there.

Going to Stanford was a genuine watershed in my life. I enrolled as an almost-junior in September of 1940, and my reaction was love at first sight. The university milieu was spirited, vital, and energizing, the campus setting idyllic, the weather superb, and my new friends were very bright, warm, witty, cheerful, and supportive. Of greatest importance for my future career was the outstanding faculty of the psychology department, which included Lewis Terman, Maud Merrill, Ernest Hilgard, Quinn McNemar, Calvin Stone, and Paul Farnsworth. The courses offered were better taught and more challenging than any I had encountered previously, and I responded with enthusiasm and dedication to my studies. Intelligence testing was taught by Merrill, a coauthor of the Stanford-Binet. She invited me to work with her in the juvenile court where she was the psychologist and her husband the judge. That brief clinical experience gave me an inkling of what it was like to work professionally as a psychologist and demonstrated that psychology had real social utility.

By the end of my first year at Stanford I was inexpressibly changed. The world had opened up; my styles of thinking and expressing myself were drastically modified; I *felt* more competent, uplifted, confident, and worldly.

World War II was declared in December of my senior year, but my student status was not immediately threatened because the draft age was twenty-one and I was not yet twenty. The academic highlight of that year was my contact with Lewis Terman, who was in his last year of teaching before retirement. He was one of the leading psychologists of his time, genuinely humane, interested in students, and impressively knowledgeable. Like other professors, he strongly encouraged me to do graduate work in psychology.

With an appointment as a teaching assistant I began graduate study at Stanford the day after I received my A.B. degree, in June 1942. Jean Macfarlane, a visiting professor that summer, gave a seminar in projective techniques and personality testing. As director of a longitudinal study, she also introduced us to the methodology and potential significance of such study. Roger Barker, new at Stanford, became an invaluable mentor and friend, a gentle, thoughtful, and creative psychologist, full of stimulating ideas. My master's thesis, under his supervision, was on the attitude of college students toward handicapped persons; we published it in

The Journal of Abnormal and Social Psychology (Mussen & Barker, 1944), my first psychological publication.

In April 1943 I received my M.A. and became an instructor in an Army Specialized Training Program (ASTP) at Stanford (through a contractual arrangement between the university and the army) designed to train enlisted men to work in army personnel. Lecturing in abnormal and social psychology and assisting in laboratory courses were excellent and rewarding teaching experiences—good preparation for my future career.

After the ASTP ended, I enlisted in the navy and was assigned to the Navy Language School to learn the Malay (now Indonesian) language. As it turned out, that language served no strategic purpose, so I was sent to the Office of Naval Intelligence in Hawaii to prepare bulletins about the geography, ecology, and culture of small South Pacific islands that might be invaded or become military targets. That reinforced my interest in cultural differences and gave me practice in writing clearly and succinctly.

I spent much of my free time in the University of Hawaii library exploring fields such as philosophy, economics, sociology, political science, and anthropology, but to me none was as engrossing as psychology. From this I concluded that I should go back to graduate school and become a psychologist, a conclusion based to a large extent on my (perhaps naive) notion that psychology could contribute most significantly to the betterment of human welfare.

The Veterans Administration had established Ph.D. programs in clinical psychology at a number of major universities, and I was encouraged to apply for admission. Accepted in several programs, I decided, to my eternal satisfaction, to go to Yale, a major center of psychological theory and research. Moreover, while many departments were enrolling great numbers of graduate students, the Yale department remained small and select; this, too, made it attractive. In September 1946, I enrolled there as a Ph.D. candidate.

The most important feature of Yale was the star quality of the faculty and their cutting-edge work and publications: Clark Hull, the most prominent figure in learning theory, the major psychological theory of the late 1940s; Carl Hovland, a leading researcher in the formation and change in social attitudes; Frank Beach, pursuing monumental work on hormones and sexual behavior; Neal Miller and John Dollard, creatively integrating concepts of psychoanalysis and learning theory (see their *Personality and Psychotherapy, 1950*); Leonard Doob, a social psychologist best known for his work on propaganda analysis and attitudes; Irvin Child and anthropologist John Whiting, using the Human Relations Area Files to test hypotheses derived from learning theory and psychoanalysis (see their *Child Training and Personality, 1953*); Seymour Sarason, a wonderfully perceptive observer of human behavior with challenging ideas about relationships between psychology, education, and social progress. Psychoanalytic theory loomed large in the thinking, teaching, and research of the psychology department, an orientation reinforced by an illustrious psychiatry department, which welcomed graduate students to case seminars.

Specialization in particular areas of psychology was much less prominent in the late 1940s than it is today; most psychologists were broadly trained. For example, the major course requirement during my first year of graduate study was a proseminar in which all members of the psychology faculty participated, providing substantial backgrounds in all major domains. Specialized aspects of the field were examined in greater depth in intensive seminars. Stimulus-response (S-R) learning, theory-driven controlled experiments, and, wherever possible, mathematical models were emphasized, and we were thoroughly indoctrinated into the notion that the most important aspects of human behavior are learned. Naive and simplistic as it is, S-R theory dominated thinking and research in psychology throughout the 1940s and 1950s. (Perhaps this reflected the zeitgeist—the optimism and prosperity of the postwar period, greater opportunities for education and advancement, and a deep-seated belief that the human condition could be improved.)

The clinical program included courses in testing and therapy as well as in theories of personality and, in addition, supervised internships in clinics and hospitals. Although I left clinical psychology a few years later, my training in that area has shaped my perspectives and research objectives—really my entire career—in highly significant and enduring ways.

My fellow graduate students were sophisticated intellectuals from diverse backgrounds who had genuine affection and respect for one another. Restaurants and coffee shops were the venues of many vigorous arguments and stimulating discussions of all sorts of issues, theories, and data—psychological and social-political—that were sometimes as enlightening as faculty lectures and seminars. Friendships with many of my peers (e.g., John Conger, Seymour and Norma Feshbach, Florence Schumer, Edna [Kaufman] Shapiro, Patricia [Pittluck] Minuchin) have been maintained since then, but some meaningful relationships of those years regrettably eroded with the passage of time and geographic distance.

My Ph.D. dissertation was an investigation of the effects of intimate contact with Afro-American peers on white boys' attitudes toward that group. (Leonard Doob as chairman, Irvin Child, and Seymour Sarason were my committee.) The research was conducted at an interracial camp where boys of both races were in intimate contact with one another for a month. Attitude tests were administered before and after the camp session, and the boys were interviewed and given Thematic Apperception Tests. As predicted by the hypotheses, those without strong aggressive needs acquired more favorable attitudes, while others retained their prejudices. The results of the study were published in *The Journal of Abnormal and Social Psychology* (Mussen, 1950) and later reprinted in several books of readings in social and developmental psychology.

I received my degree in 1949, a halcyon year for job-seeking Ph.D.s. Student enrollments in colleges and universities burgeoned, and qualified instructors were in short supply. At the same time, the number of patients at psychiatric hospitals and clinics multiplied, as did the need for clinical psychologists. Yet only a small number of Ph.D.s in psychology (200 or 250) were granted that year. (What a difference between that situation and the one faced by new Ph.D.s today!) I chose an academic career, teaching and doing research, and accepted an assistant professorship at the University of Wisconsin at Madison.

Early Years of My Career

My two-year career there began in the fall of 1949 at a salary of $3,250 per year. I taught a large undergraduate course in the psychology of adjustment, a smaller one in exceptional children, and graduate courses in testing, interviewing, and theories of therapy. All my courses had a developmental perspective, a Yale-influenced emphasis on early relationships and social learning.

The publish-or-perish philosophy was explicit at Wisconsin. I published articles based on my dissertation, as well as new studies of the personalities of politically active college students, the validity of intelligence and projective tests, and the relationships between early child-rearing practices and adjustment in later childhood. My colleagues were first-rate psychologists, most of the graduate students were excellent, and the university community was socially and culturally satisfying. In a glorious summer vacation between those two academic years I indulged my long-standing ardent interest in art by visiting museums in London, Paris, Rome, and Florence, my favorite city.

My second year at Wisconsin was marked by dissension among faculty members and the realization that the department would not substantially support what were regarded as the "softer" areas of psychology. I received several job offers from other universities, including a very attractive one from the Ohio State University (OSU), which had an excellent clinical program and paid a higher salary ($4,200 per year). I moved there in the fall of 1951.

In my four years at OSU I formed significant personal relationships and made critical decisions about my future professional life. Julian Rotter and George Kelley, the senior faculty of the clinical program, were building their own systematic theories, and close faculty-student relationships gave rise to frequent heated and enlightening debates about theoretical and methodological issues. My colleague Alvin Scodel, a recent Berkeley Ph.D., became a close friend, and together we collaborated on studies of social perceptions of authoritarians and the effect of context on responses to projective tests. Although my training and teaching were in clinical psychology and I consulted at psychiatric facilities, I was becoming increasingly doubtful about my aptitude and involvement in that field. It was also clear that my interest was in *developmental* psychology, in the study of the *antecedents* of behavior patterns.

During the summer of 1952, John Conger visited me in Columbus. We both had recently taught courses in child psychology and both of us were critical of the available texts, which we regarded as weak, restricted in coverage, and lacking in theoretical orientation. John proposed that the two of us, having similar training and interests, write a child-development text with a learning orientation. We were still new Ph.D.s, and I was skeptical about our knowledge and ability to do that, but John was persuasive, and I agreed to "give it a shot." During the next year we worked out a detailed outline for the first edition of *Child Development and Personality.*

Another event for which I am everlastingly grateful occurred during my second year at Ohio State University. Ethel Foladare, an attractive graduate student in the speech and communication department, enrolled in my seminar in group therapy. She is a UCLA graduate with broad interests in art, drama, and literature that mesh well with my own. We began dating and spending a great deal of happy time together. At the end of the summer we were engaged, and in October 1953 we got married.

By my last year at OSU I had gained some professional recognition, reflected in the reprinting of several of my articles in books of readings, as well as in invitations to present papers at colloquia at other universities, to participate in conferences, and to serve on national committees. It seemed to be a good time to identify myself as a developmental, rather than a clinical, psychologist, and the change would require further study and retooling. (In fact, many prominent developmental psychologists of my generation were trained primarily in other areas—for example, Robert and Pauline Sears in experimental, Eleanor Maccoby in social, John Conger in experimental, Harold Stevenson in experimental-learning, Jerry Kagan in physiological.)

A Ford Foundation Fellowship supported me for a year's postdoctoral work (1955–56) at the University of California, which had an excellent psychology faculty, an anthropology department with strength in culture and personality (an area of increasing interest), and, most importantly, a prestigious Institute for Child Development (now the Institute of Human Development). That institute was established in 1927 for "the promotion of the welfare of children," and its key contributions come from longitudinal studies of physical, intellectual, personality, and social development of a total of five hundred participants. It is an interdisciplinary facility that seeks to bring various social and biological disciplines to bear on fundamental issues of human development. As it turned out, the institute was to play a very important part in my professional life.

In the summer of 1955 Conger and I completed work on the first edition of our book, *Child Development and Personality.* Ethel and I moved to Berkeley that September. The institute gave me a home base, and the psychology and anthropology departments were very cordial and welcomed my participation in seminars and discussions. I immersed myself in the longitudinal data at the institute, and with Mary Jones published a few papers based on those data. During that year, I was offered a position in psychology at the university. Given my strong desire to be identified as a developmental psychologist, the impressive stature of the department (and under Clark Kerr's presidency of the university, the upsurge in the status of the social science departments), and my love of California, I could not refuse that offer.

My Career Continues

The appointment at Berkeley brought me recognition as a developmental psychologist, and my career shifted into high gear. My clinical experience had helped to focus my attention on personality development. Happily, the zeitgeist and my own interests were in synchrony; personality development was stage center in developmental psychology in the 1940s, 1950s, and early 1960s. Cognitive development has dominated the field since the mid-1960s, but there is now a marked resurgence of interest in social behavior, personality, emotion, and temperament and their impacts on cognitive functioning. Undoubtedly, developmental psychology, like other disciplines, goes through cycles determined, at least in part, by social and historical trends.

My first year of teaching at Berkeley (1956–57) was the most labor-intensive and enriching one in my professional experience, for it involved preparation for new undergraduate courses in development and in culture and personality, for graduate seminars, and for participation in the departmental proseminar. The other faculty in the developmental area were Harold Jones (who was director of the Institute of Human Development), Jean Macfarlane, who also gave clinical courses, and John McKee, a University of Iowa Ph.D. The graduate students were top-notch, and several have become leading psychologists.

During that year, the first edition of *Child Development and Personality* appeared to very favorable reviews (by Eleanor Maccoby in *Contemporary Psychology* and by Pauline Sears in *Science*), and it was adopted for use in hundreds of schools. New editions have been published approximately every five years since then, and it has been translated into thirteen other languages, including German, Spanish, Russian, Italian, Japanese, Greek, Indonesian, and Chinese.

My first years in Berkeley were joyous in other ways, too. We built a house in the Berkeley hills, and two wonderful family events occurred: the births of our daughter, Michele, in 1956 and our son, James, in 1958—two healthy, beautiful, and bright children. Observing and interacting with them has had incalculable effects on my thinking about developmental phenomena, and I cannot ever thank them or Ethel enough for all they have given me personally and professionally.

Psychology moved rapidly into the age of specialization after World War II, and graduate programs in particular domains (clinical, social, experimental, physiological) were established in many universities. Psychology became a very popular undergraduate major, and student enrollments in psychology courses burgeoned. By 1965 the developmental group at Berkeley expanded to include Jonas Langer in cognitive development, and Dan Slobin, an expert in language development. We designed and implemented a graduate program, including a series of proseminars, courses in methods and statistics, and research experience. John S. Wetson, Sue Ervin-Tripp, Mary Main, and Martin Banks later joined the developmental group and participated in the program. Over the years, the National Institutes of

Child Health and Development has awarded us generous grants to support graduate and postdoctoral fellowships, laboratory equipment, and clerical help. Judged by the number of distinguished developmental psychologists who received their Ph.D.s or postdoctoral training there, the program has been a great success: William Damon, Deanna Kuhn, Eldred Rutherford, Geoffrey Saxe, Nancy Eisenberg, Susan Sugerman, Sidney Strauss, and many others.

Programmatic research is generally more fruitful and gratifying, but my early studies and publications were quite diffuse and had no central theme. I was therefore eager to establish a fruitful program, and it was not difficult to find an appropriate focus: My clinical experience, reading (particularly of Freud, Erikson, and Mowrer), and introspection about my own development—or some combination of these—motivated me to study identification and its underlying processes. (Can the research interests of social scientists escape the influence of their personal histories?) Additionally, the topic was appealing because identification is a basic concept in most theories of personality and readily translated into terms of learning theory. (My Yale background still manifested itself!)

The process of identification cannot be measured directly, but discernible consequences of the process—resemblances in patterns of behavior, appropriate sex typing, and superego development—can be assessed. Using masculinity of interests and attitudes as the criteria of father identification, my first Berkeley studies yielded evidence supporting the validity of the developmental hypothesis, which maintains that identification is based on satisfying relationships with the like-sex parent. Although these studies were well received and are frequently cited, I now believe they are of limited value because the measure of identification, conformity with *contemporary stereotyped* masculine responses and attitudes, is a restricted one. Therefore, the findings are probably not generalizable to other cultures or eras. Research findings in developmental psychology must be interpreted in the context of their times and social settings.

The favorable reception of the textbook and my other publications catapulted me (at least I felt catapulted) to prominence well beyond my expectations. This brought numerous invitations to give seminars and colloquia, to be an editor, and to consult on television programming and advertising for children. I was appointed to be the first American psychology editor of the *International Journal of Child Psychology and Psychiatry;* co-editor, with Mark Rosenzweig, of *The Annual Review of Psychology;* and a consulting editor for *Child Development, Journal of Consulting Psychology, Journal of Educational Psychology, The Merrill-Palmer Quarterly,* and the *Journal of Genetic Psychology.*

Shortly after I came to Berkeley, the National Academy of Sciences–National Research Council's Committee on Child Development proposed publishing a handbook of research methods and asked me to be the editor. Because of the apparent need for a volume that would help accelerate the rate and raise the caliber of research, many distinguished colleagues agreed to contribute to it. It was published in 1960, and although, as anticipated, many new methods have been devised and old methods of research have been improved since then, the volume was of great value to researchers for many years.

In the early 1960s, the "cognitive revolution" turned the tide of American developmental psychology away from social and personality development. In 1959 the Social Science Research Council (SSRC), always concerned with the early detection of intellectual trends, appointed the Committee on Intellective Processes Research. This committee consisted of Roger Brown (chair), Jerome Kagan, William Kesson, Lloyd Morrisett, Kimball Romney, Harold Stevenson, and me. Although we had no clearly defined mandate, we set out to explore the state of knowledge about cognitive development and to delineate future directions of research and theory. We did this through a series of six conferences—each with its own theme—that were the most well-planned and thought-provoking—and sheer fun—of any I have attended. The international group of participants included John Flavell, Joachim Wohlwill, Herbert Simon and Allen Newell, Richard Atkinson, Herbert Pick, Noam Chomsky, Ursela Bellugi, David Palermo, Barbel Inhelder, Patrick Suppes, Lee Cronbach, A. V. Zaporozhets, Hanus Papousek, and many others. Each conference was reported in a *Monograph of the Society for Research in Child Development,* and all were published in a single volume, *Cognitive Development in Children* (Social Science Research Council on Intellective Process Research, 1970). In a sense, the conferences were riding the crest of the wave of the cognitive revolution; on the other hand, they were important in strengthening that wave.

Also in 1959 I was awarded a Fulbright Fellowship to the Harvard-Florence Project, a longitudinal study of the development of Italian adolescents directed by H. Bouterline-Young, who practiced medicine and did research in Florence. The opportunity to live there for a year, immersed in the art and culture of that fabulous city, was irresistible. Using the Italian longitudinal data, Young and I coauthored several papers related to some of my earlier investigations. For cultural enrichment, esthetic gratification, and the pleasure of living in a warm, exuberant milieu, that year in Florence could not be surpassed. In addition, the fellowship provided opportunities to visit other countries and to learn firsthand about what was going on in psychology in France, Switzerland, Greece, Poland, and Israel.

Because interest in child development was accelerating and our text was highly regarded and profitable, Conger and I were asked to prepare a second edition. For many reasons we decided to find another coauthor, and we approached Jerome Kagan, who had been a colleague at OSU and a member of the intellective development committee. He accepted primary responsibility for the second (1962) edition, accomplished the task superbly, and continued as coauthor in the subsequent editions.

Not long afterward I wrote a small book entitled *The Psychological Development of the Child* (Mussen, 1963) for *Foundations of Modern Pschology,* a series that gave concise overviews of major areas of psychology. It became popular as a supplementary text in educational psychology courses or as one of several books used in introductory courses. Two revised editions and translations into eighteen other languages were published later.

Upon my return from Europe in 1961 I resumed teaching and research, determined to link my research goals more closely with my humanistic interests. Surprisingly, I found that there were few systematic investigations of the development of *positive* social behavior; little was known about the antecedents of altruism, generosity, tolerance, and cooperation. These characteristics are generally conceptualized as aspects of the superego, also products of identification, and thus research on these variables was related to my earlier work. A grant from the National Institutes of Health enabled me and Eldred Rutherford, a former student then teaching at San Jose State University, to undertake a program of studies on prosocial orientations and behavior, the main topic of my empirical efforts and publications ever since.

My research over the next twenty years, in collaboration with colleagues and research assistants, was centered on the familial and environmental antecedents as well as personality and cognitive correlates of a number of prosocial attributes and responses (e.g., altruism, empathy, generosity, honesty, kindness, cooperation, and helpfulness). Participants in the studies ranged in age from preschool to late adolescence. Levels of prosocial behaviors were assessed by means of observations in naturalistic and structured situations, sociometric questionnaires, teacher and peer ratings, and interviews. Antecedent and personality variables were independently evaluated by child and parental interviews, ratings, projective doll play, and personality tests. Different manifestations of prosocial behavior were found to be significantly positively intercorrelated. Most important, stated in drastically abbreviated form, the findings are convergent in supporting the hypothesis that high levels of prosocial behavior in children are associated with warm, nurturant relationships and strong identifications with prosocial parental models as well as with characteristics such as self-esteem, self-confidence, assertiveness, and relatively low levels of competitiveness.

In the 1960s, my involvement with professional organizations encompassed membership in the Council of Representatives of the American Psychological Association (APA) (Division 7, Developmental), the Executive Committee of Division 7, the Policy and Planning Boards of APA, and the Governing Council of the Society for Research in Child Development (SRCD). From 1963 to 1967 I was a member of a study section of the National Institute of Mental Health, a position that required great expenditures of time and energy but that had the compensatory merits of valuable education about different research perspectives and methods.

To get some hands-on experience in cross-cultural research, I accepted a proposal from the Institute of Social Sciences at the University of Puerto Rico to spend, in the winter of 1964, a sabbatical leave there, investigating whether or not industrialization and, consequently, changes in family life transformed child-rearing practices. During that semester I was also a visiting professor at Harvard, where the teaching load was light, my proseminar students were outstanding, and the new Cognitive Center presented many dynamic seminars and colloquia. Commuting between Cambridge and San Juan made life hectic but very satisfying.

The next academic year (1965–66) was one of extraordinary social unrest at Berkeley, animated by the free speech movement. The campus was endlessly in an uproar, rife with sit-ins, riots, boycotts of classes, picket lines, and invasions by police and the National Guard. Sympathetic as I was with most of the students' protests and demands, I found the relentless (often unpleasant) action exhausting.

Sometime late in 1964 Bill Kessen, a Yale professor and a consultant to John Wiley Publishers, presented me with one of the greatest challenges of my career: editing a new (third) edition of *Carmichael's Manual of Child Psychology* to provide a comprehensive, accurate picture of the *current* state of knowledge in the field. (The second edition had been published in 1954.) With invaluable assistance from an outstanding advisory committee (Jerome Kagan, William Kessen, Eleanor Maccoby, Harold Stevenson, and Sheldon White), we composed a table of contents and a list of experts to invite to write the chapters. Almost all the invitations were enthusiastically accepted, a gratifying indication of what leaders in the field thought about the potential worth of the work. The two-volume edition (Mussen, 1970), became *the* major source book, highly valued by researchers, theorists, and practitioners in all fields related to child development.

By this time, as a member of psychology's "establishment," I spent a delightful academic year (1968–69) as a fellow at the Center for Advanced Study in Behavioral Sciences and in the next few years was elected to the presidencies of the Western Psychological Association (1973–1974) and Division 7 (Developmental) of the APA (1976–1977), in addition to an appointment to the board of directors of the Social Science Research Council (1976–1979). My two presidential addresses, essentially advocacy papers, expressed my strong and enduring belief that psychologists ought to address their research efforts to critical social problems.

From the outset of my appointment at Berkeley I held a part-time appointment as a research associate at the Institute of Human Development, which gave me some release time from teaching for my own research and writing. The institute faced a crisis in 1968 when the director, Brewster Smith, resigned to go to the University of Chicago. The chancellor of the university asked me to serve as acting director for the academic year 1969–70 while a university committee searched for a new permanent director. I was flattered by the request and felt obligated to the institute, so I agreed to do it. Considering the position temporary (and therefore manageable) and blessed with a first-rate secretary, an excellent administrative assistant, and a supportive professional staff, I did not find my administrative duties onerous. Longitudinal research continued, new projects were initiated, over sixty papers and chapters in books were published, and there were no major conflicts among the staff that year.

The year 1970–71 was a sabbatical year. I planned to work on the next edition of the textbook, to resume research, to write reports, and to travel abroad, lecturing and consulting in Kenya, Nigeria, Israel, and, of course, Florence. Meanwhile, the search committee and the ad hoc committee of the university failed to agree on a recommendation for the permanent director. The chancellor then called me, and after expressing admiration for what the institute accomplished during the year and my qualifications, asked me to continue as director, dropping the "Acting" from my title. I agreed to do so after my sabbatical leave. I certainly did not anticipate that my term would last nine more years, but it did!

The impressive professional staff I would direct was indeed an elite group—Nancy Bayley, Marjorie Honzik, Jeanne Block, Diana Baumrind, Jean Macfarlane, Jane Hunt, Wanda Bronson, John Clausen, Guy Swanson, George De Vos, Jonas Langer, Elliot Turiel, Dorothy Eichorn, Glen Elder, Norma Haan, Mary Jones, Henry Maas, Norman Livson, Arlene Skolnick, Leona Bayer, and John Watson. Furthermore, by 1970 the institute's research foci had extended considerably beyond the original, and continuing, longitudinal studies. Those studies were still of central importance, but several researchers had their own longitudinal investigations, and dozens of other projects were conducted (e.g., restandardizing the Bayley Scales, friendship patterns among preschoolers, stability of marriage, drug use, the impact of mental illness on family structure, coping and defense mechanisms, moral development). Many researchers used data in the longitudinal records, supplementing them with new data from their own studies.

In the ten years of my directorship, institute data were the bases of over five hundred publications, including many classic articles as well as original, influential books such as *Elder's Children of the Great Depression* (1974), Jack Block's *Lives Through Time (1971), The Course of Human Development* (Jones, Bayley, Macfarlane & Honzik, 1971), *Present and Past in Middle Life* (Eichorn, et al., 1981), *Coping and Defending* (Haan, 1977), *Growth Diagnosis* (Bayer and Bayley, 1975), *The Origins of Logic* (Langer, 1980), *Vital Involvement in Old Age* (Erikson, 1992), and *American Lives* (Clausen, 1993). Moreover, there was a notable increase in the number of graduate and postdoctoral students getting training in research at the institute. A professional archivist was hired to systematize the vast body of longitudinal data in our files and arrange it for efficient retrieval and computer accessibility, thus facilitating the work of investigators on our staff and in other institutions. In short, the unit continued to be active, vital, creative, and productive.

Because of the renown of the institute, its director is cast into a position of prestige—well beyond anything I ever expected my small destiny to entail. Hardly a week passed without my receiving a request to give a colloquium, consult with governmental or private organizations on research or policy, attend an important conference, or serve on the board of an institution or research center. Although this was the busiest time of my life, I was happy about these requests and consented to many of them.

On the downside were the prices to be paid. Rewarding as it was to work with such a talented group of scholars and researchers, many of my duties were complex and difficult, requiring an inordinate expenditure of time and energy. (Consider this sample: writing research proposals; preparing extensive, detailed annual reports, budget justifications, and letters of recommendation for the advancement of personnel; answering requests of investigators to use institute data in their research; negotiating with the university, which was progressively reducing its financial support; attempting to resolve or arbitrate conflicts—about space, funds, or authorship—between members of the staff.) The greatest personal cost was predictable, drastic reduction in my own research activities, and this happened just as my studies of the antecedents of prosocial behavior were getting under way.

Also, it was disappointing that some of my goals were not fulfilled. For example, I had wished to initiate more multidisciplinary projects, but although a few sociologists did research at the institute, the input from educators, cultural anthropologists, geneticists, and other biological scientists has been minimal. Furthermore, the definition of the field of human development has been appropriately extended to cover the entire life span and members of the original longitudinal studies have reached their sixties and seventies, but the institute has not yet produced much research in aging and adjustment in later life. Finally, there seems to be a marked decline in interest in the original longitudinal studies; only a few Berkeley faculty members have used these data in research recently. The National Institutes of Child Health and Human Development supported institute research well in the past, but their last grant ended in 1978 and recent applications for funds from that organization have not been successful.

After almost ten years, I felt it was time to retire from the directorship but could not do so in good conscience before obtaining funds to continue the key longitudinal studies. Fortunately, a proposal to the MacArthur Foundation was successful and yielded funds for five more years of data collection and analysis. This accomplished, I submitted a letter of resignation and it was accepted by the University administration. Guy E. Swanson, a social psychologist and a member of the institute for many years, became director in July of 1980.

In spite of some disappointments, my accomplishments as director of the institute and as (for lack of a better term) a research facilitator are undoubtedly among my most significant contributions to the discipline. I look back on those ten years without regrets; I would not exchange that experience for anything.

Although very much attenuated, my research and writing activities were not completely extinguished during that ten-year period; in collaboration with students, I conducted and published some research on prosocial behavior. Nancy Eisenberg worked with me in organizing and synthesizing the most pertinent facts and theories in *Roots of Caring, Sharing, and Helping* (1977). The book was well received and has had a seminal influence; it is cited frequently and has fostered further research and conceptualization in that domain. A second edition of the book, *Roots of Prosocial Behavior,* appeared some years later (Eisenberg & Mussen, 1989).

In the autumn of 1980 I spent three months in China as part of a Berkeley–Peking University program of exchange of scholars. My hosts were Professors Xu, Meng, and Jing, and all the members of the psychology department were overwhelmingly friendly and appreciative. With the aid of an excellent translator, I gave a series of fourteen lectures on general and developmental psychology that were well attended by both students and faculty, some of whom have since earned American Ph.D.s. Also, Professor Xu and I began to design an investigation of the relationship between child-rearing practices and prosocial behavior among Chinese children. She spent most of the following academic year in Berkeley, where we completed our research plans, which were subsequently implemented and reported in Chinese and American journals.

January 1981 marked my return to full-time teaching and reactivated research activity. The number of calls to participate in other professional activities (editing, consulting, giving papers at meetings and conferences) did not diminish appreciably; I visited many campuses and research centers in this country and in England, France, Germany, Italy, Tunisia, Japan, India, Taiwan, Malaysia, New Zealand, and Australia.

Wiley had approached me about editing a much-needed new (fourth) edition of *Carmichael's Manual,* now to be called *Handbook of Child Psychology,* in 1978. The field had changed immeasurably and progressed in many new directions since publication of the last edition and there was no comprehensive, balanced publication that reviewed the latest scientific findings, methodological advances, concepts, theories, and specialized domains. I understood the enormity of the task, but, spurred on by respected colleagues, I began to work out plans for a new edition of four volumes edited by recognized authorities: theory and history (Kessen), infancy and biological bases (Haith and Campos), cognitive development (Flavell and Markman), and social and personality development (Hetherington). The editors met to outline a table of contents that would insure coverage of fundamental issues and promote good research. With a distinguished group of contributors, the *Handbook* soon became the standard sourcebook of child psychology (Mussen, 1983). This edition is for me the capstone of my publishing career, and when it was completed I began to consider retirement seriously. In 1985, I retired from the university.

I cannot summarize my professional career succinctly or evaluate it in an objective, unbiased way. In my view, my research productivity has been greater than average, and the findings of much of my research have furthered our comprehension of development. Also, as a research facilitator, I have directly or indirectly helped others to advance the field. But the most noteworthy aspect of my career has probably been my role as an educator, broadly defined—not only as a professor, but as a coauthor of a widely used textbook and the editor of *the* standard sourcebook in the field. Insofar as these have helped raise the level of scholarship and research—and I believe they have—they have made noteworthy contributions.

For me, retirement is a delicious state; I am living one of the fantasies of my youth, that I was destined for a life of cultured leisure. I am happy to be done with large classes but frankly miss the contact with students one has in seminars and in supervising research. My few current professional activities are reading developmental literature, evaluating manuscripts, and consulting on projects designed to promote prosocial behavior. The rest of my time is spent in pleasant family activities, reading a wide range of contemporary literature, studying art history, meeting with friends, visiting art galleries, swimming, hiking, and traveling. It is an easy, contemplative, relatively unproductive and responsibility-free life, and it suits me fine.

Future Directions

This brief section offers opinions rather than facts, a mixture of applause, criticism, and some little homilies.

During the forty-plus years of my professional career, the field of developmental psychology has been radically remade and has achieved greater scientific maturity. Early in its history, the chief occupation was descriptive and normative studies; now the concentration is on the "whys"—underlying processes and mechanisms—of development and change. The volume of research has accelerated enormously: valuable new information accumulated, new questions generated, novel methods and approaches invented, and established concepts and theories have been challenged and revised. All of these changes demonstrate progress in the field, significant and praiseworthy. Yet I believe passionately that developmental psychologists ought to examine (or re-examine) their "sense of problem" and priorities, concentrating their research and theory formulation more directly on social utility; that is, the improvement of the human condition and quality of life. Ours is a field that matters, and we can make it matter more. In the present sad state of the world there is a host of problems that we could, by scientific investigation, help understand and alleviate—for example, child abuse, school dropout rates, drug abuse and addiction, prejudice, emotional maladjustment, the impacts of poverty and homelessness. What interventions are conducive to modification and improvement? What are the potentials and limitations for change in psychological attributes whose genetic bases have been scientifically established—as more of them are likely to be? What conditions promote health and adjustment in the middle and later years?

All these issues require intensive study of real people making real responses in the real world. The behavior, attitudes, motives, cognitions, and environmental conditions associated with social and personal problems—and their amelioration—are intrinsically complex and their complexity must be taken into account in research designs.

The current emphasis on contextualism is salutary because it acknowledges that the phenomena with which we are most concerned are multiply determined. Often, relevant investigations must be multidisciplinary, with inputs from specialists in health, anthropology, economics, sociology, and other disciplines. Statistical techniques such as multiple and partial correlations, as well as path analysis, are available to assess the relative contribution of each antecedent, and undoubtedly even more efficient statistical techniques will be available in the future. Enlarging our armamentarium of research methods to incorporate hermeneutic and narrative techniques, family history, psychobiography, and other creative approaches may also yield important information and ideas.

Contextualism also calls attention to the limitations of generalization from empirical findings, acknowledging that our findings may hold at a particular time or place but not have universal applicability. Contemporary research will not discover universal principles but may suggest better questions for future study.

Developmental psychology is an exciting, expanding field that holds great *promise* of achieving the objective to which it is dedicated, "the promotion of human welfare throughout the life cycle," by systematic investigation of significant issues. By focusing our efforts and expertise on the task, we can *deliver* what is promised: solid knowledge that can be applied by enlightened policymakers and authorities in ways that will greatly benefit individuals and society.

References

Bayer, L. & Bayley, N. (1975). *Growth diagnosis.* Chicago: University of Chicago Press.

Block, J. (in collaboration with Norma Haan). (1971). *Lives through time.* Berkeley: Bancroft.

Clausen, J. A. (1993). *American lives.* New York: The Free Press.

Dollard, J. & Miller, N. E. (1950). *Personality and psychotherapy.* New York: McGraw-Hill.

Eichorn, D. H., Clausen, J. A., Haan, N., Honzik, M. P. & Mussen, P. H. (Eds.). (1981). *Present and past in middle life.* New York: Academic Press.

Eisenberg, N. & Mussen, P. H. (1989). *Roots of prosocial behavior.* New York: Cambridge University Press.

Elder, G. H., Jr. (1974). *Children of the great depression.* Chicago: University of Chicago Press.

Erikson, E. (1992). *Vital involvement in old age.* New York: Norton.

Haan, N. (1977). *Coping and defending.* New York: Academic Press.

Jones, M., Bayley, N., MacFarlane, J. & Honzik, M. (1971). *The course of human development.* New York: Wiley.

Langer, J. (1980). *The origins of logic.* New York: Academic Press.

Mussen, P. H. (1950). Some personality and social factors related to changes in children's attitudes toward Negroes. *Journal of Abnormal and Social Psychology, 45,* 423–441.

Mussen, P. H. (1963). *The psychological development of the child.* Englewood Cliffs, N.J.: Prentice-Hall.

Mussen, P. H. (Ed.). (1970). *Carmichael's manual of child psychology* (3rd ed., 2 vols.). New York: Wiley.

Mussen, P. H. (Ed.). (1983). *Handbook of child psychology* (4th ed., 4 vols.). New York: Wiley.

Mussen, P. H. & Barker, R. (1944). Attitudes towards cripples. *Journal of Abnormal and Social Psychology, 39,* 351–355.

Mussen, P. H. & Eisenberg-Berg, N. (1977). *Roots of caring, sharing, and helping.* San Francisco: W. H. Freeman.

Social Science Research Council on Intellective Processes Research. (1970). *Cognitive development in children.* Chicago: University of Chicago Press.

Whiting, J. W. M. & Child, I. L. (1953). *Child training and personality.* New Haven: Yale University Press.

Representative Publications

Eisenberg-Berg, N. & Mussen P. H. (1978). Empathy and moral development in adolescence. *Developmental Psychology, 14,* 185–186.

Harris, S., Mussen, P. H. & Rutherford, E. (1976). Some cognitive, behavioral, and personality correlates of maturity of moral judgement. *Journal of Genetic Psychology, 128,* 123–135.

Mussen, P. H. (1961). Some antecedents and consequents of masculine sex-typing in adolescent boys. *Psychological Monographs, 75,* 1–24.

Mussen P. H. (1977). Choices, regrets, and lousy models. (Presidential address, Division 7, APA). *Newsletter of the Division on Developmental Psychology.*

Mussen P. H. & Beytagh, L. (1969). Industrialization, child-rearing practices and children's personality. *Journal of Genetic Psychology, 115,* 195–216.

Mussen P. H., Bouterline-Young, H., Gaddini, R. & Morante, L. (1963). The influence of father-son relationships on adolescent personality and attitudes. *Journal of Child Psychology and Psychiatry, 4,* 3–16.

Mussen, P. H., Conger, J. J. & Kagan, J. (1963). *Child development and personality* (rev. ed). New York: Harper and Row.

Mussen P. H. & Distler, L. (1959). Masculinity, identification, and father-son relationships. *Journal of Abnormal and Social Psychology, 59,* 350–356.

Mussen P. H. & Distler, L. (1960). Child rearing antecedents of masculine identification in kindergarten boys. *Child Development, 31,* 89–100.

Mussen P. H., Honzik, M. P. & Eichorn, D. H. (1982). Early adult antecedents of life satisfactions at age 70. *Journal of Gerontology, 37,* 316–322.

Mussen, P. H. & Jones, M. C. (1957). Self conceptions, motivations and interpersonal attitudes of late- and early-maturing boys. *Child Development, 28,* 243–256.

Mussen, P. H. & Rosenzweig, M. R. (1973). *Psychology: An introduction.* Lexington, Mass.: D. C. Heath.

Mussen P. H. & Rutherford, E. (1961). Effects of aggressive cartoons on children's aggressive play. *Journal of Abnormal and Social Psychology, 62,* 461–464.

Mussen P. H. & Rutherford, E. (1963). Parent-child relations and parental personality in relation to young children's sex-role preferences. *Child Development, 34,* 589–606.

Mussen P. H., Rutherford, E., Harris, S. & Keasey, C. B. (1970). Honesty and altruism among pre-adolescents. *Developmental Psychology, 3,* 169–194.

Mussen P. H., Sullivan, L. B. & Eisenberg-Berg, N. (1977). Changes in political-economic attitudes during adolescence. *Journal of Genetic Psychology, 130,* 69–76.

Mussen, P. H. & Wyszynski, A. B. (1952). Personality and political participation. *Human Relations, 5,* 65–82.

Rutherford E., & Mussen, P. (1968). Generosity in nursery school boys. *Child Development, 39,* 755–765.

Scodel, A. & Mussen, P. (1953). Social perceptions of authoritarians and non-authoritarians. *Journal of Abnormal and Social Psychology, 48,* 181–184.

10

Seymour Wapner

Although a few years ago I gave some thought to autobiography with respect to my recent work in environmental psychology (Wapner, 1990), the invitation to contribute to the present volume served as a trigger to make me focus even more sharply on my relationship to developmental psychology. I take as my task tracing the people, places, and events that guided me in adopting the holistic, developmental, systems-oriented perspective that I currently hold (e.g., Wapner, 1977, 1978, 1981, 1987a, 1991, 1992; Wapner & Demick, 1991a).[1] Such a journey must go back to family background, formal education, and professional career.

Family Background

I was born in Brooklyn, New York, on November 20, 1917, the son of warm, growth-fostering parents. When I was twelve years old my father passed away four days after the onset of a sudden, misdiagnosed illness. This traumatic event, which was not prevented by my deep, intense prayers, had a profound impact on moving me atheistically to a religion restricted to conformity to high ethical standards—a position I recognize as guiding my experience and action over these many years since my father's unexpected death. He—an excellent craftsman, an upholsterer by trade and owner of a furniture and decorating business—instilled my interest in doing things with my hands and my head, thereby fostering my ongoing aesthetic interest in creating sculpture, toying with the possibility of a career in architecture, and enjoying the challenge of fixing broken things. My mother, a loving, good-humored, tender person, instilled my interest in doing things with my heart and my head; fostered and took joy in my individual development; nurtured my respect for, interest in, and sensitivity to other people; cultivated in me the pleasure of doing creative work; infused in me my love for a job well done; fostered my skill of handling multiple tasks simultaneously and my capacity for appreciating the enjoyment derived from completing the smallest chore to the largest project that was initiated.

This home background—including the empathic support of an older brother, two older sisters, and an adoring younger sister—served well in helping me, not yet a teenager, to cope with the sudden death of my father, and despite the Depression of the 1930s to take on an attitude of "the glass is always half full."

A central ethos of the household was created by my brother Sidney, ten years older than I, who took over as head of the household after my father died. He had a group of intellectually oriented fun-loving friends who frequented our home, enjoyed my mother's hospitality, warmth, and food, and made me forget my "younger brother" status by bringing me into their philosophically oriented conversations, their not-too-serious chess games, and their general camaraderie. Despite the Depression, it was always clear that I was headed for college, and indeed the seed was planted by one of Sid's friends, who was attending graduate school at the time, that the academic life had a number of features of the good life.

Formal Education

My interests in academic life were clearly reinforced by attending Boys High School in Brooklyn, which had an unusual and outstanding faculty, many of whom had Ph.D.s. It was known for capturing awards in mathematics and other prizes when the New York City public school system was in its heyday.

When I started college, family pressure to consider the possibility of medical school brought me into early contact with the physical and biological sciences, for which I have been ever grateful. This work was buttressed by other attempts to obtain a general education, which brought me in contact with philosophy, English literature, languages, and other areas, including psychology.

My first yearlong college course in psychology, taken with E. R. Henry in my junior year, served as a precipitating event in shaping my career. I was quick to realize that psychology was an area that naturally meshed with my general interests and talents, that opened new challenges for me, and that was a field in which I was able to be creative and feel completely at home. It should not be surprising, then, that my earlier extensive work leading to a major in biology became coupled with a major in psychology through my devoting three-quarters of my program in my senior year to psychology. I took three yearlong courses: one in social psychology with Malcolm Campbell that introduced me to Lewinian theory, one in test and measurements with Edwin Henry, and the third in physiological psychology with Louis William Max.

My interest in a holistic, organismic analysis of human functioning traces back to Max's (1935) exciting work on the motor theory of consciousness that is exemplified by his studies of hearing and speaking people and deaf mutes. He found that the muscle action potentials from body parts carried out in an imagined act were also present in the action currents recorded from arm muscles of deaf mutes when dreaming or solving abstract problems. This reinforced my view that the linkage between biological changes—manifest in action potentials from muscles—and psychological phenomena such as thought processes, or more generally, the problem of the linkages between the biological and psychological levels of integration, was a significant problem of great interest that spoke to the holistic functioning of the human being.

Max's course also involved a laboratory experience—an observational study of the rat's emotional behavior (measured by place and amount of micturition and defecation) while exploring an open field. This was modeled on the study by Calvin Hall (1934) and on Norman R. F. Maier's research at the University of Michigan on abnormal behavior in the rat, for which he received the American Association for the Advancement of Science (AAAS) award in 1938 (Maier, 1939).[2] My biological, experimentally oriented background undoubtedly made Maier's approach of analyzing abnormal behavior in the rat in paradigmatic situations involving conflict and frustration extremely attractive. This experience rapidly attenuated any vague, unformed thoughts of medical school and intensified my powerful interest in doing graduate work in psychology. The next step was self-evident. I wanted to work with Professor Maier on this problem. Accordingly, I applied for admission and was accepted into the Ph.D. program at the University of Michigan.

The emphasis on the holistic/organismic levels of integration approach was advanced by my work as a graduate student with Norman R. F. Maier on the analysis of abnormal behavior in the rat by studying the impact of situations involving conflict and frustration for the rat, and on my Ph.D. dissertation, conducted under Maier's supervision and influence, which involved the impact of brain injury on what the animal learned in a discrimination task assessed by the use of equivalence of stimuli (Wapner, 1944). This work on a research problem in psychobiology brought me in contact, at the University of Michigan, with some very special biologists, including Elizabeth Crosby (cf., Ariens Kappers, Huber & Crosby, 1936), who was an outstanding scholar in comparative neuroanatomy focusing on phylogenetic development, and, in particular, Charles Judson Herrick (1949), who made significant contributions to the conceptualization of levels of organization/integration. Moreover, my work on abnormal behavior and equivalence of stimuli in the rat moved me into research on physiology and behavior with J. W. Bean of the University of Michigan Medical School. Our collaboration led to studies on the effects of exposure to oxygen of high barometric pressure on such higher psychological functions of the nervous system as maze learning and retention (Bean & Wapner, 1943; Bean, Wapner & Siegfried, 1945).

In the then-small incipient Marquis University of Michigan psychology department there were, in addition to Norman Maier, a number of outstanding faculty. Among them, John F. Shepard had a very positive effect on my development. Shepard in his courses Advanced Systematic and Comparative Psychology, in his supervision of Ph.D. dissertations, and in a personal way made his impact on psychology through his graduate students rather than from his relatively sparse but significant publications. This is evident in the careers of two of his prize students, Norman Maier and Ted Schneirla, whose treatment of animal psychology was in keeping with the comparative approach ingredient in Shepard's teaching. Moreover, Shepard conducted ingenious experimental studies—for instance, on the cues used by ants in construction of their trails (Shepard, 1911) and on reasoning in rats manifested in a maze-learning situation (cf., Shepard, 1933), which served, respectively, as the bases for Schneirla's (e.g., 1929, 1934) classic studies on behavior of ants and Maier's (e.g., 1929, 1931, 1960) programmatic investigation of reasoning and other problem areas.

It is noteworthy that my exposure to Maier and Schneirla's (1935) analysis of animal behavior brought me into early contact with an approach to the problem of development that Schneirla (1957) later formulated more systematically. He focused on development as linked to maturation (consisting of growth of the physiological systems and differentiation of the structural features of the organism), which occurs in a supportive environmental context. These organismic/holistic notions and the conception of development as a function of both maturation and the organism's environmental context were in keeping with Shepard's teaching and experimental work: for example, the studies he initiated on the development of the pecking response in chickens (Padilla, 1930; Shepard & Breed, 1913).

Other people in the stimulating Ann Arbor environment included my fellow graduate students in psychology[3] and others from related fields.[4] These people played a large role in enhancing my concern to focus on the concept of levels of organization/integration as including the biological, psychological, as well as the sociocultural level; on the role of multiple perspectives in shaping a research problem; and on utilizing multiple diversely grounded methodologies that were relevant to the particular research problem.

Perhaps the most potent event at Michigan, which had very powerful impact on my thinking, my research, and indeed my future academic career, was meeting a very special person, Heinz Werner, internationally known for his creative, broadly conceived approach to the problems of development.[5]

My introduction to Heinz Werner and some of his work took place at a departmental colloquium during the academic year 1940–41 at the University of Michigan. The presentation dealt with his conceptualization of a relationship between motion and motion perception (Werner, 1945). He used the vicariousness concept—the notion of substitutability of functioning, in this case the substitution of functioning at the psychological level for functioning at the level of motor activity—to account for the relationship between motion perception and motor activity. I was highly impressed with this example of Werner's capacity to attack a significant problem by providing an ingenious marriage between a theoretical conceptualization and an empirical study. The vicariousness concept, which was later incorporated in the sensory-tonic field theory of perception (e.g., Werner & Wapner, 1949, 1952) reinforced my interest, first stimulated as an undergraduate by Max's (1935) work linking motor activity and mental processes in the important problem of relationships between levels of organization/integration. The seeds were planted for taking advantage of future opportunities to become better acquainted and indeed to work with this prestigious, creative scientist.

My primordial relationship with Werner was further advanced with respect to another feature of his conceptualization—his concern with developmental analysis—by a personally significant event, namely, my presentation of a paper at the Michigan Academy of Science describing my Ph.D. dissertation (Wapner, 1944), which was conducted under the sponsorship of Professor Maier. As already noted, the study was concerned with a qualitative analysis of learning in the partially decorticated rat. In contrast to the studies conducted at that time that were concerned with the reinforcement history that made for mastery of a discrimination, the central concern of the study was to focus on experience. That is, the objective was to determine "what" the animal learned when a discrimination was mastered and how this differed for the partially decorticated rat as compared with the normal rat.

Using Klüver's (1931) method of equivalent stimuli in a Lashley jumping stand, it was found that for rats, a learned positive response to a card with a large black circle on a gray ground and an avoidance of a card with a small black circle on a gray ground was made on the basis of response "darker than." This response to the "darker card"—rather than to the card with a larger black circle, as humans typically saw the situation—increased after brain injury. This finding provided the seeming contradiction that a rat suffering brain injury responded to a greater degree in *terms of a relationship* than did normal rats.

It was of great interest to Professor Werner, who was in the audience, that I introduced a developmental interpretation of these findings using his notion of "analogous processes" (Werner, 1957a), which postulates three levels of abstraction: namely, relationship on a sensorimotor level (as obtains with normal and brain-injured rats and in transposition experiments with chicks); on a predominantly perceptual level; and on the most advanced level of abstraction, which consists of a mental activity where the parts of a situation are separated from the whole and these detached qualities are experienced in isolated fashion (Wapner, 1944).

During and after my presentation, Werner mentioned his approval of the study and the interpretation of the findings. My interest in the developmental aspect of Wernerian theory was reinforced both with respect to the notion of a developmental analysis being applicable to understanding the so-called regression that obtains under neuropathological insult, and to the principle of analogous functioning that may represent different processes underlying formally parallel achievements (see Werner's classic 1937 paper on process and achievement).

This event rounded out my acquaintanceship with the Wernerian perspective insofar as my earlier contact with the "organismic" aspect in Werner's colloquium dealing with motor activity and motion perception was now complemented by close contact with the "developmental" aspect of the Wernerian approach. Moreover, it undoubtedly served to foster a communal spirit between us and provided the background for initiating our joint work later on.[6]

Professional Career

University of Rochester

Having completed my Ph.D. at Michigan in the early fall of 1943, the question was, What sort of job to help in the war effort could I obtain? I had been classified as 2A, occupational deferment, by my draft board in the Bedford-Stuyvesent area of Brooklyn on the grounds that graduate school prepared me for a special military assignment during World War II. Although my long-term goal was an academic job, I was fortunate to obtain a position at the University of Rochester office of the Civil Aeronautics Administration, which was involved in the selection and training of aircraft pilots for the army, navy, and air forces.

This position was very effective in shaping my career in a number of ways by providing the opportunity to have contact with many well-known and interesting psychologists, including Jack Dunlap, John Flanagan, Morris Viteles, and Phil Rulon; to work with such special people as Len Kogan, Henry Odbert, David Bakan, Leon Festinger, Ed Ewart, Bob Walker, Morey Wantman, and David Tiedeman; to learn about the research of Witkin utilizing field dependence-independence as a selection instrument for aircraft pilots; to introduce me to the use of IBM machines for analysis of large amounts of data; to assess my ability and interest in administration when I took over directorship of the office after Odbert left; to follow Maier's dictum, "Always continue to do research no matter what the context," by working with Festinger, after hours, on studies on decision time and level of aspiration; to learn how to fly as a means of better understanding the job for which we were to carry out selection and training studies; to teach a summer-session course on learning and thereby find out how much I enjoyed teaching; to find, in keeping with my holistic orientation, that an elementaristic analysis of flight instruments to assess the reliability and validity of a flight inspector's ratings proved far less meaningful, reliable, or valid than an inspector's holistic assessment that could take into account the entire context of a flight test (Walker, Wapner, Bakan & Ewert, 1946).

This professional experience was complemented by my personal good fortune of meeting a very, very special person, Lorraine "Rainie" Gallant, through Julie Youngner, whom I knew from my Michigan days. Both were working at the Manhattan Project (in the medical section of the Atomic Energy Commission) of the University of Rochester Medical School. With the war having come to a close in 1945, I began thinking about a teaching job. I had the good fortune to be offered an assistant professorship at Brooklyn College. I proposed to Rainie by telling her that I accepted the teaching position at Brooklyn College and wanted her to join me in that venture as part of our life venture together. Happily, she said yes.

Brooklyn College

Our move to Brooklyn College was exciting despite the postwar lack of housing and especially because of the outstanding faculty that included such people as

Heinz Werner, Herman Witkin, Abraham Maslow, Herb Hyman, Dan Katz, Edward Girden, and Burton Fisher.

My stay at Brooklyn College was so full of exciting activity and new challenges that for many years I thought I had been there a dozen rather than the two years (1946–48) I actually spent. I applied for and was awarded a grant from the American Philosophical Society to continue the animal work conducted for my dissertation. My friendship and collaboration with Hy Witkin was very important—we joked about being academic cousins since he was a student of Schneirla and I was a student of Maier. Witkin's work reinforced my predilection toward holism insofar as it was based on the assumption that personality characteristics were manifest in the entire range of operations of the organism, including perception as well as other cognitive and affective processes. Moreover, our collaboration involved contact with a number of outstanding scholars dealing with broad aspects of human functioning. We collaborated on a major research project (Witkin, et al., 1954), which had a significant influence and relationship with some of my more current research (see Wapner, 1991; Wapner & Demick, 1991a, 1991b). The concern with holistic analysis was further enhanced by Alex Novikoff (1945a, 1945b), a friend of Witkin and a member of the biology department, who wrote a classic piece clearly articulating the levels of integration notion.

Further, during the academic year 1946–47, there was a significant trend developing in psychology—the "new look" in perception—linked to a particular event that fostered my collaboration with Werner. I remember very vividly one afternoon when Jerry Bruner and George Klein visited with Witkin and me in Witkin's laboratory to talk about setting up a conference at the forthcoming meeting of the American Psychological Association (APA) devoted to a symposium on the new look that focused on including subjective factors as well as autochthonous factors as determinants of perception (cf., Blake & Ramsey, 1951; Bruner & Klein, 1960; Zener, 1949a, 1949b). The planned symposium, Personal and Social Factors in Perception, that took place at the 1948 meetings of the APA in Denver involved presentations by such outstanding scholars as Heinz Werner, Hans Wallach, Jerome Bruner and Leo Postman, George Klein and Herbert Schlesinger, Edward Tolman, Gardner Murphy, and Egon Brunswik.

Prior to the occurrence of this symposium, and in keeping with our mutual interests, Werner and I began thinking about a program of research that addressed the problem of understanding perception from an organismic, holistic perspective that took into account both subjective and autochthonous factors. Our approach, which we named the sensory-tonic field theory of perception (Werner & Wapner, 1949), was born at Brooklyn College; its first formulation was completed at Clark University during 1948 and published in one of the two volumes (Zener, 1949a, 1949b) that incorporated the Denver symposium and other theoretical and empirical studies by a number of investigators.

My experience at Brooklyn College played a powerful role in shaping the rest of my career. The experience informed me that I thoroughly enjoyed teaching (even though in that undergraduate context it involved five three-hour courses per week). It involved me in three research endeavors: the completion of my animal research; participation in the major project on field dependence-independence, including its development (Rainie also worked on the Witkin project as a research assistant); and the beginning conversations with Werner about developing the sensory-tonic field theory of perception. Additionally, my experience at Brooklyn College gave me a further taste of administration, now of a psychology department (Dan Katz, chair at Brooklyn, was offered a position at Michigan and I was asked to serve as acting chair of the department at Brooklyn while he was on leave for the year 1947–48).

The two years at Brooklyn College sharpened and strengthened my views that teaching is a two-way street, where professor learns from student as student learns from professor, and that it is a great pleasure to support the growth and development of a student. Moreover, I found that it is possible to carry out a heavy load of scholarly activity while at the same time being involved in a heavy teaching load, and indeed while carrying out administrative duties as well. I also reinforced my views that the significant features of the job of department chair are to foster the development of the faculty so that its members' statuses as teachers and scholars is maximized, and to support the institution as well as the department with which one is associated. Finally, a number of principles that underpin my personal philosophy became focal: follow the Wapner twenty-four-hour, forty-eight-hour, or seventy-two-hour rule to delay before taking action, depending on how critical the issue; integrate home, work, and recreational worlds (though this may not be easy), for each, like the totality, is very special; enjoy maximizing your potential, whatever it happens to be; and always remember that the glass is half full.

Despite the positive features of the Brooklyn College experience, there was still an unfulfilled desire to work with graduate students. By January of my second year at Brooklyn College, an extraordinary opportunity arose. I was approached by Howard Jefferson, president of Clark University—a truly extraordinary, brilliant, warm person deeply concerned with his own field of philosophy—about the possibility of an associate professorship in the Department of Psychology and Education.

Heinz Werner was already at Clark, and the prospect of working with him to rebuild psychology was an exciting challenge I could not refuse. Thus, in the summer of 1948, Rainie and I moved to New England.

This move turned out to be more than a professional venture, for our two wonderful children, Jeff and Amy, were born in Worcester. Jeff, after receiving his Ph.D. in clinical psychology, is now a school psychologist for the New York City public schools and has a clinical practice in Westchester. Amy, trained as a dance therapist, divides her time between practice, consulting on dance therapy in Japan, working in an educational setting, and caring for her new husband, Peter, and five wonderful children—Jacob, Jenny, and Noah, now joined by Mirah and Ella.

Clark University

There were a number of challenges soon after arrival at Clark. I was given the choice of taking three thousand dollars to fix up the disheveled and almost nonexistent laboratory or waiting for Jonas Clark Hall to be rebuilt. My decision to renovate was a good one, for the rebuilding of Jonas Clark Hall was finally started more than forty years later. I was also asked to chair an executive committee of the then Department of Psychology and Education, which eventually led to a decision to split the department in two, with Vernon Jones as chair of education and Werner as chair of psychology.

The task of the revitalization of the psychology department was initiated. Critical in the development were various research programs and the creation of developmental, clinical, experimental, and other training programs. Revitalization was characterized by a very lively, exciting context, including such outstanding events as Anna Freud's visit to celebrate Clark's sixtieth anniversary. Her father, Sigmund Freud, made his only visit to America during Clark's twentieth anniversary in 1909. Also notable was the establishment of the Institute of Human Development in 1956, later (after Werner's retirement in 1964) renamed the Heinz Werner Institute of Developmental Psychology and most recently (1986) renamed the Heinz Werner Institute for Developmental Analysis.

I was part of the revitalization in a number of ways, including as a teacher of undergraduate and graduate students; as administrative support person for Werner in his position as chair; as chair of the department for twenty-six years (from the time of Werner's retirement in 1960 through 1986); and as investigator in three major research programs, namely, the organismically oriented sensory-tonic field theory of perception, the organismic-developmental program in cognition, and its more recent, holistic, developmental, and systems-oriented version. Let us consider these research programs, which of course are closely tied to student activity, the development of my own thinking, and some possible relations between professional and personal lives.

Sensory-Tonic Field Theory of Perception. In developing sensory-tonic field theory, the first, central question we asked was, How can we understand how essentially alien factors, such as sensory on the one side and motivational or organismic on the other, could interact? For example, if it is true that the size of a coin is perceived as bigger when it is highly valued (Bruner & Goodman, 1947), then simply assuming that the two interact is not enough. From the perspective of individuals who make a distinction between process and achievement (cf., Werner, 1937) and are devoted to process analysis, simply stating that an interaction occurs poses the further key question of *how* an interaction between so-called objective and subjective factors can be mediated. For Werner and myself, the solution of the problem of interaction rested on the grounds that the two sets of factors appeared to be heterogeneous only superficially; rather, they were of essentially the same fundamental nature. It was assumed that no matter how diverse the source of stimulation to the organism, underlying it was the common feature that it was fundamentally sensory-tonic in nature. Any stimulation, whether it comes through extero-, proprio-, or intero-ceptors is essentially a sensory-tonic entity. Thus, for example, visual factors on the one hand and valuational or motivational factors on the other interact because fundamentally they are of the same nature: That is, the unit of interaction is a sensory-tonic unit; an interaction of vectorially characterized "sensory-tonic states" is involved. Thus, organismic factors are part and parcel of every percept. That is, perception was characterized as a relationship between objective stimuli in the environment and the ongoing subjective state of the organism defined by sensory-tonic states, specifically affective, valuative, and neuromuscular. Given these and other basic assumptions,[7] a powerful research program on perception and related problems based on this theoretical conception flourished.[8]

The Organismic-Developmental Program in Cognition. The more we progressed in the theoretical analysis of perceptual functioning and in the accumulation of empirical data, the more we felt that our handling of the problems of perception was restrictive insofar as it did not provide a framework for embedding perception in the wider totality of organismic behavior.[9] Our subsequent thinking included treating aspects of cognition other than perception as well as undertaking a developmental analysis of a broad variety of cognitive processes.

The expansion toward treating cognition more generally, including perception, involved the introduction of two principles. First, the notion of *functional equivalence* of stimulation; namely, that different forms of stimulation applied to the organism make for the similarity of end product. For example, visual perception of verticality is affected equivalently by auditory stimulation and direct muscular change (see Werner & Wapner, 1952). Second, the complementary assumption of *vicarious channelization* of sensory processes: Sensory processes may come to expression in terms of muscular, visceral, ideational, and perceptual activity. This is exemplified by studies conducted in the Clark laboratories demonstrating that the introduction of motor involvement decreases perceptual movement as measured by verbal responses to pictorial material (Krus, Werner & Wapner, 1953), and by studies demonstrating that the restriction of motor activity is linked to a greater degree of autokinetic motion (Goldman, 1953). Other studies demonstrated an inverse relation between motor discharge and internalized (e.g., imaginal) activity (Hurwitz, 1954; Kruger, 1954; Misch, 1954).

Our most systematic turn toward developmental psychology occurred when we systematically undertook an empirical and theoretical analysis of the *ontogenetic development* of perception (Wapner & Werner, 1957). There we attempted to infer developmental change in perception from the orthogenetic principle, which states that development proceeds in terms of change from dedifferentiation to an increase in differentiation and hierarchic integration (Werner, 1957a,

1957b; Werner & Kaplan, 1956, 1963). In keeping with sensory-tonic field theory that treated perception in terms of object-organism relationships, differentiation had meaning for us, for example in terms of differentiation of self (body) and environment (object). Hierarchic integration, for example, had bearing on such important problems as that of hierarchically ordered developmental levels of cognitive functioning (e.g., sensorimotor, perceptual, conceptual), including the vicarious shift from the sensorimotor to the perceptual level. The relation among these levels of functioning was not restricted to ontogenesis because the organismic-developmental viewpoint adopted transcends the boundaries of ontogenesis (cf., Werner, 1957a, 1957b; Werner & Kaplan, 1956, 1963; Wapner, 1964, 1966).

A significant step in studying ontogenesis in terms of "object-organism" relationships was a study based on 237 males and females between the ages of six and nineteen years. This study threw light on the development of and on mechanisms involved in perceptual constancy and on the ontogenesis of a stable framework and world. It was found that at early stages of development, lack of differentiation between subject and object was manifest in two forms, *egocentricity* (e.g., proximal position interpreted in terms of body position) and *stimulus boundedness* (inordinate responsivity and adaptation to stimuli), which make for lack of "thing-constancy." Objective constancy is presumed to emerge when these two factors become clearly articulated and related to each other in a systematic fashion. These findings, as well as others relevant to the problem of individual differences in the development of a stable frame of reference, are described in detail in Wapner and Werner (1957).

When this ontogenetic study was conducted, both points of view—sensory-tonic field theory of perception and comparative developmental theory—guided the research. They were largely left as parallel frameworks with the relations between them unarticulated. An integration began to emerge after Werner and Kaplan (Kaplan, 1966, 1967; Werner, 1957a, 1957b; Werner & Kaplan, 1963) systematized organismic-developmental theory. Sensory-tonic field theory formulations were integrated, especially with the efforts of Leonard Cirillo, within the broader framework of organismic-developmental theory (see Wapner & Cirillo, 1973; and Wapner, Cirillo & Baker, 1969, 1971 for details).

Simultaneous with and before the incorporation of sensory-tonic theory within organismic-development theory, studies were initiated dealing with cognitive operations other than perception. For example, studies concerned with learning demonstrated that sensorimotor operations were characteristic of children's learning whereas conceptual operations were characteristic of adults (Clarkson, 1961; Kempler, 1964). In keeping with this notion, Wapner & Rand (1968) found that when learning a series of lights flashing in a horizontal array of boxes, the older the subjects (ranging in age from eight to eighteen years), the more likely they were to give attention to organization of the series as a whole; younger subjects were more likely simply to rehearse, reiterate, or identify the elements comprising the series, giving little attention to relations between elements.

Rand and Wapner (1969) also studied ontogenetic changes (seven to nineteen years) in locating a simple figure in a complex configuration. There was evidence to suggest that there is greater difficulty in younger age groups insofar as the appearance of the parts change as a function of their embeddedness in a strong gestalt. That is, they do not have a hierarchically organized percept in which parts and wholes exist simultaneously, as obtains with adults.

Another study by Rand, Wapner, Werner, and McFarland (1963) concerned a detailed functional analysis of behavior on the Stroop Color-Word Test with subjects ranging from six to seventeen years of age. From detailed study of the children's verbal behavior on the test, seven behavioral categories were defined representing deviations from an ideal performance. The frequency of occurrence of these behaviors was computed for all of the age groups tested. The function of each of these behaviors was discussed in relation to two sets of processes presumed to underlie performance: the process of *identification* of the appropriate aspect of the stimulus item and the process of *serial organization* of the responses. Overall achievement was found to be underpinned by different processes in children differing in age. For example, greater frequency of such identification responses as inappropriate color responses was more frequent in the younger age groups. Although inserted linguistic words or phrases decreased with increase in age, inserted nonlinguistic utterances increased.

The Holistic, Developmental, Systems-Oriented Perspective.   Although the integration of organismic and developmental theory accounted for considerable progress in the analysis of a wide variety of aspects of cognitive functioning, a further step occurred with the systematic introduction of the environmental context.

The importance of the environmental context in understanding human functioning was clearly recognized by Werner in his early descriptions of comparative-developmental theory, in our conceptualization in the sensory-tonic field theory of perception, in organismic-developmental theory, and in our reformulation of sensory-tonic theory as a exemplar of organismic-developmental theory. But it was not until a number of colleagues and I became strongly concerned with environmental psychology that the role of the environmental context formally entered in the formulation of organismic-developmental theory, which is now characterized as a holistic, developmental, systems-oriented perspective. How did this change come about?

The precursors underpinning the change are clearly stated in Wapner, Cirillo, and Baker's (1969) reformulation of sensory-tonic theory: "From the organismic-developmental viewpoint organisms and their environmental settings constitute systems which may be analyzed and compared with one another in formal terms" (p. 493). At this time, other general factors underpinning potential change were the immediate environmental context of psychology and the general social context of the late 1960s.

In the spring of 1956, William Ittelson, Jerome Bruner, and I presented some of the research each of us were involved in at the time at a conference on clinical psychology at the University of Kansas (Wapner, 1956). I had an opportunity to become more deeply acquainted with and interested in Ittelson's (1970) analysis of perception, which was grounded in Dewey and Bentley's (1949) transactionalist position (cf., Ames, 1951; Ittelson & Cantril, 1954). It rejected the separation between perception and action, pointing to the reciprocal relations between them as the event to be studied. These concerns were of interest to me, along with Ittelson's crucial role in developing the subfield of environmental psychology; all operated as powerful factors in bringing into sharper focus my interest in the environmental context[10] as a critical factor to be analyzed in the attempt to understand the development of human functioning.

Simultaneously, the general cultural context, namely, the university upheaval and powerful period of student unrest of the late 1960s, fed my interest in the impact of the sociocultural context on behavior. Indeed, a one-year term of service, 1969–1970, as first provost of Clark University triggered my serious concern with research problems involving transactions (experience and action) of the person with the environment. My involvement was fully with the world of the student and others in their everyday life situations. We were witness to potent change in people and their lives. Developmental change, both regressive and progressive, was striking. The "world out there" as a potential laboratory became more vivid. The highly controlled conditions of the darkroom laboratory were neglected but not abandoned. Work on such problems as the microgenetic development of the cognitive organization of the university environment by freshmen following their transition to university life (cf., Schouela, Steinberg, Leveton & Wapner, 1980) replaced studies of ontogenetic development of space perception assessed in the highly controlled conditions of a darkroom with its tilting chairs and luminous rods.

The immediate Clark University context, that is, the linkage between geography and psychology, promoted great interest in problems of environment and behavior. The union between psychology and geography was formally initiated by Robert W. Kates, geographer, and Joachim F. Wohlwill, psychologist, in a special issue of the *Journal of Social Issues* on the topic "Man's Response to the Physical Environment," which they coedited (Kates & Wohlwill, 1966). A very active, highly productive interdisciplinary group developed, as described in the special Clark University issue of the *Journal of Environmental Psychology* coedited by Canter and Craik (1987).[11]

My involvement is described in this issue in the piece titled "1970–1972: Years of Transition" (Wapner, 1987b). Central to my empirical and theoretical advances in developmental and environmental psychology was my collaboration, initiated in 1970, with Saul Cohen and Bernard Kaplan. Cohen was concerned with extending behavioral analysis to geography, Kaplan at that time had given some thought to links between architecture and psychology, and I had been thinking about the role of the environment in human functioning. The paper we wrote on transactions of persons-in-environments (Wapner, Kaplan & Cohen, 1973) set the stage for my being involved in a paradigmatic long-term research program on critical transitions of persons-in-environments, or more generally, transactions (experience and action) of persons-in-environments. This program of research continues to develop both theoretically and empirically (e.g., Wapner, 1978, 1981, 1987a, 1987b, 1988, 1991; Wapner & Demick, 1990) with the collaboration of many colleagues and students from here and abroad.[12]

Before describing this developmental program of research and others, it seems appropriate to summarize briefly the main theoretical and methodological assumptions of the perspective and then consider some work done under its aegis as well as the open problems it poses for developmental study.

Basic to the formulation of the holistic, developmental, systems-oriented perspective is the *transactionalist* assumption that the *person-in-environment*, rather than the person, should serve *as the unit of analysis*. Both person and environment are characterized with respect to three levels of integration/organization: With respect to the person, these include the *physical/biological* (e.g., health), *psychological/intrapersonal* (e.g., self-concept), and the *sociocultural* (e.g., role) aspects; with respect to the environment, these include the *physical* (e.g., natural and built), *interpersonal* (e.g., friends, relatives), and the *sociocultural* (e.g., rules, regulations) aspects. *Transactions* of the person with the environment include both *action and experience* (knowing including sensorimotor, perceptual, and conceptual processes; feeling; and valuing). The person-in-environment system is assumed to operate *holistically*, to exhibit *multiple intentionality, directedness toward goals* that can be achieved by a variety of instrumentalities, and *capacity to plan*. Underpinned by the *constructivist* assumption that the person actively shapes his or her environment, both *dynamic* (means-ends relationships) and *structural* (part-whole relationships) analyses are employed.

The developmental conceptualization assumes that person-in-environment system states are developmentally orderable in terms of the *orthogenetic principle* (Kaplan, 1966; Wapner, 1987a; Werner 1957a, 1957b; Werner & Kaplan, 1956), which defines development in terms of the degree of organization of the system: Development proceeds from a dedifferentiated to a differentiated and hierarchically integrated system state. This encompasses a shift from *interfused to subordinated functions*, from *syncretic to discrete* mental phenomena, from *diffuse to articulate* structures, from *labile to stabile*, and *rigid to flexible* modes of coping (cf., Kaplan, 1966). Moreover, the change toward the more advanced person-in-environment state is assumed to involve (1) greater salience of positive affective states; (2) diminution of isolation, anonymity, helplessness, depersonalization, and entrapment; (3) coordination of long-term and short-term planning; and (4) optimal use of available instrumentalities to accomplish personal goals. In short, the developmental ideal involves movement toward an integrated unity of the person's overt and covert actions (Wapner, 1987a, pp. 1444–1445).

This formal, organizational characterization of development permits applicability to a number of developmental series, including not only *ontogenesis* and old age, but also *microgenesis* (e.g., the course of development of a percept or concept), *pathogenesis* (both organic and functional pathology), and other developmentally orderable series such as sleeping-waking.

There is a concern with characterizing and understanding underlying conditions and the process by means of which transformation of the person-in-environment system is advanced, arrested, or reversed. A central problem concerns the process underpinning the relationship between experience (e.g., wanting to do something) and carrying out that desire into action. Both idiographic and nomothetic methods are involved, including phenomenological, naturalistic observational and experimental methodologies that are employed depending on the specific nature of the problem.

Some Current Research Problems

My research endeavors over the last two decades have been strongly influenced by the holistic, developmental systems-oriented perspective and its assumption that the appropriate unit of analysis is the person-in-environment. This emphasis brought me into contact with the subfield of environmental psychology that evolved during the last three decades and propelled me into the paradigmatic research program I shall now describe.

Research Program on Critical
Person-in-Environment Transitions

This research program, conducted with many colleagues and students, was initiated in the early 1970s (Wapner, Kaplan & Cohen, 1973) and has continued for more than two decades. Though recognizing that every moment of person-in-environment functioning involves change, our concern has been with those transitions where a perturbation to any aspect of the person-in-environment system is experienced as so potent that the ongoing modes of transacting with the physical, interpersonal, and sociocultural features of the environment no longer suffice. Such powerful changes in the person, in the environment, and in the relations between them may make for *developmental regression,* which, depending on other conditions, may be followed by *developmental progression* as characterized by the orthogenetic principle. The more or less progressive changes are expected to be manifest in various aspects of the transactions (experience and action) of the person with the environment. Functioning of any part of the person-in-environment system may impact the functioning of all other parts and thereby may influence the system as a whole. Sites of possible perturbations to the system are the three levels of operation of the person (namely, physical/biological, intrapersonal/psychological, and sociocultural), the three levels of the environment (namely, physical, interpersonal, and sociocultural), and the relations among all of these aspects (e.g., Demick & Wapner, 1988; Wapner, 1977, 1978, 1981, 1987a, 1987b; Yamamoto & Wapner, 1992).

A number of studies have been initiated and conducted on critical transitions initiated at these sites of the person-in-environment system. On the person side, at the *physical/biological* level, studies have been conducted on health (Quirk & Wapner, 1991, 1995), including such specific illnesses as juvenile rheumatoid arthritis (Quirk & Young, 1990) and prevention of HIV/AIDS (Wapner, 1994, August); on the *intrapersonal/psychological* level, some studies have been initiated on developmental regression and progression involved in onset and recovery from mental illness (Demick & Wapner, 1986, July); and on the *sociocultural* level, studies have involved such developmental change in role as the transition from work to retirement (Hanson & Wapner, 1994; Hornstein & Wapner, 1984, 1985).

A more extensive series of studies dealt with a perturbation to one or more aspects of the environment. For example, with respect to the *physical* level, studies have included an assessment of the role of cherished possessions in adaptation of the elderly following a move to a nursing home (Wapner, Demick & Redondo, 1990), and a developmental analysis of an unanticipated powerful person-in-environment system shock induced by a tornado, a hurricane, an earthquake, an atomic bomb, and a technological catastrophe (Chea & Wapner, 1995: Wapner, 1983).

With respect to the *interpersonal* aspects of the environment studies, for example, studies were conducted on development of friendships following entry into the university (Roelke, 1989, 1993) and on the development of personal networks following entrance into a new environment (Minami, 1985).

With respect to the *sociocultural* aspects of the environment, we have conducted developmental analyses of entering nursery school (Ellefsen, 1987; Wapner et al., 1983), entering and leaving college (Apter, 1976; Schouela, Steinberg, Leveton & Wapner, 1980; Wofsey, Rierdan & Wapner, 1979), entering and adapting to medical school (Quirk, Ciottone, Letendre & Wapner, 1987), and the impact of introducing legislation regarding use of automobile safety belts (Demick, et al., 1992; Wapner et al., 1986).

These studies are paralleled by others that seek to understand the conditions that underpin the initiation of action representative of a developmental advance in some aspects of functioning. Here we have been involved in the problem of the relation between experience (including intention) and action, that is, the conditions under which a person initiates a transition by in fact putting into action a desire, such as initiating the use of automobile safety belts (Demick et al., 1992; Rioux & Wapner, 1986; Wapner et al., 1986), stopping smoking (Tirelli, 1992) and stopping drinking (Agli, 1992), initiating a diet regimen (Raeff, 1990), and using an appropriate means for preventing transmission of HIV (Ferguson, Wapner & Quirk, 1993, April; Wapner, 1994, August). These studies on the developmental relations between thought and action have focused on the distinction between general factors making for change and the triggers or precipitating events that are involved. Hopefully, they not only help us understand the basis for change but can be used in intervention studies that can help the person achieve the developmental advance of moving from thought to effective health-related positive action (cf., Quirk, 1993, July; Quirk & Wapner, 1991; Wapner, 1993a).

Concurrent with these studies dealing with developmental analysis of critical person-in-environment transitions, my colleagues, students, and I have continued over the years to conduct studies dealing with cognitive, affective, and valuative aspects of ontogenetic, microgenetic, and other developmentally ordered series (cf., Wapner, 1993b). For example, a preliminary study, worth pursuing, combined ontogenesis and microgenesis. It utilized four American children (ages four and a half, six and a half, nine, and ten years) who accompanied their parents to an unfamiliar environment and drew sketch maps immediately after entering it and after two months and six months residence. In keeping with the orthogenetic principle both microgenetically and ontogenetically, sketch-map representations of an environment showed progressive differentiation of a scene into distinct objects with their spatial relations more integrated (Wapner, Kaplan & Ciottone, 1981).

A study by Dandonoli, Demick, and Wapner (1990) concerned age differences (5–7, 8–10, 11–13 years, and adults) in representations of the same room biased in two ways: furniture placed in a "part-quality" manner (similar objects near one another) and furniture placed in an "integrated" manner (parts arranged in socially relevant groupings). Whereas children produced representations consisting of groupings of isolated fragmented parts ("There are tables; there are chairs"), adults' representations were characterized by an integration of parts into a socially relevant, meaningful whole (e.g., "There is a lounge area that includes coffee tables, chairs, and sofas"). This held even following exposure to the room arranged in terms of "part-qualities."

A further study that examined individuals' affective involvement with people in their interpersonal environment utilized the *Psychological Distance Map for People* (PDM) (Wapner, 1978). The PDM uses a piece of paper with a small circle in the middle labeled "me." The subject, told that "me" stands for him or her, is asked to add other circles, each one standing for someone important in his or her life so that "those people who are close to you are placed closer to the circle that stands for you." Many studies have utilized this technique to assess the development of social networks of students during their stay in the university (Minami, 1985; Thom, 1992; Wapner, 1978). They have found, for example, with respect to microgenetic change, that the interpersonal network of first-year college students becomes increasingly dominated by college friends, and there is a shift of sources of support from home to college networks.

Still another study dealt with age differences in the relations between physical and interpersonal aspects of the environment (Wapner, Demick & Mutch-Jones,

1990). Here, two PDMs are used, one for people and one for places. The PDM for places is the same as that for people except that subjects are requested to enter places rather than people important in their world. With subjects differing in age (five and a half, eleven and a half, seventeen, and twenty-two years) it was found that there were significant positive correlations between the total number of entries on maps for people and places; the majority of places mentioned were associated with significant others; and relative to males, females included more people, places, and associations to "school" and "mother."

Finally, a recently completed ontogenetic study (Dyl & Wapner, in press) dealt with age (5–7, 8–9, 10–12, 13–14, 15–16, and 17–18 years) and gender differences in the nature, meaning, and function of cherished possessions. A number of significant findings were obtained, including: younger children are egocentric with respect to their possessions whereas older children stress social relationships; females favor items to be contemplated whereas males prefer action items; possessions that are meaningful for the enjoyment they provide decreases after age seven in females but persists in males throughout all the ages assessed; and object personification persists in all age groups for females but decreases after age seven for males.

Hopefully, the findings obtained in these and future studies on ontogenetic change when incorporated with other studies dealing with pathology will not only serve to advance developmental theory but will also contribute to praxis insofar as they will uncover information useful to parents as well as to professionals in their treatment of children with psychological problems.

Current Activity

In the fall of 1988, Clark University regulations forced me to retire from my position as G. Stanley Hall Professor of Genetic Psychology. However, from 1964, when Heinz Werner passed away, I have held the position of chair of the Executive Committee of the Heinz Werner Institute. This position as well as continued involvement in research and in teaching a research course on developmental analysis of transactions of persons-in-environments, along with involvement with graduate students on their M.A. theses and Ph.D. dissertations, have made it possible for me to ignore retirement and with the cooperation and approval of faculty and administration to be involved in departmental and university faculty meetings as well as general university activities. For example, six years ago I presented to the faculty my idea of a so-called Academic Spree Day, which involves an afternoon where classes are cancelled and undergraduate students, occasionally with graduate students, are invited by their sponsoring professors to present their research in posters and paper sessions and to showcase their creative work. This activity has been universally accepted by students and faculty and promises to remain as a university institution. Finally, during the past three years, I have been the principal investigator of a National Science Foundation Research Experiences for Undergraduates site grant that involves a ten-week summer session when ten undergraduates drawn from all over the United States work in an apprenticeship, "elbow-teaching" fashion with an individual faculty associate.[13]

I mention these activities because they are manifestations of my deep concern to help undergraduate and graduate students maximize their potential and provide opportunities to help them in their life work, whatever that would be, and to help graduate students in psychology in their growth as professionals. This is reflected not only in the large number of my joint publications with graduate and undergraduate students but also in the relationships I have with them long after they have left Clark. Of course, these relationships are somewhat easier to maintain with graduate students because they remain in the profession, and many, such as Jack Demick, have been involved in joint work with me for the last fifteen or more years. My deep, continued, ongoing involvement in the intermixture of scholarly activity and teaching with undergraduate and graduate students speaks to the good fortune I have had and continue to have in getting paid for having fun.[14] And this brings me to the future.

In reflecting on the future, I consider not only my own scholarly and teaching activity but also the status of developmental psychology. As I see it, the perspective underpinning the research described here has some striking advantages over other developmental perspectives because they are restricted to age changes. In contrast, the advantages of the holistic, developmental, systems-oriented perspective described here are many, including the definition of development in broad terms focusing on formal organizational features of experience and action, which permits applicability to diverse content areas, and the powerful heuristic value of the approach in shaping new, open problems relevant to the functioning of human beings in their everyday world.

Such work includes a more thorough systematic completion of the studies introduced in the programmatic work dealing with critical persons-in-environments transition through the life span, including processes underlying the change from regressive to progressive functioning; the problem of the development of relations between the levels of integration/organization (physical, psychological, and sociocultural) characteristic of organisms at different stages of development, both normal and pathological; the microgenesis of cognitive organizations; the analysis of individual differences from a developmental perspective; the study of parental development; the development of the linkages between cognitive, affective, and valuative processes; and the analysis of processes and conditions underpinning the occurrence of a developmental shift from one stage of organization to another.

Moreover, I believe that through a developmental psychology that is holistic and person-in-environment systems-oriented, completion of further empirical and theoretical analyses will serve to help integrate the growing isolation between subfields of psychology, thereby playing a powerful role in demonstrating the influence of a developmental psychology, broadly conceived, to move psychology from a fractionated to an integrated status that has potential to optimize human functioning in the everyday context (Wapner, 1992, 1995).

Notes

I express my deep appreciation to L. G. Wapner and J. Demick for their constructive comments on an early draft of the manuscript.

1. The approach is an extension—elaborated conceptualization and increased range of empirical study—of the organismic-developmental perspective (Werner, 1957b) that evolved from Werner's (1926) classic work on comparative development, Werner and Kaplan's (1963) work on symbol formation and related problems (Werner & Kaplan, 1956), and my work with Werner and others on sensory-tonic field theory of perception (e.g., Werner & Wapner, 1949, 1952, 1956; Wapner, Cirillo & Baker, 1969, 1971) and on perceptual development (e.g., Wapner & Werner, 1957).

2. See Dewsbury's (1993) recent article describing the controversy that developed following Maier's receipt of the AAAS award.

3. Including Jim Klee, Jane Shohl, Irwin Berg, Urie Bronfenbrenner, Harold Guetzkow, Raoul Weisman, Estefania Aldaba, and Tooi Xoomsai.

4. Ted Berlin and Bill Sleator (physics/chemistry), Esther Sleator (medicine), Julie Youngner and Herman Lichtstein (bacteriology), William Dusenbury (economics), Leonard "Jimmy" Savage and Sammy Eilenberg (mathematics), and Jane Savage (anthropology).

5. For biographic material on and descriptions of the works of this truly outstanding scholar of international stature, who broke new ground in developmental psychology and carried out programmatic research in diverse areas of psychology, including language, perception, aesthetic experience, and mental retardation and who wrote critically on broad conceptual and methodological issues, see Barten & Franklin, 1978; Glick, 1983, 1992; Kaplan & Wapner, 1960; Wapner & Kaplan, 1966a, 1966b; Witkin, 1965.

6. In 1943, Werner left Wayne County Training School, where he had completed an extensive program of research on mental retardation, for a teaching position at Brooklyn College. Our work in perception was initiated there in 1946, when I joined the faculty.

7. For example, functional equivalence (that various forms of stimulation have similar perceptual end-effects) and the summative hypothesis (simultaneous introduction of two or more functionally equivalent factors operate coactively or summatively). As to the former, evidence has been accumulated for various aspects of space perception (see Werner & Wapner, 1952, 1956); relevant to the latter is the study by Meisel & Wapner (1969).

8. The research program on the sensory-tonic field theory of perception was supported by NIMH Research Grant MH #00348 for twenty-four years and produced more than 100 publications, approximately 40 Ph.D. dissertations, 50 M.A. theses, and 150 papers presented at professional meetings. Along with completing theses and dissertations, many graduate students with other involvements in advancing the research program included: Harvey Baker, Mel Barton, Martin Bauermeister, Jan Bruell, Ken Chandler, Len Cirillo, Frank Clarkson, Bruce Denner, Joe Glick, Anna Guyette, Don Krus, Jonas Langer, Bob Liebert, Joe McFarland, Al Mehrabian, Paul Meisel, Arnie Miller, Ric Morant, Tom Mulholland, Sonoko Ohwaki, George Rand, Jerry Schlater, Csaba Sziklai, and Leon Teft.

9. In a critical article in the Festschrift for Heinz Werner (Kaplan & Wapner, 1960), Kurt Goldstein (1960) also recommended the need for expansion of sensory-tonic field theory: "I would like my article to be considered an expression of my affirmation of the sensoritonic basis of perception; I merely would like to add a hint that sensoritonic theory may need expansion in the direction of the organismic theory of behavior" (p. 122).

10. Consider the study on the effect of the environmental context on body perception (Wapner, McFarland & Werner, 1963).

11. A fuller description of the national and Clark University context is given by the contributors to the special Clark University issue: J. Anderson, J. M. Blaut, A. Butimer, D. Canter, K. H. Craik, R. A. Hart, R. W. Kates, D. Leventhal, G. F. McCleary Jr., G. D. Rowles, D. Seamon, D. Stea, S. Wapner, J. F. Wohlwill, D. Wood, E. H. Zube. Other critical people on the Clark scene at the time were: R. Beck, M. Bowden, S. B. Cohen, B. Kaplan, R. Kasperson, G. T. Moore, T. O'Riordan, and H. Prince.

12. Currently with Jack Demick, Suffolk University, and others who were on the Clark scene, including Bob Ciottone, Mark Quirk, Gail Hornstein, Ogretta McNeil, numerous graduate and undergraduate students. Other colleagues from abroad include, from Japan: Takiji Yamamoto, Masaaki Asai, Ichiro Soma, Tamotsu Toshima, Kunio Tanaka, Shinji Ishii, Hirofumi Minami, Kiyoshi Asakawa, Wataru Inoue. From Puerto Rico: Angel Pacheco, Nydia Lucca-Irizarry. From Italy: Mario Bertini, Luigi Pizzamiglio.

13. My colleagues Tom Schoenfeld (in 1991–1992) and Nancy Budwig (1992–1993; 1993–1994) have been coprincipal investigators.

14. These generally positive feelings have been complemented by recognition from Clark University (e.g., I was awarded a Clark University Centennial Medal in 1989 and an honorary Sc.D. in 1991) and the profession (e.g., I was presented with the Teacher of the Year Award by The Massachusetts Psychological Association in 1989).

References

Agli, S. (1992). *General factors and precipitating events involved in the cessation of alcohol consumption among college women.* Unpublished honors thesis, Clark University, Worcester, Mass.

Ames, A., Jr. (1951). Visual perception and the rotating trapezoidal window. *Psychological Monographs, 65* (7), Whole No. 324.

Apter, D. (1976). *Modes of coping with conflict in the presently inhabited environment as a function of variation in plans to move to a new environment.* Unpublished master's thesis, Clark University, Worcester, Mass.

Ariens Kappers, C. U., Huber, G. C. & Crosby, E. C. (1936). *The comparative anatomy of the nervous system of vertebrates, including man.* New York: Macmillan.

Barten, S. S. & Franklin, M. B. (Eds.). (1978). *Developmental processes: Heinz Werner's selected writings, Volumes 1 and 2.* New York: International Universities Press.

Bean, J. W. & Wapner, S. (1943). Effects of exposure to oxygen of high barometric pressure on higher functions of the CNS. *Proceedings of the Society of Experimental Biology and Medicine, 54,* 134–135.

Bean, J. W., Wapner, S. & Siegfried, E. C. (1945). Residual disturbance in the higher functions of the CNS induced by oxygen at high pressure. *American Journal of Physiology, 140,* 206–213.

Blake, R. R. & Ramsey, G. V. (1951). *Perception: An approach to personality.* New York: Mc-Graw-Hill.

Bruner, J. S. & Goodman, C. C. (1947). Value and need as organizing factors in perception. *Journal of Abnormal and Social Psychology, 42,* 33–44.

Bruner, J. S. & Klein, G. S. (1960). The functions of perceiving: New look retrospect. In B. Kaplan & S. Wapner (Eds.), *Perspectives in psychological theory* (pp. 61–77). New York: International Universities Press.

Canter, D. & Craik, K. H. (Eds.). (1987). Special issue. Environmental psychology at Clark University: C. 1970–72. *Journal of Environmental Psychology, 7* (4), 281–441.

Chea, W. & Wapner, S. (1995). Retrospections of Bahamians concerning the impact of hurricane Andrew. In J. L. Nasar, P. Grannis & K. Hanyu (Eds.), *Proceedings of the twenty-sixth annual conference of the Environmental Design Research Association, 26,* 87–92.

Clarkson, F. E. (1961). *A developmental analysis of the performance of children and adults on a maze learning and on embedded figures task.* Doctoral dissertation, Clark University, Worcester, Mass. (University Microfilms no. 61–4999).

Dandonoli, P., Demick, J. & Wapner S. (1990). Physical arrangement and age as determinants of environmental representation. *Children's Environments Quarterly, 7* (1), 26–36.

Demick, J. & Wapner, S. (1986, July). *Entering, living in, and leaving the psychiatric setting.* Paper presented at the 21st International IAAP Congress Symposium, Jerusalem, Israel.

Demick, J. & Wapner, S. (1988). Children-in-environments: Physical, interpersonal, and sociocultural aspects. *Children's Environments Quarterly, 5* (3), 54–62.

Demick, J., Inoue, W., Wapner, S., Ishii, S., Minami, H., Nishiyama, S. & Yamamoto, T. (1992). Cultural differences in impact of governmental legislation: Automobile safety belt use. *Journal of Cross-Cultural Psychology, 23* (4), 468–487.

Dewey, J. & Bentley, A. F. (1949). *Knowing and the known.* Boston: Beacon.

Dewsbury, D. A. (1993). On publishing controversy. *American Psychologist, 48* (8), 869–877.

Dyl, J. & Wapner, S. (In press). Age and gender differences in nature, meaning and function of cherished possessions for children and adolescents. *Journal of Experimental Child Psychology.*

Ellefsen, K. F. (1987). *Entry into nursery school: Children's transactions as a function of experience and age.* M.A. thesis, Clark University, Worcester, Mass.

Ferguson, E., Wapner, S. & Quirk, M. (1993, April). *Sexual behavior in relation to protection against transmission of HIV in college students.* Paper presented at the annual meeting of the Eastern Psychological Association, Arlington, Va.

Glick, J. A. (1983). Piaget, Vygotsky and Werner. In S. Wapner & B. Kaplan (Eds.), *Toward a holistic developmental psychology* (pp. 35–52). Hillsdale, N.J.: Erlbaum.

Glick, J. A. (1992). Werner's relevance for contemporary developmental psychology. *Developmental psychology, 28* (4), 558–565.

Goldman, A. E. (1953). Studies in vicariousness: Degree of motor activity and the autokinetic phenomenon. *American Journal of Psychology, 66,* 613–617.

Goldstein, K. (1960). Sensoritonic theory and the concept of self-realization. In B. Kaplan & S. Wapner (Eds.), *Perspectives in psychological theory. Essays in honor of Heinz Werner* (pp. 115–123). New York: International Universities Press.

Hall, C. S. (1934). Emotional behavior in the rat: I. Defecation and urination as measures of individual differences in emotionality. *Journal of Comparative Psychology, 18,* 385–403.

Hanson, K. & Wapner, S. (1994). Transition to retirement: Gender differences. *The International Journal of Aging and Human Development, 39* (3), 189–208.

Herrick, C. J. (1949). A biological survey of integrative levels. In R. W. Sellars, V. J. McGill & M. Farber (Eds.), *Philosophy for the future* (pp. 222–242). New York: Macmillan.

Hornstein, G. A. & Wapner, S. (1984). The experience of the retiree's social network during the transition to retirement. In C. M. Aanstoos (Ed.), *Exploring the lived world: Readings in phenomenological psychology* (pp. 119–136). Carrollton: West Georgia College Press.

Hornstein, G. A. & Wapner, S. (1985). Modes of experiencing and adapting to retirement. *International Journal on Aging & Human Development, 21* (4), 291–315.

Hurwitz, I. (1954). *A developmental study of the relationships between motor activity and perceptual processes as measured by the Rorschach test.* Doctoral dissertation, Clark University, Worcester, Mass. (University Microfilms no. 9011).

Ittelson, W. H. (1970). *Visual space perception.* New York: Springer.

Ittelson, W. H. & Cantril, H. (1954). *Perception as a transactional approach.* New York: Random House.

Kaplan, B. (1966). The comparative developmental approach and its application to symbolization and language in psychopathology. In S. Arieti (Ed.), *American handbook of Psychiatry, Volume 3* (pp. 659–688). New York: Basic Books.

Kaplan, B. (1967). Meditations on genesis. *Human Development, 10,* 65–87.

Kaplan, B. & Wapner, S. (Eds.). (1960). *Perspectives in psychological theory. Essays in honor of Heinz Werner.* New York: International Universities Press.

Kates, R. W. & Wohlwill, J. F. (Eds.). (1966). Man's response to the physical environment. *Journal of Social Issues, 22* (4), 1–140.

Kempler, B. (1964). *Developmental and level serial learning.* Doctoral dissertation, Clark University, Worcester, Mass. (University Microfilms no. 64–13156).

Klüver, H. (1931). The equivalence of stimuli in the behavior of monkeys. *Journal of Genetic Psychology, 39,* 3–27.

Kruger, A. K. (1954). *Direct and substitutive modes of tension reduction in terms of developmental level: An experimental analysis by means of the Rorschach test.* Doctoral dissertation, Clark University, Worcester, Mass. (University Microfilms no. 9013).

Krus, D. M., Werner, H. & Wapner, S. (1953). Studies in vicariousness: Motor activity and perceived movement. *American Journal of Psychology, 66,* 603–608.

Maier, N. R. F. (1929). Reasoning in white rats. *Comparative Psychology Monographs, 6,* 93.

Maier, N. R. F. (1931). Reasoning and learning. *Psychological Review, 38,* 332–346.

Maier, N. R. F. (1939). *Studies of abnormal behavior in the rat.* New York: Harper.

Maier, N. R. F. (1960). Selector-integrator mechanisms. In B. Kaplan & S. Wapner (Eds.), *Perspectives in psychological theory.* New York: International Universities Press.

Maier, N. R. F. & Schneirla, T. C. (1935). *Principles of animal psychology.* New York: McGraw-Hill.

Max, L. W. (1935). An experimental study of the motor theory of consciousness. III. Action-current responses in deaf mutes during sleep, sensory stimulation and dreams. *Journal of Comparative Psychology, 19,* 469–486.

Meisel, P. & Wapner, S. (1969). Interaction of factors affecting space and localization. *Journal of Experimental Psychology, 79* (3), 430–437.

Minami, H. (1985). *Establishment and transformation of personal networks during the first year of college: A developmental analysis.* Doctoral dissertation, Clark University, Worcester, Mass.

Misch, R. C. (1954). *The relationship of motoric inhibition to developmental level and ideational functioning: An analysis by means of the Rorschach test.* Doctoral dissertation, Clark University, Worcester, Mass. (University Microfilms no. 9016).

Novikoff, A. B. (1945a). The concept of integrative levels and biology. *Science, 101,* 209–215.

Novikoff, A. B. (1945b). Continuity and discontinuity in evolution. *Science, 101,* 405–406.

Padilla, S. G. (1930). *Further studies on the delayed pecking of chicks.* Doctoral dissertation, University of Michigan.

Quirk, M. (1993, July). *Facilitating lifestyle change to promote health.* Paper presented at the International Conference on Health Psychology, Tokyo, Japan.

Quirk, M., Ciottone, R., Letendre, D. & Wapner, S. (1987). Critical person-in-environment transitions in medical education. *Medical Teacher, 9* (4), 415–423.

Quirk, M. & Wapner, S. (1991). Notes on an organismic-developmental, systems perspective for health education. *Health Education and Research, 6,* 203–210.

Quirk, M. & Wapner, S. (1995). Environmental psychology and health. *Environment and Behavior, 27* (1), 90–99.

Quirk, M. & Young, M. (1990). The impact of JRA on children, adolescents and their families: Current research and implications for future studies. *Arthritis Care and Research, 3,* 37–43.

Raeff, C. (1990). *General factors and precipitating events influencing action: Initiation of a weight loss regimen.* Unpublished master's thesis, Clark University, Worcester, Mass.

Rand, G. & Wapner, S. (1969). Ontogenic changes in the identification of simple forms in complex contexts. *Human Development, 12,* 155–169.

Rand, G., Wapner, S., Werner, H. & McFarland, J. H. (1963). Age differences in performance on the Stroop Color-Word Test. *Journal of Personality, 31,* 534–558.

Rioux, S. & Wapner, S. (1986). Commitment to use of automobile seat belts: An experiential analysis. *Journal of Environmental Psychology, 6,* 189–204.

Roelke, D. T. (1989). *A comparison of close and non-close friendships: Shared worlds and contributions to social support.* Unpublished master's thesis, Clark University, Worcester, Mass.

Roelke, D. T. (1993). Essential relationships: The shared world of friendships. In J. Demick, K. Bursik & R. DiBiase (Eds.), *Parental development* (pp. 119–133). Hillsdale, N.J.: Erlbaum.

Schneirla, T. C. (1929). Learning and orientation in ants. *Comparative Psychology Monographs, 6,* 143.

Schneirla, T. C. (1934). The process and mechanism of ant learning. *Journal of Comparative Psychology, 17,* 308–328.

Schneirla, T. C. (1957). The concept of development in comparative psychology. In D. B. Harris (Ed.), *The concept of development.* Minneapolis: University of Minnesota Press.

Schouela, D. A., Steinberg, L. M., Leveton, L. B. & Wapner, S. (1980). Development of the cognitive organization of an environment. *Canadian Journal of Behavioral Science, 12,* 1–16.

Shepard, J. F. (1911). Some results in comparative psychology. *Psychological Bulletin, 8,* 41–42.

Shepard, J. F. (1933). Higher processes in the behavior of rats. *Proceedings of the National Academy of Sciences, 19,* 149–152.

Shepard, J. F. & Breed, F. S. (1913). Maturation and use in the development of an instinct. *Journal of Animal Behavior, 3,* 274–285.

Thom, F. (1992). *Relationship between people and places important in the freshmen's and senior's experiential world.* Unpublished paper, Clark University, Worcester, Mass.

Tirelli, L. (1992). *General factors involved in smoking cessation: A cross-cultural study.* Unpublished manuscript, Clark University, Worcester, Mass.

Walker, R. Y., Wapner, S., Bakan, D. & Ewert, E. S. (1946, October). *The agreement between inspectors' observations as recorded on the Ohio State Flight Inventory and instrument readings obtained from photographic records.* Report no. 67. Washington, D.C.: CAA Division of Research.

Wapner, S. (1944). The differential effects of cortical injury and retesting on equivalence reactions in the rat. In J. F. Dashiell (Ed.), *Psychological monographs, 57* (262), 1–59.

Wapner, S. (1956, August). *Sensory-tonic theory and the developmental approach to psychopathology.* University of Kansas Workshop in Clinical Psychology.

Wapner, S. (1964). Some aspects of a research program based on an organismic-developmental approach to cognition: Experiments and theory. *Journal of the American Academy of Child Psychiatry, 3,* 193–230.

Wapner, S. (1966). An organismic-developmental approach to perceived body-object relations. In N. Jenkin and R. H. Pollack (Eds.), *Proceedings of a conference on perceptual development: Its relation to theories of intelligence and cognition* (pp. 250–288). Chicago: Institute for Juvenile Research.

Wapner, S. (1977). Environmental transition: A research paradigm deriving from the organismic-developmental systems approach. In L. van Ryzin (Ed.), *Wisconsin Conference on Research Methods in Behavior Environment Studies: Proceedings* (pp. 1–9). Madison: University of Wisconsin.

Wapner, S. (1978). Some critical person-environment transitions. *Hiroshima Forum for Psychology, 5,* 3–20.

Wapner, S. (1981). Transactions of persons-in-environments: Some critical transitions. *Journal of Environmental Psychology, 1,* 223–239.

Wapner, S. (1983). Living with radical disruptions of person-in-environment systems. *IATSS Review, 9,* June, 133–148. In Japanese. English translation available.

Wapner, S. (1986, November). *An organismic-developmental systems approach to the analysis of experience and action.* Paper presented at the Conference on Holistic Approaches to Analysis of Experience and Action at the University of Catania, Sicily, Italy.

Wapner, S. (1987a). A holistic, developmental, systems-oriented environmental psychology: Some beginnings. In D. Stokols & I. Altman (Eds.), *Handbook of environmental psychology* (pp. 1433–1465). New York: Wiley.

Wapner, S. (1987b). 1970–1972: Years of transition. *Journal of Environmental Psychology, 7,* 389–408.

Wapner, S. (1988). Unifying psychology: Strategies from a holistic, developmental, systems perspective. *Hiroshima Forum for Psychology, 13,* 1–15.

Wapner, S. (1990). One person-in-his-environments. In I. Altman & K. Christensen (Eds.), *Environment and behavior studies: Emergence of intellectual traditions* (pp. 257–290). New York: Plenum.

Wapner, S. (1991). Some relations between field dependence-independence and a holistic, developmental, systems-oriented perspective. In S. Wapner & J. Demick (Eds.), *Field de-*

pendence-independence: Cognitive style across the life span (pp. 353–383). Hillsdale, N.J.: Erlbaum.

Wapner, S. (1992). Theory, empirical study, and praxis. *The General Psychologist, 28:2* (63), 29–32.

Wapner, S. (1993a). *From thought to action: Theoretical implications of the holistic, developmental, systems-oriented perspective to health issues.* Paper presented at the International Congress of Health Psychology, Tokyo, Japan.

Wapner, S. (1993b). Parental development: A holistic, developmental, systems oriented perspective. In J. Demick, K. Bursik, & R. DiBase (Eds.), *Parental development* (pp. 3–37). Hillsdale, N.J.: Erlbaum.

Wapner, S. (1994, August). *AIDS: The holistic, developmental systems-oriented approach.* Presented in a symposium World Views: Focus on AIDS at the 102nd annual convention of the American Psychological Association, Los Angeles.

Wapner, S. (1995). Toward integration: Environmental psychology in relation to other subfields of psychology. *Environment and Behavior, 27* (1), 9–32.

Wapner, S., Ciottone, R., Hornstein, G., McNeil, O. & Pacheco, A. M. (1983). An examination of studies of critical transitions through the life cycle. In S. Wapner & B. Kaplan (Eds.), *Toward a holistic developmental psychology* (pp. 111–132). Hillsdale, N.J.: Erlbaum.

Wapner, S. & Cirillo, L. (1973). *Development of planning.* Public Health Service grant application. Clark University, Worcester, Mass.

Wapner, S., Cirillo, L. & Baker, A. H. (1969). Sensory-tonic theory: Toward a reformulation. *Archivio di Psicologia Neurologia e Psichiatria, 30,* 493–512.

Wapner, S., Cirillo, L. & Baker, A. H. (1971). Some aspects of the development of space perception. In J. P. Hill (Ed.), *Minnesota Symposium on Child Psychology, Volume 5* (pp. 162–204). Minneapolis: University of Minnesota Press.

Wapner, S. & Demick, J. (1990). Development of experience and action: Levels of integration in human functioning. In G. Greenberg & E. Tobach (Eds.), *Theories of the evolution of knowing. The T. C. Schneirla Conference Series, Volume 4* (pp. 47–68). Hillsdale, N.J.: Erlbaum.

Wapner, S. & Demick, J. (1991a). Some relations between developmental and environmental psychology: An organismic-developmental systems perspective. In R. M. Downs, L. S. Liben & D. S. Palermo (Eds.), *Visions of aesthetics, the environment & development: The legacy of Joachim F. Wohlwill* (pp. 181–211). Hillsdale, N.J.: Erlbaum.

Wapner, S. & Demick, J. (1991b). Some open research problems on field dependence-independence: Theory and methodology. In S. Wapner & J. Demick (Eds.), *Field dependence-independence: Cognitive style across the life span* (pp. 401–429). Hillsdale, N.J.: Erlbaum.

Wapner, S., Demick, J., Inoue, W., Ishii S. & Yamamoto, T. (1986). Relations between experience and action: Automobile seat belt usage in Japan and the United States. In W. H. Ittelson, M. Asai, & M. Carr (Eds.), *Proceedings of the 2nd USA/Japan Seminar on Environment and Behavior* (pp. 279–295). Tucson: Department of Psychology, University of Arizona.

Wapner, S., Demick, J. & Mutch-Jones, K. (1990, March). *Children's experience of people and places.* Paper presented at the Eastern Psychological Association annual meeting, Philadelphia, Penna.

Wapner, S., Demick, J., & Redondo, J. P. (1990). Cherished possessions and adaptation of older people to nursing homes. *The International Journal of Aging and Human Development, 31* (3), 299–315.

Wapner, S., & Kaplan, B. (1966). Heinz Werner: 1890–1964. *American Journal of Psychology, 77*, 513–517.

Wapner, S. & Kaplan, B. (1966). *Heinz Werner: 1890–1964.* Worcester, Mass.: Clark University Press.

Wapner, S., Kaplan, B. & Ciottone, R. (1981). Self-world relationships in critical environmental transitions: Childhood and beyond. In L. Liben, A. Patterson & N. Newcombe (Eds.), *Spatial representation and behavior across the life span* (pp. 251–282). New York: Academic Press.

Wapner, S., Kaplan, B. & Cohen, S. (1973). An organismic-developmental perspective for understanding transactions of men in environments. *Environment and Behavior, 5*, 255–289. [Reprinted in G. Broadbent, R. Bunt & T. Llorens, (Eds.). (1980). *Meaning and behavior in the built environment.* New York: Wiley.]

Wapner, S., McFarland, J. H. & Werner, H. (1963). Effect of visual spatial context on perception of one's own body. *British Journal of Psychology, 54*, 41–49.

Wapner, S. & Rand, G. (1968). Ontogenetic differences in the nature of organization underlying serial learning. *Human Development, 11*, 249–259.

Wapner, S. & Werner, H. (1957). *Perceptual development.* Worcester, Mass.: Clark University Press.

Werner, H. (1926). *Einführung in die Entwicklungspsychologie.* Leipzig: Barth. (2nd ed., 1933; 3rd ed., 1953; 4th ed., 1959).

Werner, H. (1937). Process and achievement. *Harvard Educational Review, 7*, 353–368.

Werner, H. (1945). Motion and motion perception: A study in vicarious functioning. *Journal of Psychology, 19*, 317–327.

Werner, H. (1957a). *Comparative psychology of mental development* (rev. ed.). New York: International Universities Press. (First copyright, 1940).

Werner, H. (1957b). The concept of development from a comparative and organismic point of view. In D. Harris (Ed.), *The concept of development* (pp. 125–148). Minneapolis: University of Minnesota Press.

Werner, H. & Kaplan, B. (1956). The developmental approach to cognition: Its relevance to the interpretation of anthropological and ethnolinguistic data. *American Anthropologist, 58*, 866–880.

Werner, H. & Kaplan, B. (1963). *Symbol formation.* New York: Wiley.

Werner, H. & Wapner, S. (1949). Sensory-tonic field theory of perception. *Journal of Personality, 18*, 88–107.

Werner, H. & Wapner, S. (1952). Toward a general theory of perception. *Psychological Review, 59*, 324–338.

Werner, H. & Wapner, S. (1956). Sensory-tonic field theory of perception. *Revista di Psicologia, 50*, 315–337.

Witkin, H. A. (1965). Heinz Werner: 1890–1964. *Child development, 30*, 308–328.

Witkin, H. A., Lewis, H. B., Hertzman, M., Machover, K., Meissner, P. & Wapner, S. (1954). *Personality through perception.* New York: Harper and Brothers.

Wofsey, E., Rierdan, J. & Wapner, S. (1979). Planning to move: Effects on representing the currently inhabited environment. *Environment and Behavior, 11*, 3–32.

Yamamoto, R. & Wapner, S. (Eds.). (1992). *A developmental psychology of life transitions*. Kyoto: Kitaoji. In Japanese.

Zener, K. (Ed.). (1949a). Interrelations between perception and personality: A symposium. Special issue, Part I. *Journal of Personality, 18* (1).

Zener, K. (Ed.). (1949b). Interrelations between perception and personality: A symposium. Special issue, Part II. *Journal of Personality, 18* (2).

About the Book and Editors

The ten original essays presented here chart the personal and professional life experiences of these remarkable contributors from the discipline of developmental psychology. Employing the autobiographical approach, the book provides a unique view of how research and scientific inquiries are conducted while adding the human dimension generally absent from textbooks or journal articles.

This book will be of interest to students in history or developmental psychology courses as well as to the general reader looking for first-person accounts of the emergence of contemporary developmental psychology.

Dennis Thompson is associate professor of educational psychology and special education at Georgia State University. **John D. Hogan** is professor of psychology at St. John's University.